JOHNSTOWN BASKETBALL

The Cambria County War Memorial Invitational Tournament

BRADLEY A. HUEBNER
FOREWORD BY GENE BANKS

THE
History
PRESS

Published by The History Press
Charleston, SC
www.historypress.com

Copyright © 2024 by Bradley A. Huebner

All rights reserved

First published 2024

Manufactured in the United States

ISBN 9781467156042

Library of Congress Control Number: 2024941855

To Dad,

The kid from Allentown who played baseball
at Point Stadium in Johnstown
in front of 15,200 fans in the early 1950s.

The man who taught me
the lessons and benefits gained
from playing competitive sports.

To my Father in Heaven,

Thank you for showing me the beauty of places
like Johnstown, Pennsylvania,
a mini-city that persists and endures.

CONTENTS

FOREWORD

When we think about basketball regions, basketball aficionados always talk about New York, California and Illinois. Great high school players have come from those states, but the one state that has produced some of the greatest scholastic basketball players is Pennsylvania. There is a lengthy list. One of the greatest of them all, Wilton Norman Chamberlain, was a Pennsylvania product, born and raised on the west side of Philadelphia, who went on to be one of the greatest basketball players in the history of the game, if not the greatest. Another was Larry Miller from Catasauqua, who left the Keystone State to become one of the greatest players in University of North Carolina basketball history as a two-time ACC Player of the Year and a first-team Parade All-American along with playing in the ABA and making the all-rookie first team. Other names such as Kenny Durrett, Henry Williams, Norm Van Lier, Len Chappell and Sam Clancy, whom I played against, gave Pennsylvania nationwide recognition of the style of gritty play that was Pennsylvania's stamp. I, Gene Banks, am proud and honored to have journeyed and be noted as a player who is recognized as one worthy of high praise due to my Pennsylvanian heritage and my accolades during my time.

Brad Huebner has done an amazing job telling, sharing and giving accurate accounts of the moments that are remembered and archived. Reading this book brought back memories along with being proud of being a Pennsylvania basketball player. The gladiator battles and the rivalries within the state are historic and etched in basketball history throughout America. Yes, we Pennsylvanians made history with such tenacity, intelligence and grit

Gene Banks, daughter India and former Duke coach Mike Krzyzewski. *Courtesy of Gene Banks.*

that other states envied and wished they had such experience. My team—
the 1977 National USA Champions West Philadelphia Speedboys—had the
nation on notice and even had the local and national media covering our
every move, day to day. The Johnstown Tournament stamped our prowess
and legitimized our national claim as the best high school team in America
after we had the "Greatest Game" played there against Sam Clancy and
Brashear High School, which was ranked No. 3 in the nation. After this
game, which we won in a classic battle, many throughout the nation started

to go into the history of Pennsylvania basketball regarding the many talented players who traveled along the path of history that made Pennsylvania a place of such a rich tradition in the sport.

To be named the national Player of the Year against such other scholastic greats as Earvin "Magic" Johnson (Michigan) and Albert King (New York) was a highlight that stays with me more than ever to this very day, but representing the state of Pennsylvania was my greatest fulfilment. To be named in the same breath as Durrett, Williams, Chappell and Miller as a great Pennsylvanian is one of my greatest accolades. To be among such great people who influenced my life and others—such as Sonny Vaccaro, Herb Sendek Jr., Joey Goldenberg and even James "Bruiser" Flint, just to name a few—helped mold me into the man I am today and helped propel my career after high school.

Reading the stories and highlights of such wonderful competitive battles that went on in Pennsylvanian basketball and reading about the accomplishments of everyone made it hard to put down this book. There was a thread that bonded us all then and now, in the history of representing the great Keystone State and the Johnstown Tournament.

The greatest high school All-American game (Dapper Dan) was created by Sonny Vaccaro, who was from Trafford, Pennsylvania. It became *the* high school All-American game before the now prestigious McDonald's All-American high school classic came into existence; it was formed and played in Pennsylvania, pitting the USA All-Stars against Pennsylvania's best. Pennsylvania held its own for many years, not winning the multitude of contests, but in my year of 1977, along with Sam Clancy and now Iowa Hawkeye head basketball coach Fran McCaffery, we took to the task of standing Pennsylvania proud and came away with the victory. Afterward, I was booed winning the MVP of the classic, due to the partisan sellout crowd. I quickly grabbed the mic and respectfully turned the trophy over to Sam Clancy from Pittsburgh. It was because I was Pennsylvania proud and happy to have won the game for our state against the best in America, and a fellow Pennsylvanian was the key to such a victory—not just me.

This book will give you many more names and stories of feats and unbelievable moments. It can be considered the Bible of our heritage of Pennsylvanian high school tournament basketball history at its best. I am honored to be mentioned among the many great players who made history and were Pennsylvania proud!

—GENE "TINKERBELL" BANKS

ACKNOWLEDGMENTS

Kudos to all the people who committed to interviews and making sure that the accounts of Pennsylvania high school basketball and beyond in this book are accurate. As always, my team of Dave Burman, Don Canzano and Mike Toth were invaluable for their help acquiring information and documents. The people at DeMatha Catholic—from Tom Ponton to Pete Strickland, from Johnny Jones to Mike Brey and Dereck Whittenburg and others—directed me to the many great coaches and players who were part of Morgan Wootten's Hall of Fame program. I thank the librarians and researchers for their help in running down past feature and game stories, historic photos and timely statistics, as well as Johnstown sportswriter Mike Mastovich. I learned that acquiring photos from the mid-1900s is tougher in a town washed out by floods.

West Philly's Gene Banks and Joe Goldenberg, Dobbins Tech's Darryl "Heat" Gates, Overbrook's Ricky Tucker and Whit (Dereck Whittenburg) are people I met during this process who repeatedly answered my questions or verified details. McKeesport High alumnus Lanny Van Eman reminded me of all the great achievements of his high school coach, Cornelius "Neenie" Campbell, and provided his memories of the night he watched DeMatha take on the great Lew Alcindor and the night Sonny Vaccaro pieced together the Dapper Dan Roundball Classic. To Bo Ryan, a fellow Wilkes alumnus and a Chester Clipper icon, I thank you for taking time to support this project while you were waiting to see if you made the Hall of Fame and as the movie about your Division III decade of dominance neared its release.

I pestered Dunbar High coach Bob Wade many times for information and photos about his elite program. All he did was deliver what he had with a smile. I apologize for my intrusions anyway. War Memorial Arena staffers and General Manager Jean Desrochers answered all my questions and unearthed the old tournament posters for me. Jean, a hockey guy, scrounged old newspaper clippings in eight giant collections and made his 1st Summit Arena available on multiple occasions. On one visit, I was encouraged to see the arena's locker rooms gutted, partway through a fresh refurbishing.

I've expanded my resource network to New Yorkers like Joe DeSantis and Gary DeCesare, two valuable connections who made it possible for me to get in touch with men like Len Elmore, Tony Fiorentino and New Jersey community leader and rising politician Jerry Walker, a man who works for others every day.

As usual, I utilized newspapers.com to obtain historical newspaper stories about the great Johnstown Tournament and its teams. My mentor, Dr. J. Michael Lennon, continues to advise and inspire me to write creatively and capture the human and historical sides of sports.

Every writer needs a few reliable historians, and I had great ones in Ben Jenkins and Ken Zaremba, who redirected me as needed. I thank those willing to read a chapter, hoping to eliminate errors of all kinds before the manuscript was published. Writing about a tournament that spanned 1949 to 1994 with teams from all over the East Coast can be a massive undertaking, especially when it's set in the Flood City. But like the people of Johnstown, I persisted to completion. Thomas Slusser from the *Johnstown Tribune-Democrat* photographed all the tournament posters so they might be useable in this book. Kudos.

As always, thank you to my family, the support system that sustains me, from my sister, Heidi, whose meals and generosity light up every holiday, to my brother, Mike, who made it possible to reunite in Myrtle Beach. I love you all!

PART I

1949–1959

The Beginning

FLOOD CITY

To enter Johnstown, Pennsylvania, you'll likely use the Johnstown Expressway or Menoher Boulevard and descend into the commercial downtown. You will arrive at a flattened grid of businesses, libraries and stadiums. Follow the decline toward the action like a homeowner retiring to a playroom. Encounter this once-thriving steel town, with its beautiful baseball stadium and four-thousand-seat multi-purpose arena. Tour the town, where you'll see charcoal water marks six feet high on some façades, scars from three historic floods. Notice Johnstown's naked, idle, tubular mills and factories where men once sweated their way to financial stability. The infrastructure for a once-thriving mid-sized city remains, but like many of the brick façades on buildings, neglect, decay and Mother Nature have effaced some of the shine.

For most entering Johnstown, the pathway is the same one the 1889 Johnstown Flood took when the South Fork Dam burst and 20 million tons of water traveled fourteen miles, smashing the collected, rushing flotsam against the Stone Bridge, killing more than 2,200 in a town of 30,000.[1] Gravity and topography conspired to form chutes that carried raging waters to where they could uplift houses and trains and trees, twist them into wreckage and haul them amid the forty-foot rushing wall of water to where the landscape flattens, down near where Point Stadium sits today. The waters charged forth until some structure fortified firmly enough could absorb the thrust without being toppled or eviscerated. In all, more than 1,600 buildings were obliterated. Old sepia-tone photos show the second stories of downtown structures impaled by giant oaks.

Left: War Memorial Arena (now 1st Summit Arena) in 2024. *Photo by Bradley A. Huebner.*

Below: 1st Summit Arena. *Photo by Thomas Slusser, of the* Tribune-Democrat.

And even with that, despite that tsunami of wreckage and the carnage left by that regenerating liquid fist that repeatedly socked the region, Johnstown recovered. Locals who survived rebuilt the town from cataclysm. Rather than refill the valley by South Fork Dam, where the first flood began, it was better to leave it alone in its natural state, as a verdant reminder, a now-lush green valley bisected by an innocuous creek winding its way through the terrain, the water deep enough only to submerge your ankles. Tough and true as steel, Johnstown's natives fought to keep their town humming. They built it back once…twice…but would it ever be as good as the Shangri-La of the early 1900s or the postwar 1950s?

"The streets were once paved with gold," one local lifer said in 2023. "A land of milk and honey. The town once had everything you could want.… Everybody had good jobs. There was entertainment.…Of course, it's nothing like that today."

Over the years, locals and visitors have traveled down, down, down into Johnstown proper for parades, for the annual All-American Amateur Baseball Association (AAABA) summer tournament at Sargent's Stadium at the Point near the confluence of the Stonycreek and Conemaugh Rivers. The AAABA tournament is still the highlight of the social season. In winter, they used to travel to downtown for the annual basketball showcase tournament at War Memorial Arena (now called 1st Summit Arena). From 1949 to 1994, War Memorial Arena hosted some of the greatest basketball players in history, from Wilt Chamberlain to Wali Jones, Kenny Durrett, Hawkeye Whitney, Tom McMillen, Gene Banks, Hank Gathers, Bo Kimble, Muggsy Bogues and Rasheed Wallace. America's best teams—from Morgan Wootten's DeMatha to Bob Wade's Baltimore Dunbar, Bob Hurley's St. Anthony's and Bill Ellerbee's Simon Gratz—ventured here for four-team December tournaments.

They played mere blocks from Point Stadium, where baseball greats like Babe Ruth, Lou Gehrig, Al Kaline, Joe Torre and Orel Hershiser once had played, either in the AAABA or as part of a barnstorming exhibition. How many Pennsylvania cities had two sports venues on par with what Johnstown boasted?

Eventually, Hollywood brought its cameras to capture this sporting oasis. Paul Newman starred in the minor-league hockey comedy *Slap Shot*, filmed here in the 1970s. Tom Cruise starred in the 1980s high school football movie *All the Right Moves*. Locals felt like Hollywood royalty themselves, buying beers for Blue Eyes and meeting Cruise. Johnstown, however, has since gone the way of the Rust Belt. The steel industry (U.S. Steel and Bethlehem Steel) started to dry up after World War II, taking away local jobs and hope. By the 1990s, most of the jobs in the mill had vanished.

In between *Slap Shot* and *All the Right Moves*, the third major flood hit Johnstown. A twenty-four-hour storm parked over the town and dumped almost a foot of rainwater, ravaging the downtown yet again, forcing lifers to relocate to higher ground, to the 'burbs.[2] We should have seen it coming. Hollywood tried to warn us. *Slap Shot* chronicles a struggling semipro hockey franchise in a dying town. Fictional Ampipe High in *All the Right Moves* centers on teenagers desperate to land football scholarships to get the hell out of town, to escape the grime and drudgery of the mill—or worse, a town without a mill.

But like that former lover who clings to bygone, amorous days, when the flame was hot and emotions were simmering, eventually he must accept the new reality: It's over. It's time to relocate. Find something, someone or someplace new.

Johnstown residents have either moved to higher ground or relocated well beyond Cambria County walls to evade the floods and the diminishing job prospects. And that's how the recent generations have progressed. They've accepted the new reality and fled.

Today, there's a curious loyalty among the diehards who remain. While the younger generations have departed, their parents and grandparents remain behind to finish out their days. They share the town with 777 victims of the May 31, 1889 flood, who reside in Grandview Cemetery's Plot of the Unknown, arrayed in precise rows like you would see honoring war heroes in Arlington National Cemetery. More than 70,000 are buried here in a tranquil setting ideal for reverence and reflection.[3] Those buried here built this town and made it a destination, but who will maintain what they created from the resilient community that survived not one, not two, but three floods?

Walk through town in the modern era and you'll feel as if most of the citizenry has been whisked away in the Rapture. An eerie quiet, an emptiness, fills visitors like me who stroll the streets where so much happened. On streets where fifty or so passersby once nodded and waved, there might be a half dozen today. There's a palpable cacophony of silence in the quiet solitude of vacant streets. Next to a fancy men's clothing store with high-end silk ties and sport coats is a vacant storefront with tattered cloth and crumpled newspapers left by the entrance, a vagabond's bed.

A walk down the street is an intrusion back in time. Brick façades like the one promoting Roudabush Paint Supply Company still offer remnants of advertisements for bygone businesses; many are faded and barely legible.

Drive beyond the downtown to the steel mills. They are neatly aligned uniformly, like Hollywood movie studios. You'll notice rusted brown and orange metal that once encased the production of the very beams that built America into a world power. Now they're mostly skirted by chest-high weeds and pocked by broken windows, melancholy reminders of a different era, like old and idle vintage cars plopped onto a farmer's front yard, home now to nesting birds and untamed overgrowth.

Research the demise. Go online and examine the chart revealing population trends in Johnstown from 1910 to 2021. Like the downtown's entryway, the graph slopes down gradually, from more than fifty-five thousand residents in 1910 to just over eighteen thousand today.

Will Johnstown streets ever again be coated with gold, as one man recalled? Will the town ever cough to life behind some new company willing to relocate to the middle of bucolic central Pennsylvania to make some new technology the world demands? Can this mountainous oasis become a thriving, self-sufficient mini-city between Pittsburgh and Harrisburg? Do locals with keen memories dare chance to believe it—or even hope for it anymore?

Through everything, the cataclysmic tumult and jarring events, Johnstown has been lifted by its sports. Maybe the town can't produce tons of steel anymore, but the local athletes and teams have always found a way to compete and impress the locals. The town's forefathers erected a top-tier ballpark and an arena to showcase the town's ambitious youth who—given the chance—could match America's best. The town's forefathers were dreamers and visionaries who brought mid-sized city amenities to a small city. Among their success stories was the Cambria County Johnstown War Memorial Invitational Basketball Tournament, which ran every December for forty-six years. Somehow, the Johnstown dreamers lured basketball royalty to drive here and showcase their talents for the locals for nearly half a century. It remains a mini-miracle conceived in the minds of a few Renaissance men.

THE IMPETUS

Shortly after World War II, a few locals hatched the idea for an elite basketball tournament involving Johnstown boys. The rationale? Well, if we could beat Germany and Italy and Japan in a worldwide war, why couldn't Johnstown boys hold up against America's best athletes?

Opportunities for Pennsylvania athletes to test themselves against the best proliferated in the middle of the twentieth century. Johnstown's famed AAABA baseball tournament started by crowning the Amsterdam Rugmakers of New York as its first champion in 1945. Teams from New Orleans, Detroit, New Jersey, Ohio and Maryland were early repeat winners.[4]

The 1950s also brought about the Big 33 football showdown between Pennsylvania's best high school players and a United States All-Star team, or one from another state. In 1958, Pennsylvania won by scoring the game's only touchdown. Uniontown High quarterback Sandy Stephens plunged from the 1. The late Hall of Fame defensive coach Monte Kiffin, whose son Lane is an elite college football coach today at the University of Mississippi, was on the national squad.[5]

Famed sportswriter Jim Dent would memorialize the Big 33 game in his book *The Kids Got It Right* about the 1965 Texas All-Star team that came to Hershey to down Pennsylvania, to avenge an earlier defeat.[6] The Big 33 All-Star game would evolve and change over the decades. For years it pitted talent-rich Ohio stars against Pennsylvania's best. Today, it matches Pennsylvania against Maryland's finest. The game may have changed and even downsized, but it has endured. The Big 33 website—which calls its event "The Super Bowl of High School Football"—boasts that a Big 33 alumnus has played in fifty-seven straight National Football League Super Bowls. The names of past stars read like a litany of Canton, Ohio busts: Montana, Namath, Marino and Kelly. And those were just quarterbacks from Pennsylvania.

In between the AAABA's inception and the beginning of the Big 33 game in Hershey, Johnstown locals began a four-team December basketball tournament so local teams could test themselves against elite competition. Locals credit a multi-sports star named Charles Kunkle Jr. and town leaders Clayton Dovey III and Howard Picking for starting the event. These were Renaissance men who touched the world in copious ways—rare men who lived the life of ten successful people. They were fashioned from the mold of Philadelphia's Ben Franklin, who wrote, published, invented, politicked and imagined a better world, or Italy's Leonardo Da Vinci, who painted the *Mona Lisa* and *The Last Supper*, sketched the *Vitruvian Man* and then developed early designs of canals, parachutes and guns.

In Johnstown, Charles Kunkle Jr. was such a man. He was an officer on the first night aircraft carrier, the USS *Independence*, in the South Pacific during World War II. From there, his obituary captures his life best:

> *"Kunk" was founder and Chairman of Laurel Holdings, Inc. and Laurel Management Company as well as founder of Laurel Technologies, Inc. and Vice President of the Johnstown Water Company and The Manufacturers Water Company 1955–1964. He was Chairman of the Cambria County War Memorial Corporation, 1948–1951; the University of Pittsburgh at Johnstown, 1968–1979, the Johnstown Area Regional Industries, 1973–1985, when Metropolitan Life Insurance and Abex Wheel Plant opened operations in Johnstown; a Board Member of Johnstown Savings Bank for 34 Years and of Conemaugh Memorial Hospital for 36 years. He also was President of the Johnstown Jets (hockey franchise), 1949–1952 and served on the United States Olympic Hockey Committee in 1964 and 1968. Kunk was the Johnstown City Tennis Champion, a ten-time Sunnehanna Country Club Golf Champion, a five-time participant in the United States Amateur Golf Championship and played in the 1956 Masters. He was instrumental in the founding of the Sunnehanna Amateur. Kunk was a member of Westmont Presbyterian Church.*

Kunk was also captain of the 1936 Duke University men's basketball team. In three years of playing college basketball for Irwin, Pennsylvania native and Duke coach Eddie Cameron in the Southern Conference, Kunk's Blue Devils won fifty-six and lost only twenty. Kunk couldn't take his hometown with him to Durham, North Carolina, to share top-shelf basketball, so he brought the basketball world to Johnstown.

"Kunkle and Howard Picking always thought we had great athletes in Johnstown," said Carl Sax, a starter on the Johnstown High basketball teams in the 1950s.[7]

Many remember Kunk's class and kindness. "I knew him as well as a teenager could know a gentleman in his '60s," Todd Thiele posted on Facebook.[8] "He was very good to me. He only got angry at me once, and I felt like I was being scolded by God, but it was the disappointment he showed when I turned down a scholarship from his alma mater Duke to go to UNC. Can you blame me? Carolina girls were much prettier! They don't make men like this anymore."

Boys avoided trouble and discovered glory by playing sports in the Flood City. Johnstown native Jack Ham would star for the Pittsburgh Steelers in the NFL. He would win three Super Bowls and make the Hall of Fame. Pete Vuckovich pitched for the Brewers, Blue Jays, White Sox and Cardinals in Major League Baseball. Vuckovich would win the 1982 Cy Young Award with Milwaukee.

In basketball, Johnstown produced Pat Cummings, a six-foot-nine forward who played twelve years in the NBA for five teams. So, yes, Johnstown had athletes, especially in the 1970s and 1980s. Ham, Vuckovich and Cummings watched baseball and basketball played locally at the highest level during their childhoods.

Along with Kunk and Picking, local outdoorsman Clayt Dovey Jr. also helped run the Cambria County Johnstown War Memorial Invitational Basketball Tournament. Dovey wrote outdoors columns for the *Johnstown Democrat* and maintained a presence well beyond the town. Better known for his outdoors column and TV show, Dovey made huge contributions to Johnstown basketball as well.

As his own playing career faded, Kunk needed new outlets for his raging competitiveness. The talented amateur golfer didn't want his athletic career to end after securing dubious records in the Masters golf tournament in Augusta, Georgia: highest score in a round (95) and highest overall score (340 in 1956). Both records still stand.

Maybe he wouldn't compete in the basketball tournament at War Memorial Arena, but Kunk could help provide the cavernous venue for outstanding hockey and basketball players to test their mettle against the best. He had seen local boys assemble for pickup games at the outdoor court just up the hill from Johnstown's business district.

"Clayt Dovey was the person who ran the Johnstown Night Tournament," said Sax. "He was also TV's old angler. Clayt also had a lighted basketball court at his house and invited many of the players to participate in a tournament. [Coach Paul] Abele wasn't too fond of that. He didn't want us playing there and risk getting hurt."

Local outdoor basketball games weren't enough for Kunk, Picking and Dovey. They wanted to broaden the competition to include the best squads in high school basketball, wherever they might find them. Kunk needed that competitive fix, that athletic purpose. After all, as an athlete himself, the man had won championships in tennis, golf and basketball. If he could do all that....

THE HOMEBOYS

The premise of the Johnstown basketball tournament was twofold:

- Expose locals to high school basketball at the highest level.
- See how the local boys stacked up.

If local teams like Johnstown, Johnstown Catholic, Bishop McCort, Conemaugh and Richland weren't competitive against these visiting elite teams and players, the foundation of the four-team field would crumble. Would residents pack War Memorial Arena to watch their boys get annihilated in a shiny new arena? Not likely.

Johnstown funded the foundation to make the tournament go. When the plans for the proposed War Memorial Arena were made public in the late 1940s, thousands of locals ponied up. A drive to raise $750,000 began. Bethlehem Steel chipped in $100,000 almost immediately. Another business topped that amount. Smaller businesses pledged a few thousand dollars. Wallets popped open like cash jack-in-the-boxes. The result: a big-time showplace to entertain the locals through elite events, including its marquee sport: minor-league ice hockey.

"Basketball games—scholastic, collegiate and pro—hockey, ice shows, and other sports of interest will be held at the arena, which can seat a crowd of 5,500," *Williamsport Sun Gazette* columnist "The Sports Mike" professed. "There are 3,865 permanent fixed chairs with folding seats and arm rests. At the right end of the floor there are 147 plank seats while an additional 1,500 additional loose folding chairs can be placed on the main floor."9

There were also five concession stands and six public bathrooms, making the ambitious venue ideal for showcase tournaments. And for concerts featuring performers and bands like Duke Ellington, the Supremes, the Rolling Stones, Springsteen, Kansas, Kiss, Willie Nelson and, in recent years, Alice Cooper, the venue was spacious yet quaint. Other events included ice shows, circus shows, professional wrestling and, of course, the Harlem Globetrotters.

Answers as to whether the high school basketball tournament would attract fans came quickly. In the first tournament—held at Johnstown High School in 1949 because War Memorial was under construction—local Conemaugh High defeated McKeesport on opening night, giving the locals a victory to cheer, which plenty did. Reading High won the tournament, which was fitting because in 2024 the Berks County school had the most total basketball victories of any school in Pennsylvania history.

In year two, 1950, with the tournament permanently relocated to the new $1.5 million War Memorial Arena, Johnstown Catholic defeated Johnstown and then won the tournament with a 34–31 victory over Ed McCluskey's emerging Farrell High dynasty. Dovey and Kunk were further justified when Johnstown Catholic went on to win the parochial schools state title in March. Hometown basketball teams were, in fact, elite! Tournament organizers made it a goal to have state champions—past and future—in the tournament field.

Local fans were relieved and proud. Their boys could match up with Pennsylvania's best and even beat them. The tournament had legs. McCluskey's Farrell squad would reach the 1951 Class A state final, losing to Allentown High.

HERB SENDEK JR. WAS a boy growing up in central and Western Pennsylvania back then. He was one of many young athletes who benefited from having elite basketball and baseball tournaments in the Flood City.[10] "My father [Herb Sr.] is from Windber, Pennsylvania," he said. "That is right next to Johnstown. Ironically, my dad played in the first basketball game ever played in the War Memorial Arena. It was a high school game, Windber High vs. Johnstown Catholic. My dad became a teacher and a coach, so I was not surprisingly tagging along to games here and there and everywhere."

Herb Sr.'s high school teammate Phil DePolo might have scored the first basket at the arena, but Johnstown Catholic won the first game. Herb Jr. would become a highly successful college basketball coach at Santa Clara, Arizona State, North Carolina State and Miami of Ohio.[11]

Back in 1905, neighboring Windber also had been home to another talented young athlete. Johnny Weissmuller, the famous five-time gold medal–winning Olympic swimmer, would famously play Tarzan in the movies and go on to set sixty-seven world records. Weissmuller's family stayed in Windber only three years before relocating to Chicago, where "Tarzan" grew to be six-foot-three. Frank Kush was a standout lineman for Windber High in the 1940s before playing football at Michigan State University and later coaching at Arizona State University and for the Baltimore Colts. The football field at ASU was named Frank Kush Field. Playing sports and being active was expected in Pennsylvania.

"I can remember going around Christmas time to the War Memorial Arena for the annual high school tournament that has such a rich history through the years," said Herb Sendek Jr. "At that time, when I walked into War Memorial Arena, I thought it was the biggest arena in the world. That was like being in Heaven, going with my dad to the Johnstown War Memorial, watching the best high school teams and players compete."

Pottsville's historic Martz Hall, today considered the finest high school gym in the state, wasn't built until 1970. In the 1950s, the Penn Palestra was the signature arena, with a capacity of 10,000 seats. South of Johnstown, you had the Hershey Sports Arena (now Hersheypark Arena), capacity 7,225.[12] In 1961, Pittsburgh built its Civic Arena, which held more than 17,000. For big-time basketball events in the old days, you traveled to college or high school gyms. So a venue like War Memorial Arena stood out and was worthy of being a showcase arena.

LOCAL WESTMONT HIGH, KUNK'S alma mater, went 0-2 in the 1951 tournament, losing to Farrell and two-time tournament Most Valuable Player Julius McCoy by 20 and to Swoyersville by 6. Farrell would pound Ford City by 33 in the championship game and then in March 1952 win the Class A state championship. By December 1952, Farrell had started its own four-team holiday tournament aimed at bringing elite teams to the Shenango Valley. The Steelers took Johnstown's winning concept and adopted it for themselves.

In 1952, Johnstown's local teams needed to bounce back in the Cambria County Johnstown War Memorial Invitational Basketball Tournament with a strong showing. The rising Johnstown High varsity squad held promise. "In junior high," said forward Carl Sax, "we went undefeated. I think we did in junior varsity, too."

These were the boys whom tournament organizers had seen playing on summer playgrounds in Johnstown and in Westmont. Expectations for the local teams were high without a powerhouse like Farrell in the mix. Johnstown returned plenty of height after an 18-4 campaign. Farrell neighbor Sharon High faced the Trojans on opening night. Those two teams and Greensburg High entered the tournament undefeated, while Old Forge had one loss from opening night when some of its players were trickling in from a stellar football campaign.

Against Sharon, Johnstown thwarted a third-quarter rally that saw the Tigers tie the game at 40. The Trojans regrouped with an 18–9 final quarter for a 58–49 victory. That against a team the *Scrantonian Tribune* had anointed as a likely state finalist candidate. Johnstown's center Jack Keelan scored 14 points, Jerry Lashley 13.[13]

"Coach Paul Abele worked the daylights out of you," said Johnstown's Sax. "Our job was to get the ball inside to the big guys" in the three-out, two-in offense.

When Greensburg edged Old Forge 61–58, the final was set. The 1952 championship game remained close throughout, with Greensburg's Jack Kalbfus scoring a game-high 30 points. Kalbfus would eventually team up with Johnstown's Paul Schmidt at Duke University. Johnstown countered with Dave Niel's 20 and Lou Robson's 12. The Trojan's 9-point edge in the even quarters gave them a 57–51 victory. The home fans exulted at seeing their boys become champions.[14]

It would take local baseball teams nearly three quarters of a century to win the AAABA baseball tournament title at Point Stadium. Basketball, playing against a much smaller field, recorded a title inside of two years for the Catholic school and inside of four years for the public school. Johnstown High's basketball team remained undefeated through its first 27 games. In the Pennsylvania Interscholastic Athletic Association (PIAA) western semifinal, the Trojans met that same Sharon squad (21-3) that had been predicted to reach the state final. The *Pittsburgh Post-Gazette* preview story suggested that the survivor would likely win the state title.[15] A furious Johnstown rally late cut an 11-point deficit to 2, but Sharon prevailed 42–40. The Tigers then won the western final game before losing in the state final to Yeadon High.

JOHNSTOWN GRADUATED MOST OF its talent heading into 1953–54. But that young cohort that had registered unbeaten seasons growing up had the talent to make another run. In the opening game of the tournament, six-foot-five center Paul Schmidt scored a game-high 20 points. New Kensington from Western Pennsylvania actually led 37–35 entering the fourth quarter. The Trojans closed with a 20–12 spurt to finish off a 55–49 victory. The homeboys were heading back to the championship game. In the other opening game, powerful, quick Chester High from Delaware County outlasted New Castle 60–54 behind Marty Miller's 22 points. In the final, Johnstown edged Chester by 2 to become the tournament's first repeat champion. If competition was the goal of tournament organizers, they found it in 1953. No game was decided by more than 6 points, the average margin being 4.

With Johnstown securing consecutive titles, tournament organizers hoped to make an even bigger splash when it dipped into a Philadelphia basketball hotbed for the biggest individual catch in the tournament's history in 1954.

THE DIPPER

Voted as the outstanding player in the Sixth Annual Tournament and the Invitational's top star ever, 7'2" Wilt Chamberlain is most everyone's choice as the greatest prospect alive.
—caption under the photo of Chamberlain on the cover of the seventh annual Johnstown Tournament program

By the time Wilt Chamberlain flew west to Pittsburgh to compete in the renowned Farrell High and Johnstown basketball tournaments in December 1954, he was already a national name. He was seven-foot-one, coordinated and competitive in an era when six-foot-five players were deemed abnormally tall.

Luring the great Wilt Chamberlain to compete in Johnstown was tantamount to landing the hot couple of 1954—the Yankees' Joe DiMaggio and pinup queen Marilyn Monroe—to chaperone prom. You didn't, by chance, come across A-list pop icons in the Flood City.

Chamberlain's Overbrook High team had won all but two games his sophomore year in 1952–53, claiming the Public League title but losing to West Catholic in the city title game. Chamberlain's junior year, the Panthers went undefeated, easily winning both the Public League and city championships. Wilt scored a combined 103 points in three postseason games. He was bigger in every way.

Chamberlain entered his senior season of 1954–55 regaled as the most highly prized college recruit in America, probably in the brief history of high school basketball. Another undefeated season in his senior year seemed

Wilt Chamberlain. *1955 Johnstown Tournament program.*

likely. Johnstown Tournament organizers as well as the Farrell Tournament Committee both signed Overbrook to play over the Christmas break. The Philadelphia Athletic Council signed off too. Unfortunately, its members thought they were agreeing to one tournament, not two. They didn't want their athletes playing in two consecutive tournaments that would require days of games with no break. Upon realizing their mistaken consent, the council withdrew support.[16]

Wanting Wilt Chamberlain's presence at any cost, Farrell and Johnstown adjusted their tournaments to place Overbrook automatically into their finals (on December 28 and December 30, respectively), forgoing the Panthers' need to play semifinal games. In Johnstown's case, that meant telling Meadville High that it was no longer in the tournament. Meadville became a casualty of Wilt. The adjusted formats resulted in a one-day break between the two tournament "championships" for Overbrook.

The Panthers were on a 26-game winning streak coming into the Farrell Tournament. Farrell (8-0) sported a 22-game winning streak overall and 75 straight at home. The Steelers had played in state championships in 1951, 1952 and 1954, winning the latter two.

In the Farrell Tournament, available today on low-res video via YouTube, Overbrook fails to get Chamberlain the ball late with the game on the line after Farrell's Paul Gustus hit two free throws to give them a 59–56 lead.[17] Overbrook tips in a rebound to pull within one and then gets the ball back, but a thirty-five-footer rims out in the final seconds.

Chamberlain is everywhere in the video. It shows Overbrook attacking Farrell's full-court press by inbounding the ball to him at the foul line with Farrell's six-foot-five center, Don Jones, playing behind him. Farrell then forces Chamberlain to dribble the ball up court himself. The biggest controversy came in the first half when Chamberlain picked up three fouls, and—as the story goes—Farrell representatives told the referees not to foul out the giant. McCluskey didn't want excuses for why Farrell had beaten the Philadelphia Public League power if it happened. Such disputations could taint an otherwise colossal victory.

Nonetheless, Chamberlain and his Panther teammates felt like victims of hometown refereeing. Yes, Wilt scored thirty-three points, more than half of his team's total. But that wasn't outrageously more than Farrell star Jim McCoy's nineteen points. McCoy was the younger brother of two-time Johnstown MVP Julius McCoy. Don Jones—who had transferred into Farrell from Indiana High in Pennsylvania despite his parents and younger sibling remaining behind—scored twelve.

In the opening matchup of the Johnstown Tournament for the right to face Overbrook in the finals, McKeesport High trailed Johnstown by 8 at halftime. The Tigers exploded for 27 third-quarter points and cruised to a 71–54 victory, earning the right to face Chamberlain.

Basketball and football were embedded into McKeesport culture, as children of the local steel mill workers aspired to greatness. Enough McKeesport alumni went on to play professional football to start their own squad. In 2024, the PA Football History website tabulated that among all Pennsylvania high schools, McKeesport had the most players drafted into the National Football League with twenty-two (Johnstown tied for third with Uniontown at sixteen).[18]

The Tigers basketball program in the 1950s funneled players to college programs under the direction of Coach Cornelius "Neenie" Campbell, who cut players good enough to make college rosters because the Tigers were stacked with so many talented athletes. Prior to coming to McKeesport, Campbell had won sectional titles at Ford City High. That program produced basketball notable Zigmund "Red" Mihalik, a future referee who would work Olympic Games and make the Naismith Basketball Hall of Fame. Campbell was another of those multitalented Renaissance men like Charles Kunkle. He boxed professionally, played baseball in the minor leagues and played high school football well enough to be recruited by Pitt when they were the best program in America. As an adult basketball player, Campbell barnstormed through Ohio and Pennsylvania with the likes of Jim Thorpe. So highly did the sports world think of Campbell that he was offered the head basketball coaching position at Clemson University.

"He was offered and accepted the Clemson basketball coaching job before turning it down after a week because of personal family issues," said former McKeesport High guard Lanny Van Eman.[19] "He then had to recommend Press Maravich to Clemson's athletic director and football coach Frank Howard as a substitute. Howard had already recruited a bevy of McKeesport football players and decided that he might also develop a pipeline with basketball as well. Campbell's legacy is amazing."

Campbell's 1954–55 McKeesport basketball team opened with a win over Johnstown as Stu Heller and Gene Danko each scored seventeen points. The strong performance earned Danko the opportunity to participate in a television publicity shot with Chamberlain before the championship game. McKeesport had already suffered a loss earlier in the season to Farrell, so Campbell knew by comparison what he was facing in Overbrook.

When the six-foot-two Danko arrived for the television interview, the producers took him and Chamberlain to a hill for a majestic vantage point. The stars formally introduced themselves to each other.

"Hi, Wilt, it's really great to meet you," Danko said.[20]

"I can tell you right now I'm gonna like you," Chamberlain said. "You're the first person on this trip who didn't call me 'Wilt the Stilt.'" Chamberlain hated that moniker. "Wilt" was fine. "The Big Dipper" was fine. "Dip" or "Dippy" was passable. But "Wilt the Stilt" rang out like he was some vaudeville act or a promotion espoused by a circus ringmaster—*Step right up and see the giant who walks on stilts!*

The seven-foot-one phenom would jump center against the six-foot-six Stu Heller. The pressure was all on Chamberlain and Overbrook after losing to Farrell. They certainly didn't venture 350 miles west to go 0-2. What would that do to Chamberlain's celebrity? Two months later, he would be featured with other seven-footers in national *Life* magazine, the issue with Princess Margaret on the cover. The basketball article begins on page 59 with the headline, "The Giants of Schoolboy Basketball."[21] Chamberlain and seven other "giants" are photographed reaching high with two hands, clutching the net together at the bottom so the basketball inside it can't slip through. Another shot shows Chamberlain dunking in a game in which he scored forty-four points. Giants don't go 0-2 in in-state Christmas tournaments. Chamberlain and Overbrook coach Cecil Mosenson *needed* to beat McKeesport.

Wilt played like his reputation was on the line as a record 3,819 people watched in awe. Wilt was magnificent, prodigious, setting the tournament record with forty-six points to go with his thirty rebounds.[22] The extra boards allowed the Panthers to attempt a whopping seventy shots. Even his teammates were impressed.

"Dippy," teammate and two-handed set shooter Doug Leaman said, "he's my idol. He was a natural. He had a sixth sense."[23]

Overbrook, who also had future NBA player and six-foot-five forward Vince Miller, had built a six-point lead by halftime. And yet, late in the game, McKeesport rallied to take its own six-point lead. It didn't take a clairvoyant to know that Chamberlain needed to rescue the Panthers. He scored a few baskets, uncharacteristically drained a few underhand free throws and positioned Overbrook for the win.

McKeesport misses also contributed to the Panther comeback. "We were ahead by 4 or 5 and missed 5 of our last 6 free throws," said Van Eman, an underclassman then. Overbrook coach Cecil Mosenson, in his early twenties, would ride his early success to author the book *It All Began with Wilt*.[24] He claimed that Wilt's legend, his competitive dominance, began in Johnstown. Trailing McKeesport by four late, with under two minutes remaining, the dominant Wilt emerged. Coach Mosenson shared this recollection:

> *During the last 1:10 seconds of the game with the jammed field house in a complete uproar, the teams scored a total of 19 points, and somehow Wilt broke loose to score 10 of them. We took the lead with twenty seconds left and went on to win 75–74. He scored forty-six points and played with courage when we needed him. I have always thought of that game as the high point of Wilt's career. His tremendous competitive spirit and greatness under pressure came of age that night. It was a pleasure to be his coach—most of the time.*

The irony is that Chamberlain's lifelong kryptonite—free-throw shooting—was the skill he used to overcome McKeesport. For Van Eman, who would become a star player in the coming years, he was seeing his future. He would go on to coach in college and in the NBA, including on the Boston Celtics staff in the 1980s. The giant monster Wilt Chamberlain whom he was watching in Johnstown would dominate the NBA soon enough.

Wilt's NBA career finished spectacularly, his numbers far beyond what the best of his day or after his career could muster. He posted more fifty-point games than any NBA player—by more than triple! His 118 dwarfs the total of second-place Michael Jordan, who did it 31 times.

McKeesport would have to regroup following the disappointing loss to Overbrook. They'd lose only one more game the rest of the season. In the PIAA state playoffs, the Tigers would dispatch Johnstown and Pittsburgh South by the same 76–54 score. In the state final, they'd meet another eastern power in Chester on a twenty-six-game winning streak. State runners-up in 1954, Chester had opened the season with a loss and arrived at the state championship at the Penn Palestra without any other defeats. By virtue of its losses to Farrell, Overbrook and Washington High, McKeesport had three setbacks. Having already played for a championship in Johnstown, the Tigers' players felt big-game tested.

"For me and for many of our players, we'd never been in a hotel before Johnstown," Van Eman said. "All of our high school basketball was pretty local. I bet that was the same with Overbrook. That they felt like they were traveling. I do remember being in a hotel. When we went and played in the

VICTORY SMILES

McKeesport High celebrates a 1955 title. *Courtesy of Lanny Van Eman.*

state championship, the hotel we stayed in was in Philadelphia. That was the first time I'd ever flown in an airplane."

McKeesport's two post players who had been assigned to bracket Chamberlain back in December—six-foot-six Stu Heller and six-foot-four tough guy Tom Markovich—scored 19 and 15 points, respectively, in the 54–48 victory over Chester. It clinched McKeesport's first state title since 1921, when the Tigers defeated Williamsport 24–21 for the second ever state title in Pennsylvania history.

McKeesport coach Cornelius "Neenie" Campbell, who schemed the 1955 state championship, had played on the 1924 Homestead High team that won the state title over Nanticoke, 32–21. That single-class final was held at Penn State in State College, where the teams were housed in dormitories. Johnstown and Philadelphia hotels were a huge upgrade in 1954–55.

"The Johnstown Invitational Tournament is the last word in basketball," Campbell wrote in a tournament program article. "It is by far the best tournament of them all….My players will never forget the thrill of playing against the best teams in the [s]tate. Much of the credit for McKeesport's winning the state title in 1955 must go to the experience gained in [the] Johnstown tournament."

After McKeesport clinched the state title, the team flew once again, this time back to the Pittsburgh Airport to be feted by one thousand exuberant fans. First hotel, first flight, second state title.

Chamberlain and Overbrook weren't eligible to compete for a state title. Philadelphia Public League schools like Overbrook were kept separate until 2004. The Public League title and then the city title against the Catholic League champs were as far as they could go. When Overbrook won its second-straight city title in 1955, Wilt finished with 35 points, and his childhood best friend, Vince Miller, had 31. Overbrook annihilated West Catholic 83–42. Wilt set what Overbrook believed to be the state scoring record with 2,252 points despite playing just three varsity seasons. Two weeks later, Wampum High's Don Hennon would reset the mark at 2,376 after a 31-0 state championship season in Class B.

In his high school career, Chamberlain lost only three games. In his final two seasons, the only loss came against Farrell—and nearly McKeesport. How good was Pennsylvania high school basketball in the middle 1950s? Consider that Cecil Mosenson took his Overbrook team to scrimmage the Villanova University varsity team over six quarters. "We did very well against them," he told Will Mega TV in a YouTube clip.[25] "I don't want to embarrass Villanova, but we had a great scrimmage, and they were excited to meet Wilt."

In one three-game stretch his senior year, Wilt flexed his dominance. He scored 74, 78 and 90 points, setting the stage for that historic night on March 2, 1962, when he would score an unprecedented and since unmatched 100 points in an NBA game in Hershey, Pennsylvania—150 miles from Johnstown—for the Philadelphia Warriors. For Johnstown fans, the star-studded standard for their tournament will always be Wilt's 46 points and 30 rebounds in December 1954.

MCKEESPORT'S GENE DANKO WOULD encounter Wilt a few times in his life. One summer, the two players (along with Overbrook's Vince Miller) went to the Catskills in New York State to work at Kutsher's Resort and play night basketball with college and NBA coaches in attendance.

"We would play each other every day," said Danko. "There was a Borscht Belt League because all these country clubs were all Jewish people, and that's why they called it that. I was on Wilt's team. Red Auerbach was his coach. That was our team. We played Grossinger's and places like that. Wilt was a nice person. He was a bellhop, and I was a waiter. The only time I would see him was when we played basketball. The last time I saw him was at a Charlotte, North Carolina airport about a month before he died. [My family and I] went to a Pitt basketball game in the NCAA

Tournament. All of a sudden I hear this voice: 'Hey, Gene! Hey, Gene! My friend Gene!'"

It was Wilt. The friends had met on a hillside in Johnstown, on the court at War Memorial in a classic game, on outdoor courts in the Catskills and in an airport in North Carolina. Their paths—and the history of basketball—sporadically intertwined.

Danko's McKeesport teammate Tom Markovich,[26] who helped guard Chamberlain in Johnstown despite being six-foot-four, nearly faced Chamberlain with the 1957 NCAA title on the line. Markovich's Michigan State Spartans team reached the Final Four, where they met North Carolina. The Tar Heels defeated the Spartans 74–70 in three overtimes. Had the Spartans won, they would have faced Chamberlain's Kansas Jayhawks in the national championship. Markovich did not get court time in the Final Four games. But that same North Carolina team went three overtimes again to top Chamberlain and Kansas and prevent Wilt from winning a national title, one of the lingering regrets of his life.

McKeesport coach Neenie Campbell would win twenty sectional titles at Homestead and McKeesport—ten at each school—in thirty-eight seasons. He won a few more before Homestead at Ford City. Toward the end of his coaching career, Campbell had begun his next adventure coaching McKeesport Serra Catholic in 1968. He was driving to a game at the Connellsville Geibel Holiday Tournament. Campbell began to suffer chest pains, pulled over and died of a heart attack on the way to the game, which Serra Catholic would lose to Mount Pleasant, 71–69. Serra Catholic did not play the next day. Campbell was sixty-two.

When Red Mihalik gave his induction speech into the Naismith Basketball Hall of Fame in 1978,[27] he twice admonished those driving home after the ceremony to be careful, saying he'd be holding a rosary and hoping for their safety. You'd have to think that was a result of losing one of his former high school coaches on a highway. Ford City High named its gym after Mihalik, just like McKeesport had named its gym after Campbell. Ford City has a third special connection to the history of basketball that appears on the borough website.

In 1886, Ford City submitted and received its charter from the Commonwealth of Pennsylvania. One of the men who delivered the original charter to Harrisburg was Robert Naismith, basketball inventor James Naismith's brother. Previously part of Manor Township, Ford City Borough became one of the fastest-growing boroughs in the United States, gaining over three thousand in population in only ten years.[28]

Chamberlain forever held Johnstown in high regard, as seen in this letter to Johnstown Tournament officials, from tournament archives:

University of Kansas
1246 W. Campus Rd.
Lawrence, Kansas
December 4, 1956

Dear Sir,

It was indeed a pleasure hearing from you, and I feel it gives me great pleasure to relate to you my feelings on that wonderful Holiday Tournament.
I believe the game in which our high school played at Johnstown, in the Holiday Tournament of Dec. 24 [actually December 30], *1954, was the most exciting game in my high school career. I also believe it is a tournament of this nature that helps give young men the incentive to play a clean great sport like basketball.*

Yours in sports,
Wilt Chamberlain

The letter was a thank-you note to tournament director Clayt Dovey.

THE CLIPPERS

Chester is the oldest town in Pennsylvania. It dates back to William Penn's visit in 1682.

The industrial city that produced cars to navigate the highways and ships to travel the Atlantic Ocean became too big too fast. Around 1900, the town boasted about thirty-four thousand residents. By 1950, with Chester at its peak, that number had nearly doubled to more than sixty-six thousand. "Chester was known as a freewheeling destination for vices such as drugs, alcohol, numbers rackets, gambling and prostitution. Chester was widely known as Greater Philadelphia's 'Saloon Town,'" according to Wikipedia. Chester routinely ranks as one of the most violent cities in Pennsylvania, as well as in the United States. In 2020, Chester was ranked twentieth among the most violent American cities.[29]

Chester also produced great men and leaders. Martin Luther King Jr. attended Crozer Theological Seminary there, where he developed his peaceful means of social justice. "It was here that Martin Luther King strengthened his commitment to the Christian social gospel and ideas about nonviolence as a method of social reform which later played a huge role in his fight for equality," wrote Alana Winkler in an article titled "Crozer Theological Seminary."[30] From 1948 to 1951, King studied in Chester, becoming the valedictorian for the class of 1951. King broke away from his father's firebrand preaching and found his own niche, a softer, more mellifluous delivery that rose to the mountaintops in his "I Have a Dream" speech. The natives of Chester, nonetheless, haven't always adhered to King's nonviolent approach.

When Pennsylvanians think of Chester today, they often think of its community pride in the great basketball teams and the inherent dangers of the city. One of the famous cheers performed by the spirited dancing, stomping, split-finishing Chester cheerleaders flowed like this: "You made a baaaaddddd mistake, you messed with Chester!"

The line admonished teams foolish enough to challenge Chester's litany of talented basketball players and teams, but it could have applied to everything else that went down when the sun went down. Chester High basketball was the welcome diversion. Tryouts pitted nearly three hundred boys against each other for twenty-four varsity and junior varsity roster spots. In December 1953, the survivors of that Bataan-style tryout would travel to remote Johnstown in the tournament's fifth year. On opening night, the Clippers defeated New Castle from suburban Pittsburgh by 6 to reach the final against the hometown Johnstown Trojans. Johnstown locals filled the arena, while Chester might have had a dozen fans or so on hand to shout support and witness Marty Miller scoring 22 points. The game was twice tied in the final minute before George Hanna's heroics lifted Johnstown to a 48–46 victory. Hanna had messed with Chester—scoring a basket and two free throws in the final twenty-five seconds—and won.

Chester natives, nonetheless, treated their boys to a hearty welcome home, the near-conquering heroes showing well in an elite basketball tournament far from home. The team received a fire engine escort. By season's end in March 1954, the Clippers were playing in their first state championship game, losing by six to the great Farrell program.

"We put Chester on the map," said guard Benny Walker. "We had gone the furthest, going to a state championship game in 1954. That was the first time we ever went there. And we lost a close game in the championship at Johnstown."[31]

In March 1955, Chester would return to the Pennsylvania state championship game. They'd lose to McKeesport. Chester led in the fourth quarter until McKeesport stormed ahead in the final three minutes to steal the crown before nine thousand fans. "I thought we were in good shape four points ahead with only four minutes left," said Chester coach Bob Forwood, "but then some crucial rebounds got away from us, and that was the game."[32]

John Laszek scored eighteen points and Horace Walker fifteen for Chester. Stu Heller scored nineteen points in what Coach Cornelius "Neenie" Campbell called his "greatest game." Campbell became what many believed to be the third Pennsylvania baller to win a state title as a player and as a coach.

Walter Mangham poster. *Photo by Thomas Slusser,* Johnstown Tribune-Democrat.

NINE MONTHS AFTER FINISHING second in the PIAA playoffs, in December 1955, Chester returned to Johnstown with another talented group led by six-foot-three scorer Horace Walker, Benny's younger brother and an all-state talent who would later become Chester's first All-American at Michigan State University. On opening night, Walker matched up with New Castle High's six-foot-three leaper Walter Mangham, who had set a national interscholastic high jump record at six feet, nine and three-fourths inches. Mangham had averaged 22 points a night as a junior. Both teams were undefeated. The Clippers raced to a 20–8 second-quarter lead.

Horace Walker finished the game with 18 points and 24 rebounds in an impressive victory.

Bo Ryan, who was a boy living in Chester then, dreamed of becoming a Clipper. His father and youth coach, Butch Ryan, would sneak him into playoff games—state playoff games, even at the Palestra—just to see Chester's latest squad. Ryan remembers Horace Walker as being "smooth and cerebral, somebody who just flowed."[33]

Chester had entered the season favored both to win in Johnstown and to capture the PIAA state title that March. The Clippers nearly doubled the host Trojans (29–15) in the first half, but Johnstown and the cacophony of its awakened fans elevated in the third quarter. Chester's inspired defense held George Hanna to 10 points. Moreover, whenever a shot went up and failed to flirt with the net, Horace Walker went up and snatched it into submission. His 32 rebounds surpassed Wilt Chamberlain's tournament record of 30. Walker also scored 14 points. Teammate Gerry Gilbert scored 18 points and grabbed 11 more rebounds in the Clippers' 49–45 victory. The 3,500 fans had witnessed the Clippers' coming out party. Another parade back to Chester would signal to locals that the conquering heroes had completed the mission. This time, Walker was named tournament Most Valuable Player. Coach Forwood and his boys celebrated a rare title, even if it was only a four-team December invitational.

Chester would lose in the state final again in 1957 to Sharon. Overall, the Clippers would lose their first *seven* PIAA state championship games. They were somehow cursed, confined to a purgatory of runner-up finishes and big-game heartache—before finally breaking through in 1983. In 1954, 1955, 1957, 1959, 1966, 1967 and 1972, the Clippers finished one game short of a state title. As for the Johnstown Tournament, Chester would split two games in 1957 and drop both in 1960. When they finally returned to War Memorial Arena again in 1972, they would reach the championship game against Johnstown. Again.

After Chester's loss in the 1959 state final, the Clippers would not make the PIAA playoffs again until 1965. This was during a decade when Chester produced some of its greatest legends. The all-state lineage went from Horace Walker in the middle 1950s to Jerry "Chubby" Foster in 1958, Granny Lash in 1959 and Emerson Baynard in 1960–61. Lash was voted the ninth-best player in America in high school by *Dell* magazine before his careers at the University of Utah and with the Harlem Globetrotters. Baynard might have been even more talented. According to sportswriter Rich Pagano with the *Spirit* (www.myspiritnews.com), "Baynard became a member of the 1,000-point club and broke six [Delaware County] all-time county records: most points in one game (60); best average in one season (32); most field goals in one season (261); most field goals in a career (615); most points by a freshman (205); and most points by a sophomore (516)."[34]

Pagano noted that the night Baynard scored 60 points in Chester's gym, he went to the bench completely exhausted to the roar and respect of the Clipper fans. Baynard's average of 32 points per game eclipsed Foster's 30.5 average. After high school and a brief junior college stint, Baynard played in the Eastern Professional Basketball League, starting in 1962–63. He earned unanimous Rookie of the Year honors after averaging nearly 22 points and 10 rebounds per game against men—transitioning from high school senior to EBL rookie sensation playing against professionals. Just four years earlier, Farrell High legend Julius McCoy—another Johnstown Tournament alumnus and a two-time tournament MVP—had won the EBL Rookie of the Year award, but only after a stellar career at Michigan State. That's the company in which Baynard found himself.

Baynard's basketball teammate at Chester High in 1960–61 had even more impressive credentials…on the baseball field. Lew Krausse Jr., son of a former major-league pitcher, tore up the local baseball circuit with a plethora of no-hitters. After he graduated in 1961, Krausse Jr. signed a contract for $125,000 with the Kansas City Athletics. This was one year after Wampum High slugger Dick Allen—a veteran of the Johnstown Tournament himself—had signed his first contract with the Phillies for $70,000.[35]

Krausse and the Clippers lost to Johnstown on opening night of the 1960 tournament, 52–51. In the consolation game, Nanticoke downed Chester, sending the Clippers home without a win. On the same sports page, another headline lauded Chester native Danny Murtaugh for being named National League Manager of the Year for the Pittsburgh Pirates. In two tournament games, Baynard and Krausse Jr. combined for forty-eight points, with Baynard getting forty-seven of them to win tournament MVP honors. The game saw Nanticoke shoot twice as many free throws as Chester. Mike Sudler of Chester was the victim of the most vicious foul. He "slammed into the stands and was sprawled out on the floor for more than five minutes, awaiting the arrival of a doctor and stretcher. Sudler was carried to the arena's first-aid station where a thorough examination was made. The prognosis: a cramp in the hip."[36]

Two weeks after graduation, Krausse Jr. took the mound in Kansas City to make his first major-league start against the expansion Los Angeles

Angels. He matched his father, who also had reached the major leagues as an eighteen-year-old. Krausse Jr. was instantly masterful, tossing a nine-inning, three-hit shutout before 25,869 fans. One of the hits he surrendered came off the bat of Nanticoke High legend Steve Bilko. Krausse walked five and struck out six, igniting a twelve-year career.[37]

IN 1962, CHESTER LOOKED to Johnstown High—this time to hire its next basketball coach. Ron Rainey, a member of those great 1950s Trojan teams that had played in the Johnstown Tournament, was hired to succeed Bob Forwood. In 1953, Rainey had scored 5 points in Johnstown's 48–46 tournament championship victory over Chester. Now he'd try to make Chester into state champions. One of his young ball-handlers was a feisty scholar named Bo Ryan. In 1965, Ryan helped Chester to a 24-0 start. In the opening round of the state tournament—back at the Penn Palestra—they faced a Steelton-Highspire squad led by future Michigan Wolverine Dennis Stewart. The Rollers had just polished off two other unbeaten teams in the District 3 playoffs and were looking to do it again. Stewart tallied 39 points. The Rollers won 84–82 in overtime.

"He has to be the best in the state," Rainey told *Lancaster New Era* scribe Bill Fisher about Stewart. "We made five different defensive changes, but nothing stopped him. I didn't think it was possible he could hurt us that much."[38]

Ryan and his teammates broke down in the locker room after losing, an ode to disappointing their beloved city. *Delco Daily Times* scribe Rich Wescott described the gym as "a tomb of tragedy, sealed by a kid named Dennis Stewart." Rainey wondered out loud, *What had gone wrong? What lesson could be culled?* "All that work," Rainey vented. "What good was it? You beat your brains out and look what happens. Five months of work."[39]

For Ryan, it was a lifetime of work, a lifetime of watching Chester High fall just short. What hurt even more was that Steelton-Highspire went on to win the eastern final by 21 points against one-loss Mahanoy Area despite Stewart missing considerable time due to foul trouble. Surely Chester would have beaten Mahanoy Area. In the state final, the Rollers faced yet another unbeaten team. Midland High was 27-0, which meant that Steelton-Highspire's last five opponents had a combined one loss! The Rollers, however, were drummed by one of Pennsylvania's finest teams ever, a Midland High squad featuring Simmie Hill and Norm Van Lier, 90–61. Chester likely would not have beaten Midland either. Hill and Van Lier both would get drafted into the NBA by the Chicago Bulls, with Van Lier spending a decade in the league.

Maybe Chester's loss to Steel-High was preordained. Rollers coach Marty Benkovic and Midland coach Hank Kuzma had grown up on the same street in Steelton as kids. The state final matchup was decades in the making, a shared dream from the same block in the same steel town neighborhood.

When Bo Ryan graduated as Chester's class president later that spring, he became what some believe to be the last white player to start for a Clipper squad. When Coach Rainey left town to take the Wilkes University coaching job, Ryan and teammate Reuben Daniels went with him to play for the Colonels. Ryan would notch the Wilkes home court scoring record by a Division III player with forty-three points against Susquehanna. If nothing else, Chester's reputation as a basketball mecca was secure.

From 1976 to 1985, Ron Rainey coached the University of Delaware basketball team. Ryan went into coaching too, where he'd win four Division III national titles at Wisconsin-Platteville in the 1990s. Eventually, Ryan brought Rainey to Wisconsin to assist him in three of the four D-III national titles. Ryan also nearly won a Division I title with the University of Wisconsin in 2015, falling to Duke in the national championship game, 68–63. To reach that national final, Wisconsin first had to beat John Calipari's 38-0 Kentucky squad. For all of his impressive accomplishments, Ryan took all of Chester with him in his heart to the Naismith Memorial Basketball Hall of Fame in 2024.

In 1983, the Chester Clippers finally made it through a state bracket victorious, topping McKeesport 82–66. Since 1983, Chester has claimed seven more state titles in basketball: 1989, 1994, 2000, 2005, 2008, 2011 and 2012. They lost in three other finals (2003, 2007 and 2013). The orange and black has become a statewide attraction.

GO BACK TO CHESTER in the mid-1960s. Young Bo Ryan works his way up to being a varsity point guard. When he chooses his uniform number, he opts for No. 42—the same number his hero, Emerson Baynard, wore for the Clippers. The same number color barrier–breaker Jackie Robinson wore for the Brooklyn Dodgers in Major League Baseball. One generation follows the previous one in Chester and tries to make it proud.

Jump ahead to the twenty-first century. Chester-area author John Jack Lemon interviews Ryan for a book about Clipper great Emerson Baynard.

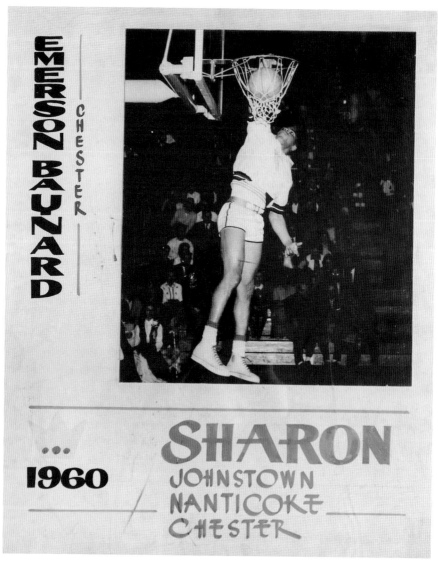

Emerson Baynard poster. *Photo by Thomas Slusser,* Johnstown Tribune-Democrat.

He tells Ryan where Baynard is buried at Haven Memorial Cemetery, as Ryan couldn't locate Baynard's grave without precise directions.

"They tell me there's nothing saying 'Emerson Baynard is buried here,'" Ryan said, incredulous. "They tell me there are no markings. His body is just buried in a plot in the ground. No headstone of any kind. That's no way for a human life to be buried."

Horace Walker poster. *Photo by Thomas Slusser,* Johnstown Tribune-Democrat.

Ryan, local historian Jim Vankoski, Lemon and a committee of Chester alumni collaborated to raise the money to give Baynard a respectful sendoff, a marker denoting the value of a human life. Ryan advised the Chester locals to raise what they could; he would match that amount with his own money. Ryan stepped up as a leader to right a wrong, befitting a class president and former captain of the football, basketball and baseball teams. It could

Bo Ryan walks on the campus at Chester in high school. *Courtesy of Bo Ryan.*

have been anybody in the ground, but it was Emerson Baynard. His name would be etched once more for posterity. The younger Clipper making the older one proud, as is always the case in this tight-knit town. And most appropriately, Baynard and Horace Walker are buried an overhead outlet pass away from each other.

SCOUTING PAYNE

Johnstown organizers, mostly Clayton Dovey in the early years, scouted All-American players and elite teams a year ahead before extending tournament invitations. The committee wanted teams that might wind up playing for state titles in March, three months after visiting Johnstown, teams that were strong the year they were being scouted, with several players returning for the following season. Or marquee players who might wind up playing big-time basketball and, perhaps, make it to the NBA. So their mission, as with all talent scouts, was projection.

Like a high school sophomore on the hunt for a serious girlfriend, you wanted someone who looked good now, but you also had to project how they might look in a year or two. In that critical, judgmental vein, organizers knew that Farrell High fit the bill. The Steelers were working on an epic home winning streak. Heck, everybody knew that. They were a great team today, but the Steelers could turn into an epic selection with time.

Life magazine, a national weekly, was casting projections of its own, similar to those made by Johnstown Tournament organizers. *Life* writers and photographers were planning on visiting Farrell, near Pittsburgh, to feature Ed McCluskey's Steelers in its pages. As a program, Farrell already looked enticing, having upset Wilt Chamberlain's Overbrook squad by one point when the Panthers visited in 1954. Farrell would look prom queen pretty once it hit the century mark for consecutive home wins. Should they falter, *Life* generated a backup plan, as gentlemen suitors must. They would visit Wampum High and its tiny dynasty, where Coach L. Butler Hennon used out-of-the-box training methods to develop championship teams. In March 1955, the Indians capped a 31-0 state championship season with Hennon's five-foot-ten son, Don, establishing a new state record for career points, topping even Wilt Chamberlain's three-year total.

"That created a lot of interest in 1955," Hennon remembered. "Each Tuesday and Friday the TV stations would report his points and mine for a comparison of the race."[40]

In 1958, Hennon and Chamberlain would both be first-team NCAA All-Americans at Pitt and Kansas, respectively, along with Guy Rodgers, Bob Boozer, Elgin Baylor and Oscar Robertson.

The projections for the 1956 Johnstown Tournament wouldn't include Farrell since the Steelers had broken away to host their own December invitational that continues to this day. But another local power, Altoona, returned a strong team. Organizers were gifted a lucky clover when Altoona upset Farrell, ending the Steelers' home winning streak at ninety-nine games. Jim Swanner paced Altoona with 25 points, making each of his lucky 13 free throws in a 57–56 stunner. Altoona's six-foot-eight center Jim Ingram added 20 points.[41] Both players would compete at War Memorial Arena in the 1956 Johnstown Tournament.

After Farrell failed in its bid to win one hundred straight home games, *Life* settled on featuring Wampum's program with a pictorial spread of its innovative drills that would be adopted by the Soviet Union's national team. Don Hennon's father and coach, L. Butler Hennon, was decades ahead of his time. He would win three state titles at a tiny school near Beaver Falls.

Charleroi High, a school atop a hill along the Monongahela River near Pittsburgh, would open against Johnstown. Charleroi was situated near athletic royalty, including Joe Montana's Ringgold High (formerly Monongahela High) as well as the Donora High of Stan Musial, Ken Griffey Sr. and former Army quarterback Arnold Galiffa fame in the Monongahela or "Mon" Valley. Charleroi's rival, Monessen High, had lost in the 1923 state final. Between 1919 and 1959, Monessen High won twenty Mon Valley basketball titles. Charleroi was second with thirteen. Donora earned three.[42]

The Mon Valley was a steel-tough region where football made boys into warriors who became responsible men. Basketball rated second among Western Pennsylvania sports. Fathers and World War II veterans coached these boys with a stern hand and a furrowed brow but nary a compliment.

"My father never told me he was proud of me," said Charleroi High's All-State player Jim "Mouse" Chacko. "He never told me, 'Good job!' Not once. I don't even remember him smiling back then. That's how all the coaches were back then. You accepted it. That's how they were raised. They had survived through the Depression and a world war. I guess they always knew that life could go back to being bad."[43]

These were families who worked in the Earth's-core heat of the Monessen steel plants that ran along the Monongahela River the length of Monessen—three hundred acres—or in Pages Wire Mill, which sat on what today is called "Josh Gibson Way." If George "Beans" Chacko needed a reminder of tough times, he could see the Negro League teams playing in town, watching Hall of Famers forced to compete on the fringe rather than in huge ballparks, legends like slugger Josh Gibson and hurler Satchell Paige.

Beans coached Charleroi's youth teams, the junior high contingent, where he stressed fundamentals. Beans Chacko had been a noted athlete in his day. As a reserve on the 1926 Charleroi basketball squad, he had helped his team win the school's first sectional title. He tried out for the Cubs in baseball but opted to attend Duquesne University to play football for one of the famed Four Horsemen, Notre Dame alumnus Elmer Layden. After college, the iron-forged defensive back did what many did in that era—he returned home to raise a family and coach the next generation of athletes. Chacko would project the athletic potential of neighborhood boys and set about sharpening their talents.

"In junior high, we won 95 in a row at home," Beans' boy Jim "Mouse" Chacko said. "He had 355 wins and 58 losses overall. We won several Western Pennsylvania Interscholastic Athletic League (WPIAL) championships. We won the last one, and they cut [the junior high playoffs] out after that because they thought it was too much pressure on ninth graders and below. The next year we went 22-0 when we had myself and Ollie Payne."

Two of Charleroi's greatest athletes from that era—Mouse Chacko and Ollie Payne—grew up two blocks apart. Payne was Black and at six-foot-three, two hundred pounds built like a Division I middle linebacker, or a Sherman tank. Chacko was White, a five-foot-eleven three-sport star who, when trailing rival Monessen late in a football game, was switched to running back.

"I've never played halfback," Chacko protested to his coach.

"Yes, you did. You played it all week in practice, and they couldn't tackle you." Chacko took the next handoff and broke a seventeen-yard run for the winning touchdown.

"That's how the Good Lord works sometimes," said Mouse.

For thirty years, Beans trained Charleroi's boys to become winners through rigorous drills and exacting effort. Johnstown Tournament organizer Clayt

Dovey knew Beans Chacko, heard about the athletes coming through—notably Mouse Chacko and Ollie Payne and a bullish football standout named Myron Pottios—and extended tournament invites in 1956 *and* 1957. On opening night in 1956, Charleroi was matched against Johnstown High, who'd nearly won the tournament in 1955 for the third time in four years. Payne scored 24 points in a 65–57 victory. All-State football halfback and muscular teammate Myron Pottios added 11 points.

In the other Johnstown Tournament opener, Altoona's football hero—All-State quarterback Jim Swanner—put up 34 points to edge Yeadon 76–75. Swanner outdueled Yeadon's five-foot-ten guard Bobby Parker, who tallied 22.[44]

In the tournament final, Charleroi employed the football adage that "defense wins championships." The Cougars hounded Swanner, limiting him to 5 points. Charleroi rolled to a 48–33 title. Payne scored 22, Pottios 10 and Chacko 8. That trio would become part of the school's first Hall of Fame class in 2005.

"If you had a Mount Rushmore of the school's best athletes," said Charleroi historian Ben Jenkins, "they would definitely be three of the four."

Despite the Johnstown championship and scoring forty-six points over two games, Payne did not win the Most Valuable Player award. That went to Yeadon's Parker, who combined for fifty points in a win and a loss.[45]

The latent test of how strong the Johnstown field would prove to be was how these teams would fare in the postseason in March. In the WPIAL semifinal, played at the Pitt Field House, undefeated Sharon (23-0) met Charleroi (24-1). Both teams shot poorly, as the Bengal Tigers eked out a 41–37 victory to advance to the WPIAL final and—ultimately—to the PIAA playoffs. Payne led the Cougars with 19 points, and Chacko added key points late. But Sharon rode its balanced scoring to end Charleroi's dream of a state title.

In the WPIAL final, unbeaten Sharon faced fellow unbeaten McKeesport (23-0) at the Pitt Field House. McKeesport led by six entering the fourth quarter, but Sharon rallied. Mark DuMars scored a game-high twenty-two points for the Bengals. The battle of the unbeatens was a true elimination game, as only the WPIAL champion advanced to the state playoffs.

Chester (26-2) from the east would advance all the way to the state championship. Sharon High would be waiting. Bill Wilson of Chester scored a team-high 20 points in the 59–50 finals defeat. Chester had dropped its third state final in four seasons, perennial runners-up. Sharon coach Bud Laycock became the first person to win a state title as a player and as a coach for the same school. Laycock had played on Sharon's 1930 squad that defeated Lower Merion 18–14 to capture the single-class championship.

What a school year 1956–57 was for the Bengals. Sharon went unbeaten in both football (10-0) and basketball (28-0). It was the best of times for the Mercer County school, just like it was for Charleroi in Washington County.

In the December 1957 Johnstown Tournament, the Charleroi Cougars opened against Chester. Pottios was at Notre Dame University playing football by then; Payne was now a six-foot-four senior and an All-State football end, and Chacko was a junior standout. Chester also featured quite a gaggle of talented players on its roster: Chubby Foster, Granny Lash, Reggie Lawson and Bill Wilson. The Clippers outrebounded Charleroi 38–7 despite being on average three inches shorter than the Cougars starters. With the game tied at 56 with forty-eight seconds remaining, Chacko made the winning free throws in a 62–58 victory that felt like a state championship game.

Payne was spectacular, totaling thirty-seven points, thirteen from the free-throw line. Chester's Foster had twenty-three before fouling out midway through the final quarter. Clipper players broke down in the locker room after the game, as reported by the *Delco Times*' Matt Zabitka. Lawson personally apologized to his coach and his native Chester community for the loss, folding his hands as if in prayer when he said to Bob Forwood, "Coach, please forgive me for letting Chester down tonight. I am terribly sorry and ashamed of myself."[46]

Never mind that Lawson snatched more rebounds (ten) than Charleroi's entire team (seven). Chester's dissatisfaction with potentially letting down the townspeople, a hometown allegiance to their roots, is unmatched in Pennsylvania basketball. In the other opening night game, Philadelphia's Overbrook High returned to Johnstown, this time without Chamberlain. The Panthers were loaded nonetheless, with a roster that included stars Walt Hazzard, Wali Jones, Wayne "The Cane" Hightower and Ralph Heyward. Jones, only a sophomore then, said that his Overbrook team is among those mentioned as the finest in Philadelphia high school history.

"We had four All-Americans," he reasoned. "We used to scrimmage college freshman teams."[47]

Overbrook rode a train to Johnstown, the first excursion of considerable distance for most of the players. They would face a small-town, coal region team called Portage High, which had a massive forward named Lenny Chappell. Chappell and Hightower matched up in a classic showdown of six-foot-eight future stars. Chappell led all scorers with 19 points, but

Overbrook's depth overwhelmed the boys from the mining town twenty miles east of Johnstown, 60–57. Wake Forest recruit Len Chappell held Kansas-bound Hightower to 11 points.[48]

Hightower later selected Kansas as his college. His announcement came shortly after Chamberlain had decided to leave school and play for the Harlem Globetrotters. One newspaper headline made the obvious Overbrook superstar connection: "Kansas Lures Another Wilt."[49] Talk about pressure. Hightower was half a foot shorter than Chamberlain but would be asked to be his equal. Both Hightower and Lenny Chappell would enjoy NBA careers, long after their showdown in War Memorial Arena.

In the 1957 Johnstown championship game, Overbrook had another superstar to try to slow down. Ollie Payne was coming off a 37-point night for Charleroi in a close win over Chester. Overbrook assigned Heyward to defend him. Heyward held Payne to 14 points. Hightower didn't disappoint on offense either, scoring 36 points. He converted 13 of 18 field goals and 10 of 12 free throws, according to the *Philly Inquirer*. Wayne "The Cane" put on a show for the Johnstown fans, who gave him a standing ovation when he left the game midway through the fourth quarter. Their admiration all but appointed Hightower tournament MVP. Overbrook stayed undefeated with a 72–58 romp.

In the consolation game, Chappell scored 30 points to help Portage to a lead over Chester, but the Clippers rallied back for a 56–50 victory. The 1957 Johnstown Tournament was as star-studded as any in its history.

CHARLEROI'S OLLIE PAYNE WOULD go off to Arizona State, where he would play basketball for the Sun Devils. Payne graduated with Charleroi High's basketball scoring record for a career (1,391) and for one game (49). He was a two-sport All-American who would start in basketball all three years at ASU.

Mouse Chacko graduated from Charleroi a year after Payne, giving him time to establish the basketball program's new single-game scoring record of fifty points. Chacko's seven hundred points in one season still stands as the school's high mark. In addition to his football heroics, Chacko also reportedly hit the longest home run at Charleroi Stadium. After Charleroi shortstop Dave Filak blasted a home run that measured 410 feet, Chacko one-upped him in the same game against Elizabeth Forward High, which featured future Pittsburgh Pirate Bill Robinson. Robinson left the mound shortly before Chacko's tape-measure blast.

"He hit it over the fence, over the houses, and it landed on the road," said Jenkins. "It's still an empty lot there. Josh Gibson had played there. Yeah, Mouse hit one of the longest ever hit in that stadium. It was estimated at 429 feet on the fly. It went over the houses beyond the stadium fence and landed on Hussey Road against a fence of the Lock Fold Paper and Box Company. Terrific athlete. He could do everything at 5-foot-10."

In Chacko's senior year, Charleroi's basketball team traveled to the Farrell Tournament in December, where Chacko scored 28 points to upset the host Steelers 66–56. The Cougars won the tournament title, prompting Farrell not to invite them back. Charleroi went on to tie Monessen for the Section 5 title, winning a tiebreaker for the section title, Charleroi's third straight. Charleroi reached the WPIAL final, where Farrell was waiting with stars Brian Generalovich and Willie Somerset, bent on revenge. The Steelers pounded the Cougars 70–47 for the WPIAL title. An era of three straight twenty-four-win seasons would end in Charleroi—the golden age gone for good.

In the 1958 PIAA western semifinal, Altoona beat Charleroi 49–47. With the game tied, Chacko went to take a charging foul. Altoona got the call, Dick Lynch hit both free throws and Charleroi's bid for a state title was over.

By 1960, Myron Pottios was working toward becoming Notre Dame's football captain, his talents landing him in the National Football League, where he would be recognized as Rookie of the Year for the Pittsburgh Steelers. Pottios fashioned a twelve-year career as linebacker. Today, Charleroi's football field bears the name Myron Pottios Stadium.

Myron's brother Ray Pottios became the winningest football coach at Lewistown High. The youngest Pottios brother, Mickey, was adopted by his aunt and took her last name, Bitsko. Mickey would play football at Notre Dame too.

"If you ever look in *Mad Magazine*, they use his name a lot," said Jenkins. "They liked the name, and they used it a lot in the magazine. They contacted him for permission, and I guess they used it. I have one of the magazines here." Apparently freckle-faced Alfred E. Neuman liked Bitsko more than most.

Nearby Uniontown High, thirty miles southeast of Charleroi, took over Section 5A in the 1960s, going 78-1 in a six-year span with six straight section titles. A throng of future college and even professional basketball and football athletes packed the Uniontown rosters. The NFL got Bennett

Myron Pottios Football Stadium at Charleroi High. *Photo by Bradley A. Huebner.*

Gregory (Buffalo), Ray Parson (Detroit), Gene Huey (Cardinals) and Ron Sepic (drafted by the Redskins of the NFL and the Royals of the NBA). Stu Lantz would play in the NBA for the Lakers. "Dunkin'" Don ("Ham") Yates and brother Pat "Doc" Yates would dominate the high school hardwood using quickness and Coach Abe Everhart's 1-2-2 trapping press. Somehow, Uniontown never competed in the Johnstown Tournament.

Charleroi faded from elite status, making its final appearance in Johnstown in 1961. The boys would lose by four to eventual champion Norristown and Jim Williams and then fall to Altoona by eight.

Beans Chacko, who had coached and mentored the finest athletes in Charleroi history, would spend the rest of his life in that pursuit. He coached all the way up to his last day, to the last out, so to speak, when the hometown Charleroi High baseball squad was playing Donora High at Vets Field in Charleroi. The end came on April 8, 1963, two years after Charleroi's final basketball appearance in Johnstown. While coaching third base, Beans collapsed on the field. He was carried to the dugout.

"He died in the dugout," said Mouse. "He had a cerebral hemorrhage and passed away in the dugout. They were behind. There was a train at the game, and it blocked the traffic to the hospital. They came on to win the game, finished it; the Cougars won 9–7. Die with your boots on, buddy. That was the attitude."

Mouse was on the other side of the country when it happened. After going to the University of Maryland to play college basketball as a freshman, he had transitioned to play college baseball for Los Angeles State University.

"We were playing Brigham Young University that day," Jim Chacko said. "I was running in from the outfield when I saw my brother Rich sitting in the dugout. He came to a lot of my games, but that was the first time he was in the dugout. As I got closer, I could see he was crying, and I asked him what was wrong. He said, 'Daddy's dead.' I was in shock. I was still a kid, only 22, and I was speechless."[50] Beans was fifty-five.

TWO-TIMERS

Most likely it started out as a kind gesture, but it developed into a brilliant marketing ploy. Johnstown officials would name an MVP after each tournament and create a poster of that player with a photo, the tournament year, the four teams that competed in the tournament and the player's name on it. Each year, those posters would hang in the concourse to remind everybody of the talented athletes from years past. Putting Wilt Chamberlain's mug on one of those posters certainly didn't hurt the marketing of the tournament.

Johnstown had its share of two-time Most Valuable Player award winners, players so scintillating that they topped a four-team field of stud athletes multiple times. In years two and three of the tournament, Farrell star Julius McCoy—whose family had moved north from South Carolina to work in the steel mills—won consecutive MVP awards. Despite Farrell losing in the Johnstown Tournament final to Johnstown Catholic 34–31, McCoy was awarded the MVP trophy.

His Farrell team would reach the public school state finals, where they would once again lose a heartbreaker, this time to Allentown High, as the six-foot-one "Hooks" McCoy scored eighteen points.

In December 1951, Farrell and McCoy returned to Johnstown. More experienced and deeper, the Steelers pounded local Westmont by 20 and then hammered Ford City in the championship game 76–44. McCoy, a smooth left-hander who could score inside with his running hook shots, left no doubt in the championship game, scoring 40 points—4 shy of Ford City's total! He made 14 field goals and 12 free throws in what would be Farrell's last appearance in the Johnstown Tournament. The next year, Farrell would start its town tournament, sponsored by the Lions Club. The Farrell Ralph Dresch/Ed McCluskey Tournament continues to this day.

In the 1952 state championship later that season, Farrell returned to the Penn Palestra for the third time, hoping for its first gold medal. McCoy turned up sick before the game. Three times Farrell coach Ed McCluskey had to pull him from the game so McCoy could catch his breath. An early 11–0 Farrell start gave McCluskey the cushion to rest his six-foot-two superstar.

Nonetheless, McCluskey put the ball in McCoy's hands against Coatesville when the Red Raiders pulled to within five points late in the game. "McCoy stole the show," reported Ben French of the *Oil City Derrick*, "collecting 18 of his 29 points in the final period to stave off a determined rally by the suddenly revitalized Coatesville Raiders."[51]

The 63–55 championship was the first of seven for Farrell and McCluskey from 1952 to 1972. In 2024, McCluskey was enshrined in the American Basketball Hall of Fame as a coach in a class that included his protégé, Bob Huggins.

McCoy, whom locals took to calling "Hooks" both for his signature shot and for his oven mitt hands, left Farrell for Michigan State University. Michigan State assistant football coach Duffy Daugherty recruited McCoy for football, but McCoy chose basketball. Daugherty had grown up in Barnesboro, Pennsylvania, two hours east of Farrell. Michigan State was well ahead of many northern schools in recruiting Black athletes.

McCoy's 1,417 points remained the Steelers record up to McCoy's death in 2008. In college at MSU, he worked his scoring average up to 27 points per game as a senior, earning him third-team All-American honors. Then he became the most valuable player of the Eastern Professional Basketball League.

Duffy Daugherty and assistant coach Frank Kush from Windber, Pennsylvania, used their Michigan State pedigree to mine Pennsylvania talent. Kush became an All-American lineman at MSU in 1952 under line coach Daugherty despite measuring five-foot-seven and weighing 160 pounds. Coaching under Clarence "Biggie" Munn, Daugherty helped the Spartans to the 1952 national title. After Daugherty became the head coach, Michigan State won shares of national titles in 1965 and 1966. Kush spent a minute in the military and then joined former MSU assistant coach Dan Devine at Arizona State University. At MSU from 1954 to 1972, Daugherty ran a Spartan football program that tapped into talent of all races in Pennsylvania and also in the South, where Daugherty established his "underground railroad."

Julius McCoy poster. *Photo by Thomas Slusser,* Johnstown Tribune-Democrat.

In the middle 1950s the Spartan basketball team lured Chester baller Horace Walker to East Lansing, Michigan. Walker had been MVP of the 1955 Johnstown basketball tournament. He would join McKeesport's Tom Markovich, a 1954 participant in the Johnstown Tournament, on Michigan State's roster. Walker became a third-team basketball All-American for MSU. It isn't much of a leap to say that central Pennsylvania natives Duffy

Daugherty and Frank Kush followed the Johnstown basketball tournament every December.

In the late 1950s, Kush recruited Charleroi star Ollie Payne to come to Arizona State. Payne had his choice of playing football or basketball or both. He chose basketball, which must have disappointed Kush. Payne very easily could have been named Johnstown basketball tournament MVP in 1956 and 1957, when he lost out to Yeadon's Bobby Parker and Overbrook's Wayne Hightower, respectively. Payne scored 1,391 points in high school. At ASU, he finished 43 points shy of 1,000 for his career, averaging 12 points per game over three seasons.

JIM CURRY, ALTOONA HIGH, 1958, 1959

For some lives, the end tells as much of the story as the middle. For Altoona High football and basketball star Jim Curry, jump ahead to his induction into the Blair County, Pennsylvania Sports Hall of Fame in 1998.

Curry's friend when he attended the University of Cincinnati was All-American basketball player Oscar Robertson. Although Curry played football in college, he and Oscar would play basketball against each other during the summers.

"Jim was a tremendous basketball player as well," Oscar said in his speech to honor Curry at the Hall of Fame induction. "I've often wondered why he didn't play basketball [at Cincinnati] as well….He was a very great basketball player—he played with a lot of style and flair. Jim was a tremendous team player in both sports."[52]

Like he did for Johnstown's first two-time Johnstown Tournament MVP Julius McCoy, Michigan State coach Duffy Daugherty also tried to lure Curry to play football in East Lansing after Curry had led Altoona to a 9-1 season in 1959. Curry was an elite quarterback with modern-day NFL size. Although he would switch to play receiver at Cincinnati, at six-foot-four, two hundred pounds, he was that top-shelf program athlete that every coach coveted, for any sport.

Curry's life, it seemed, was following McCoy's as Michigan State seemed a likely destination out of high school.

In the 1958 Johnstown Tournament, which spilled over into January 1959, Altoona pounded North Catholic by 18 in the opener. Curry, a junior, scored 22 (or 27, depending on the source) points. Against Overbrook's seeming all-star roster, Curry scored 14 points, including two key baskets late in a

Jim Curry poster. *Photo by Thomas Slusser,* Johnstown Tribune-Democrat.

huge 47–44 upset that halted the Panthers' thirty-six-game winning streak. Future pros Wali Jones (19) and Ralph Heyward (15) outscored Curry for Overbrook, but down the stretch Curry made the deciding plays to break a 38–38 deadlock.

In 1959, Curry scored 53 points as the Lions split games against Camden of New Jersey (66–63 loss) and Wampum (74–64 win). Camden came in as the unbeaten defending state champions from New Jersey. When you ask old-timers if they remember Curry, they usually have the same response: "Was he the big kid with the red hair and freckles?" That was Jim Curry. At

Cincinnati, Curry became an all–Missouri Valley Conference end. As his success grew, Curry revealed that he never really liked football until late in his career at Cincinnati. Basketball, he said, was his first love. Nonetheless, Curry was drafted by the Dallas Cowboys of the NFL.

LARRY MILLER, CATASAUQUA HIGH, 1962, 1963

The best basketball player ever produced by the Lehigh Valley, Larry Miller was a left-handed jumping jack built like a college football tight end. He was equal parts springy and solid, with a nose for finding the basketball as he posted prodigious rebounding numbers, a six-foot-four guard/forward who also jumped center.

Miller grew up just outside of Allentown in a tiny borough called Catasauqua, where the United States first manufactured anthracite iron, so you knew that Miller would be tough. In the dense neighborhoods, you could find plenty of outdoor basketball courts and playgrounds for summer workouts. Here Miller became a schoolboy superstar.

In the 1962 Johnstown Tournament, Miller was matched up against the host Johnstown Trojans. Miller the Stat Stuffer scored 28 points, pulled 26 rebounds and doled six assists in a scintillating 57–49 victory. A tall and talented Darby squad from the Philly suburbs handled Western Pennsylvania's Aliquippa—the district that produced football legend Mike Ditka and where Press Maravich had coached basketball—to reach the final. The win was Darby's thirtieth straight.

In the finals, Darby shadowed Miller everywhere he moved, extending the Rams' rangy 1-3-1 zone to place two players in Miller's area. This was the breakout Darby team that started two standout guards in Pee Wee Coleman (Villanova) and Sonny Realer, forwards David Kennard and Adrian Harmon and the six-foot-nine centerpiece, Hal Booker. Darby would go 50-0 over two seasons, repeating as Class B state champions. And although Miller and Catty played up in Class A, they were actually a similarly sized school, but not a similarly sized squad to match Darby's height.

Miller was held to 12 points in a 70–49 defeat. Nonetheless, Johnstown honored his talents with the Most Valuable Player award. Maybe they knew what time would soon reveal: this Darby outfit was among the best teams in Pennsylvania history. Three of the players would follow Darby coach Hal Blitman to Cheyney University and make a run at a college national title.

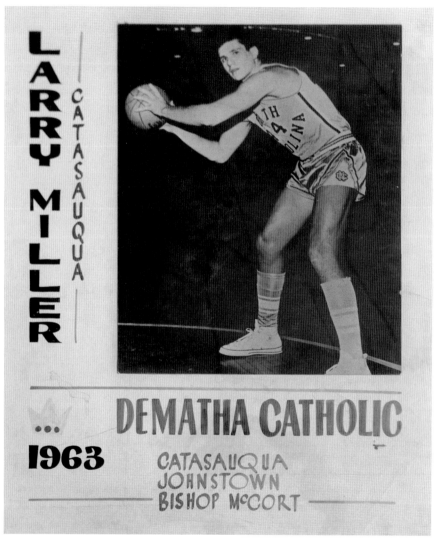

Larry Miller poster. *Photo by Thomas Slusser,* Johnstown Tribune-Democrat.

Johnstown fans couldn't wait to see Miller again in 1963. He opened with a 77–72 overtime win over nearby Bishop McCort High. More than 3,500 fans watched Miller become the fourth player in Pennsylvania history to eclipse 2,000 career points as he scored 29. Miller's 31 rebounds were one shy of the tournament record, held by Chester High's Horace Walker.[53] Miller would bring the ball up against the press, handle much of the scoring load and then rebound at both ends. He dominated like a Keystone State Oscar Robertson.

Despite Miller's dominance, the Rough Riders nearly gave the game away. Miller's local newspaper reported that Catty yielded a 5-point lead in the last minute and then squandered the last twenty-eight seconds, believing that they were in the lead and didn't need to shoot the ball. Catty salvaged the game with a 9–4 overtime advantage.

Once again Miller met a behemoth in the Johnstown Tournament final. A loaded DeMatha Catholic squad jumped out to an 18–0 lead against Catty. Morgan Wootten's team rotated players throughout the game thereafter. So talented were those DeMatha teams that the previous spring the Stags repeated as Eastern States Catholic Invitational champions despite starting five new players.

Miller would ultimately electrify the Johnstown crowd with 40 points, registering 17 of his team's 20 field goals. Brendan McCarthy led DeMatha with 27 points despite leaving the game midway through the third quarter. The 29-point defeat couldn't temper the Johnstown organizers' and fans' Miller Mania. They honored with him with a second MVP award after he'd scored a record 69 points in two games.

Charles "Hawkeye" Whitney, DeMatha Catholic, 1974, 1975

Charles "Hawkeye" Whitney, the DeMatha star who won tournament MVP honors in 1974 and 1975 as the Stags coasted to consecutive tournament championships against the Trojans, became a can't-miss, blue-chip recruit. In the middle 1970s, as tournaments proliferated and the Johnstown model was replicated and advanced throughout the country, newspaper coverage of the tournament diminished. So, of Whitney's four games over two years in Johnstown, his highest reported point total at War Memorial was a mere fifteen.

DeMatha Catholic director of development Tom Ponton attended the school during part of Whitney's era and works at the school today.

"Morgan, much like Dean Smith at North Carolina, was a proponent of teamwork," Ponton explained. "Nobody was going to score 40 a game for DeMatha. He obviously won a lot of games. If Hawkeye only scored 15, it's because Hawkeye only needed to score 15."[54]

In two tournaments that both ended with championship blowout victories over Johnstown, DeMatha was only moderately tested in a fourteen-point win over Abington High. Whitney developed into a six-foot-five, 235-pound senior the next year.

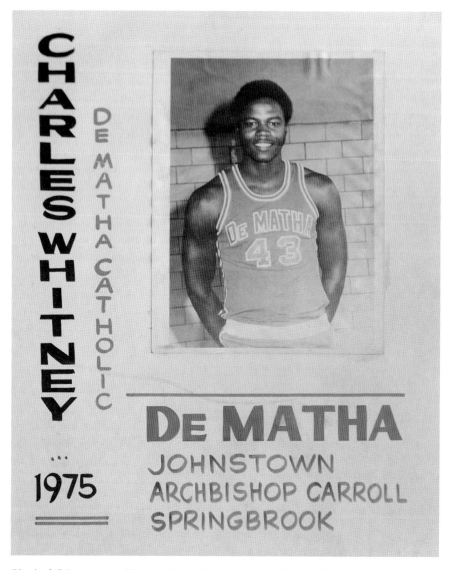

Charles Whitney poster. *Photo by Thomas Slusser,* Johnstown Tribune-Democrat.

Said teammate Bill Ruback, "He had an NBA body and an NBA game. During my high school years, we had three NBA first-round draft picks at DeMatha: Adrian Dantley, Kenny Carr and Hawkeye Whitney."[55]

Just how good was Whitney? As good as Catasauqua High product Larry Miller, who would set an ABA single-game scoring record with sixty-nine points in 1972? As good as Jim Curry, who became besties with Oscar

Robertson while playing football at Cincinnati? As good as Julius McCoy, who became a Michigan State All-American and Eastern League MVP? As good as Adrian Dantley, said to be the greatest player ever to suit up for Morgan Wootten and his first four-year starter?

"Hawkeye was a man-child among boys," said Ponton. "In 1976 when Indiana won the national title [at the Spectrum in Philadelphia], the next morning Bobby Knight was at DeMatha recruiting Hawkeye."

College coaches were in the gym every day. Wootten kept his practices open, so everybody from Dean Smith to Digger Phelps to the trombone player in the band was welcome. Whitney chose North Carolina State, where he would team up with former DeMatha teammate and friend Kenny Carr, a junior and former Parade All-American like Whitney. Carr was the leading scorer for the Wolfpack during Whitney's first year. Carr averaged 21 points and 10 rebounds. Hawkeye was right behind at 14.6 and 6 to earn Atlantic Coast Conference Rookie of the Year. Over his four years, he would finish 36 points shy of 2,000, a three-time All-ACC selection. While Carr had been drafted sixth overall out of N.C. State in 1977, Whitney went sixteenth overall in 1980. Everything was going according to plan for the boy who grew up in one of the poorest sections of Washington, D.C., as the last of thirteen children. Whitney was chasing his dream.

Hawkeye grew up on the other side of Washington, D.C., from DeMatha. He led Johnson Junior High to victories over St. Anthony's and DeMatha to claim the championship, which put him on Morgan Wootten's radar. He wrote Wootten a letter expressing his interest in attending DeMatha, and the school provided a scholarship.

"I used to catch the bus outside of my apartments at 5:00 a.m.," said Whitney. "I had to catch three to four buses to get to school in time. In summer I would ride my bike to school. One day Morgan said, 'How did you get here?' I said, "My bike. I do it every chance I get.' He set it up that one of my teammates started picking me up. At that time, you did what you had to do."[56] Some nights—to avoid that arduous commute—Whitney would sleep at Wootten's or assistant coach Jack Bruen's house.

In the NBA, he played seventy games over two seasons for the Kansas City Kings, scoring a total of 404 points before a knee injury halted his career. Without basketball, Whitney's life spiraled. A drug addiction sidetracked him. Eventually, he and some friends kidnapped a man on the street and drove him around to ATM machines so the man could withdraw money for them.

"They just saw a person that looked reasonably well-dressed," said Ponton. "The limit now is $300 on a machine. I think they went to three of them. When Morgan was interviewed about it, he said that Hawkeye was a good guy." Whitney considered Wootten a strong father figure, and Wootten reciprocated his loyalty and affection.

The man whom Whitney and company had kidnapped—who just happened to be the personal attorney for First Lady Hillary Clinton—testified that Hawkeye had been kind during the ordeal. Whitney had provided him cab fare to get home.

Not everybody backed Coach Wootten for supporting Whitney. "Somebody went by Morgan's house and put toilet paper all over his lawn because they felt he had gone too far," said Ponton.

Whitney was sentenced to jail for sixty-nine months. He had set a school record with 166 steals at N.C. State, but it was the 167th beyond the court that forced him to get the help he needed and pointed him toward the Bible, which he credits for saving his life.

"I went through some physical and mental challenges in life," he said. "It was a hard bounce back. I got back on track when I got out of prison. Going to prison saved my life. This is how God opened up my eyes. In my darkest days God was trying to get my undivided attention. And I was running, running, running away. That hard stone and coldness in my heart, he forgave me. And the most important thing of all was that he allowed me to forgive myself. I live for him every day; I can't do nothing without him."

DeMatha men like Pete Strickland, Toney Ellis, Bill Ruback, Mike Brey, Ponton and others formed a support system that helped Hawkeye bounce back. They are the link to before Whitney got sidetracked. He fondly remembers the pregame routine in Johnstown when players were celebrated as a high point in his early career.

"I saw when the Wizards were the Washington Bullets," he remembers, "I would see how when they bring the star players out and read the accolades. I always saw that but never experienced it until I went to Johnstown. They always made it bigger than the year before. When it was time to come to the games, the whole town was into the tournament. Everywhere we went people were so nice to us. Even though we beat their guys in their town, it was so amazing how nice the people were. There was no nastiness; people weren't coming at you sideways."

PART II
THE 1960s

Tournament Expansion

BASKETBALL CITY

By 1960, Nanticoke natives were expecting their basketball teams to be among the state's best. The Rams (and later the Trojans) had won state titles in 1923 and 1926. Nanticoke, south of Wilkes-Barre, became Pennsylvania's first dominant program—a dynasty. To add to that regional basketball dominance, neighboring Newport Township won a state title in 1936. One year later, the Newport Buffalos returned to the state final.

Nanticoke historian Chester Zaremba credits, ironically, local church leagues for the rise of public school basketball in Nanticoke. "Every Catholic church had a team," said Zaremba. "They were all self-contained. You had kids playing all around Nanticoke. They all fed into the high school."[57] Boys could play for Holy Trinity, Saint Mary, Saint Stanislaus, Saint Joseph or Saint Francis. This was a time when 73 percent of Americans attended church, according to Gallup, a percentage that has dipped to under 50 percent.

If you had five Catholic churches in town, that's fifty to seventy players who would funnel into one high school squad. Nanticoke native Jack Dudrick was one of many public school students who had a basket in the alley behind his house, a go-getter who would also shovel out the snow on the public court down the hill just to stay sharp. Dudrick came late to basketball, but he developed into Nanticoke's sixth man.

Signs of another championship started manifesting in the 1950s. In the 1959–60 season, the Rams started out 26-0. Fans carried signs that read, "Have Champs, Will Travel." Fans who weren't alive for the two prior state championships wouldn't miss this run.

Because of that history of success, the Rams were an easy team for Johnstown organizers to target for their December event. In March 1960 in the PIAA playoffs, Nanticoke had won its first-round game against undefeated Shamokin. In Round 2, however, Nanticoke got pounded by York High 62–47. One loss and the season was over. Specifically, York scored the first 15 points on the second quarter to begin its assault. Nanticoke's unbeaten season was over, and York's one-loss campaign would extend only one more game.

For the 1960–61 season, Nanticoke coach Sylvester "Syl" Bozinski returned three starters. Johnstown Tournament officials fit them into a stacked field with another strong Sharon High team, a Chester team led by Emerson Baynard and Johnstown. It was another strong and balanced foursome, and it needed to be, as other holiday tournaments began competing with Johnstown to land the best programs. Farrell was in the ninth year of its Lions Club Tournament and was hosting Camden High from New Jersey, the defending 1959 Johnstown Tournament champion on a fifty-one-game winning streak. In Scranton, the Lynett Tournament was playing its tenth rendition, with Nanticoke having won the 1959 version. Johnstown, per usual, was typically loaded in its twelfth season.

"Johnstown was a higher tournament," said Dudrick. "It was our first exposure to big-time basketball. We stayed over in a hotel. We were a little overwhelmed."[58]

Duane Ford was a sophomore on that Nanticoke squad. He remembers a climate issue at the start of the first game. "I remember they were making ice for the hockey game," he said. "My legs were frozen up to my knees."[59]

Nanticoke played poorly against Sharon in the opener. In 1960–61, Sharon was returning five of its top six players. Newspaper headlines didn't mince words. They wrote that Sharon "trounced," "walloped" and even "rapped" ice-cold Nanticoke in the 55–37 decimation. Meanwhile, on the same night, Sharon neighbor Farrell High annihilated defending Johnstown champion Camden by 30 points in the Lions Tournament, thus ending Camden's 51-game streak. Shenango Valley powers Sharon and Farrell were potent as usual. After Johnstown edged Chester 52–51 in the other Johnstown opener, Nanticoke faced a possible 0-2 weekend in the Flood City.

"We walked into the hotel, and we see Chester," Dudrick recalls. "We had never played against an all-Black basketball team. We see their size. They all wore coats and ties, and the ties would go down to their knees, and they were tall. We thought, *What are we getting ourselves into?* We just knew that they were a powerhouse in those days."

Jack Dudrick, former Nanticoke basketball player. *Photo by Bradley A. Huebner.*

Nanticoke, all white, responded to the Sharon humbling by gathering for a motivational team meeting. "Kenny Legins was our center," Dudrick recalls. "He was the leader of our team, for sure. We just decided we didn't play our game against Sharon. That meeting settled us down."

And it might have thwarted an apathetic consolation-game showing. "I think we were kind of surprised when we went in there and got dumped," said Ford. "The thing with the third-place game, if you can't win the championship, are you still going to go out and do your best the next day? I think we wanted it more than Chester."

Unlike the prior season, Nanticoke could do something to bounce back after its first loss. They would have to control Baynard. Baynard would score 21, and future major-league pitcher Lew Krausse added 11 for Chester, who jumped to a six-point lead after one quarter. But a tournament record–setting 27–9 second quarter propelled Nanticoke to a 69–57 victory. Chester must have felt jinxed. The Clippers' Mike Sudler got injured late in the first quarter when his momentum took him off the court and into the stands.

Early in the second quarter, Chester's six-foot-five center LaFenus Northern picked up his fourth foul and left the game. Coach Bob Forwood told the *Delaware County Times* that he wondered what else could go wrong. He got his answer when a dog wandered onto the court.[60]

Nanticoke's Legins scored a game-high twenty-five points. Nanticoke shot more than twice as many free throws as Chester (41 to 19), making 27 of them. Bozinski stuck to his system of playing only five players; Chester rotated eleven, partially due to foul trouble. Nanticoke sat in its typical 2-3 zone and found a way to outscore the taller Delaware County foes. Chester would lose two straight games for the first time in eight seasons under Forwood. Nanticoke salvaged a respectable tournament.

"Stretch didn't substitute," Dudrick said of Bozinski, who stood six-foot-five. "He had his ironman five. We would pound the ball inside to Kenny, get it to Kenny. He was like six-foot-five, and in those days that was something.… Stretch was a very successful and a very positive person. You went into the game confident you were going to win."

After Sharon nipped Johnstown for the tournament title by a point, it was clear that any of the four teams could have beaten any other—and that Nanticoke may have been given a gift: a midseason wakeup call. The Rams didn't lose another regular-season game. They won the District 2 title for the second straight season and once again faced undefeated Shamokin High (24-0) at Bucknell University, where three thousand fans roused support. Renowned coach Howie Landa was in charge of Shamokin. When he wasn't coaching his boys, he was playing in the respected Eastern Professional Basketball League. After a 20–20 tie at the half, Legins caught fire for Nanticoke, which coasted to a 52–33 romp. In the second half, Nanticoke outscored Shamokin 32–13, a significant achievement when you consider that Landa would soon move on to coach at Trenton (New Jersey) Junior College (now Mercer County Community College), where he would win two national titles.

Next up for Nanticoke: Radnor, a 1960 state finalist and then unbeaten at 25-0. Nanticoke led 43–40 in the second half. The Rams, just like they had against Shamokin, turned up the defense late. Nanticoke outscored Radnor 16–0 to close out the game for a 59–40 victory that sent the Rams into the eastern final. They would play Reading High, the program that had won the very first Johnstown Tournament but now was coached by future Princeton University guru Pete Carril.

UNDEFEATED BETHLEHEM HIGH HAD hammered Reading by thirty early in the year and then drew the Red Knights again in the state playoffs. Bethlehem's Don Rodenbach was one of five starters who could go for twenty points any night. He had grown up watching his idols Billy Packer and Al Senavitis lead Bethlehem to a standout season in 1958.

"I went to every game Packer played," Rodenbach said. "My cousin lived next door to him. I used to watch him play baseball, too. He and Senavitis were our boyhood heroes, part of a great Bethlehem sports tradition then."[61]

Rodenbach, regrettably, watched the unraveling of Packer's 19-5 Hurricanes team against York High at the Penn Palestra in March 1958. Bethlehem enjoyed a 13-point lead midway through the third quarter. Leading 46–38 heading into the final quarter and in control, Bethlehem changed its approach.

"We had ended the third quarter with momentum," said Packer. "Our coach said, 'We have enough points; let's run the air of out of the ball.' I think we were outscored 31–2 in the fourth quarter. I think we only scored 2 points, and that was on a meaningless basket I made when it didn't really count."[62]

With Bethlehem stalling, unbeaten York ramped up its defensive pressure and scored 15 straight points. The Bearcats (also called the Orange and Blue) dominated the last quarter (actually 17–2, although it must have felt like 31–2) to notch the 55–48 upset in the PIAA quarterfinals. That Bethlehem team, like the 1960–61 squad, featured a balanced attack.

"We were all good jump shooters from 15 feet," Rodenbach said. "We could all shoot. When we played Reading the second time, they played a 1-2-2 zone, the perfect defense to stop 15-foot jump shooters. We had practiced against it, and our second team was beating us. We knew it could give us trouble."

Those fears seemed overblown as unbeaten Bethlehem led 26–19 at halftime against Bethlehem alumnus Pete Carril's Reading squad. In 1961, Carril faced a Hurricanes squad that hadn't lost all season under Coach Johnny Howard. And Reading star Joe Natale was playing with a cracked bone in his right wrist on his shooting arm. He'd landed on it the previous game after being fouled driving in for a layup. Natale tried everything to overcome the injury.

When he went to the hospital after breaking the wrist, Natale fielded the doctor's grim prognosis. He advised Natale to secure his right hand and wrist with a cast.

"If you put a cast on it," Carril informed Natale, "we're done. Joe, it's up to you."

An alternative was to shoot the wrist with Novocain to temper the pain and affix a "soft" half cast.

"It was leather," said Natale. "They would tie it like old combat boots with a leather strap."

He experienced limited mobility due to the cast. He couldn't spin the ball off the backboard with his fingers like he preferred on his twisting drives. Reading High's trainer then fashioned a better, looser cast.

"He cut old tube rolls in half lengthwise," said Natale. "Then he cut that in half horizontally. He put it under my hand where my wrist began and wrapped it with an ace bandage and tape. I could move my hand and fingers."

At practice before the Bethlehem game, Carril ordered Natale to hold out his right hand to test Natale's pain threshold. He ordered a teammate to hurl a basketball at Natale's injured wrist.

"It hurt," said Natale, "but they put some analgesic balm on it." And Carril inserted Natale into the starting lineup against Bethlehem.

Against the Hurricanes, Reading rallied as Natale scored 16 despite sporting the "homemade cast." The Red Knights took the lead for good on a foul shot by Grant Jackson with twenty-five seconds left for a 49–48 victory. Bethlehem never had a better shot at a state basketball title. Its former All-State guard Pete Carril (class of 1948) would be moving on with Reading High in the PIAA playoffs.

WHEN READING AND NANTICOKE faced off at the Harrisburg Farm Show Arena in the eastern final, the Rams led after each of the first three quarters. Trailing 38–32, the Red Knights rallied to claim a 47–40 cushion with just under three minutes to play. The 15–2 run all but buried Syl Bozinski and his boys. Bozinski was notorious for insisting that his players determine the outcomes of games. Rarely would he resort to calling a strategic timeout. As Reading spurted ahead, Nanticoke players kept looking to Stretch on the bench, all but begging for a timeout to regroup like the boys had after losing to Sharon in Johnstown. Finally, Rams player Billy James called the timeout himself.

Despite their suddenly dire predicament, the Rams didn't quit. This was a town that had produced major-league baseball player Pete Gray, who, as a boy, fell off a wagon and mangled his right arm in the spokes of the wheel. Gray would lose his arm above the elbow following an amputation. Nonetheless, Gray swung a baseball bat with only his left arm and managed to hit .218 in the majors for the St. Louis Browns during 1945, when many big leaguers were overseas in World War II. In 1944, before reaching the major leagues, Gray had batted .333 and stole 68 bases to become the Southern Association's Most Valuable Player. If Pete Gray didn't quit....[63]

All year, Bozinski had Nanticoke practice a full-court zone press that they'd never used in games. It was installed for a desperate situation such as this one. The people of coal mining Nanticoke—Bozinski included—understood the need for backup plans. Crisis and tragedy haunted the men in the mines, from cave-ins to workplace accidents to lethal black lung. If the Rams basketball players were to rally, they would need a suitable backup plan—a desperate, stifling defensive effort like the ones that had propelled them into the PIAA eastern final.

"All of a sudden," said Dudrick, "the press started to work, and [Reading] started throwing the ball away."

A series of Red Knight miscues against the trapping press led to points, the crowd became energized and the momentum swung. A kernel of hope and belief metastasized into a dogged quest to triumph any way possible. Nanticoke scored the final 11 points of the game to steal a 51–47 victory that became the bane of Coach Pete Carril's basketball career and—possibly—his entire life. The loss stung Carril even more than when his 1948 Bethlehem team had lost in the opening round of the state playoffs when Carril was an All-State guard. That was against Norristown, who went on to win the state championship.

"I never won a state title," Carril would say months before his death. "That's the one regret I had. I go back to that Nanticoke game."

The year 1961 was the one to win the state title in Pennsylvania. The tournament field included neither Sharon nor Farrell. In their place, neighboring Hickory Township was the western representative. Nanticoke couldn't afford to overlook them, however. Hickory had pounded WPIAL champion Mount Lebanon by eighteen in the western final. That Mount Lebanon team had pounded Johnstown by twenty-one in the western semifinal. That same Johnstown team had been on par with Nanticoke, Sharon and Chester back in December in the Johnstown Tournament. The pre-PIAA tournament favorites—Bethlehem in the east, Uniontown in the west—already had been vanquished.

But championships are never easy. Nanticoke didn't know it then, but Hickory coach Fran Webster was a defensive wizard who would conceive the Amoeba Defense that he took to the University of Pittsburgh, which later made its way to the University of Nevada–Las Vegas. Coach Jerry Tarkanian used it to win an NCAA national title in 1990.

Playing before nearly nine thousand fans at the Harrisburg Farm Show Arena, Nanticoke had to acclimate to a stage twice the size of the one they experienced in Johnstown. "It was overwhelming," Dudrick confessed. "It was hard to get your composure. Guys were throwing up in the locker room before the game. When I went into the game in the second quarter, my knees were shaking."

Nanticoke broke an early 2–2 tie and never looked back. The 56–46 championship victory was the Rams' third overall, their first since 1926. Senior Bill James scored 19 points and grabbed 12 rebounds. Legins scored 16 points despite the Hickory defenders surrounding him. Coach Syl Bozinski's record improved to 141-30 in seven seasons, winning consecutive state tournament games against future Division I coaches who would author books about coaching.[64] For those too young to remember the Rams titles in the 1920s, the 1961 version would suffice.

"We put Nanticoke on the map," Billy James said. The downtown filled with well-wishers for the celebration, both local and from surrounding districts. Almost all of Nanticoke's sixteen thousand residents were there, along with many, many others.

"I bet there were close to 70,000 people there," said Nanticoke historian Chet Zaremba. "It was the greatest day in Nanticoke history." Nanticoke took on the name "Basketball City."

STRETCH BOZINSKI'S MOST TALENTED team came along in 1968–69. The stars were Steve and Tom Bilko. The brothers, one year apart, were the sons of Steve Bilko Sr., a Nanticoke High alumnus who had played for six major-league baseball teams from 1949 to 1962, but not before posting astronomical statistics in the Pacific Coast League. "Stout Steve" Bilko won the triple crown there by batting .360 with 55 home runs and 164 RBIs. He made it to the majors, just like local icon Pete Gray had. Teaming with Stout Steve's sons on the 1969 basketball team were Bob Yatko, Dave Washinski and Dave Morgan.

In the second round of the PIAA playoffs, Nanticoke (24-0) played six-loss Steelton-Highspire. "That was the first year you could finish second in the league and still make the district playoffs," said Steelton sports historian Nick Conjar. The Rams led 39–23 at halftime after making 17 of 23 shots from the field, according to *UPI* reporter Burton W. Siglin. Nanticoke led 46–31 late in the third quarter, so the Rams' fans scurried to purchase tickets for the next game, the eastern final game against Penncrest. Backup plans are more reliable than hasty ones, however.

Steel-High changed its tactics to full-court pressing after halftime, and slowly the game changed. Slowly, consistently, then drastically. The Rollers pressured Nanticoke's guards into turnovers. At one point, Steel-High scored fourteen straight points. Nanticoke players were repeatedly called for traveling violations that hadn't been called in the first half. Some players admitted that they became fearful of handling the ball because they thought the referees would blow their whistles regardless of what they did.

Steel-High came all the way back to win the game, 57–54. Stretch Bozinski and the Nanticoke townspeople called foul, just not as often as the District 1 referees who worked the game. The Nanticoke Chamber of Commerce and the Athletic Club of Nanticoke demanded an investigation. Their claims as printed in the *Wilkes-Barre Times Leader*: "Thirty-one violations called on Nanticoke, of which 23 were walking infractions. Of the 31 violations, a total of 27 were called by one official."[65]

After playing a nearly perfect first half, Nanticoke players were said to have traveled with the ball twenty-three times. The most talented team in school history finished 24-1. "We had the game taken away from us in the second half," Bozinski told *Hazleton Standard-Speaker* writer Ray Saul. "It was unbelievable. Our kids didn't lose it; they just had it taken away from them."[66]

THE OTHER POST-1969 SAVING grace for Nanticoke fans, if you can call it that, was provided by the Nanticoke girls' basketball team in 1990. That squad made a mockery of its schedule, regularly pulverizing teams by an average of 71 points. *Four* seniors from that team scored over 1,000 career points. The records show that John S. Fine won the state title that year because that was Nanticoke High's name, briefly, before it became Greater Nanticoke Area. The girls concluded a 30-0 season with a 77–67 victory and a No. 25 ranking in *USA Today*. No referee's whistle could derail the perfect season, as it may have for the boys in 1969.

DUANE FORD, A BACKUP on the 1961 boys' state championship team, carried the successful Nanticoke lineage into his own coaching career. The former Dickinson College football player was hired to teach and coach at Central

Columbia High. His 1981 boys' basketball team won the Class AA state championship behind six-foot-eight Brian DeWitt and Doug Davis. Ford coached boys' basketball at Central Columbia for eighteen years and girls' for fourteen, amassing 584 combined wins. That total fell far short of his softball production, where Ford won state titles in 1994 and 2014 on the way to 805 wins over forty-seven seasons, leaving him second all-time behind Southern Lehigh's Brian Neefe (847 wins in fifty-two seasons).

BETHLEHEM HIGH STANDOUT DON Rodenbach never played in Johnstown. He didn't make it to a state championship game either. But he would go on to play at Princeton University for Coach Butch van Breda Kolff, Pete Carril's former coach at Lafayette College. Rodenbach would team up with Bill Bradley and take the Tigers to the NCAA Final Four in 1965. They would lose to Michigan and Cazzie Russell, who would lose to UCLA in the national championship game. Despite not reaching the championship game, Bill Bradley would be recognized as tournament Most Valuable Player after averaging more than thirty-five points per game in the Final Four. The finest of Princeton seasons resulted in Van Breda Kolff getting hired to coach the Los Angeles Lakers in 1967. To replace him at Princeton, Van Breda Kolff recommended a former Reading High coach: Pete Carril from Bethlehem, Pennsylvania, who had gone from Reading High to Lehigh University.

RODENBACH'S GREATEST OFFENSIVE OUTPUT of his career happened to connect to a prior Johnstown Tournament MVP. As a boy, Rodenbach went to Bethlehem High's spacious Memorial Gym to watch Wilt Chamberlain play for the Philadelphia Warriors against the Detroit Pistons. On January 25, 1960, Chamberlain scored fifty-eight points, setting an NBA rookie record and a Memorial Gym record.

"I remember when I stood next to him," said Rodenbach, "my eye level was at his belt buckle."

Two years later, in his final home basketball game for Bethlehem High, Rodenbach pursued Chamberlain's Memorial Gym milestone in a game against Tamaqua High. It came down to the final seconds:

The last shot, I take it from the right side of the top of the key. It goes up. If I make it, I break the record. The shot misses. It comes off the front of the rim. I'm not done. This is the basketball gods being good to me. The ball

Author Bradley A. Huebner holds up his first book, *Titles for Our Town*, while standing in historic Hersheypark Arena. *Photo from Bradley A. Huebner.*

> *bounces back into my hands; this is no bullshit. I turnaround almost with my back to the basket and throw up a hook shot. The ball is in the air, the buzzer goes off, and the ball goes in! The fans storm the court and carry me off. I have a picture of that. Last home game as a senior.*[67]

Down went Wilt's Memorial Gym record—by one point. One year into Van Breda Kolff's tenure as Lakers coach, they traded for Wilt Chamberlain. Together Van Breda Kolff and Chamberlain took the Lakers to the next two NBA finals. So many people and careers began in Johnstown or Nanticoke or Bethlehem and would flourish elsewhere.

WOOING WOOTTEN

In the Johnstown Tournament's first decade, organizers succeeded in landing some of the top basketball programs in the state: Chester, Overbrook, Reading, McKeesport, Farrell, Sharon, New Castle, Altoona, Williamsport and Wampum. Local Johnstown High, Johnstown Catholic, Conemaugh and Westmont all got to test themselves against the Keystone State's best teams, coaches and players.

In the second decade, tournament organizers expanded the recruiting base to include more powers from other states. In 1959, they dipped into New Jersey and got powerful Camden High. In 1961, however, they landed perhaps the biggest fish in the ocean, at least one of the biggest on the East Coast, when they persuaded Morgan Wootten to bring the DeMatha Catholic Stags to Johnstown. Wootten had taken over the program based in Hyattsville, Maryland—which competed in the vaunted Washington, D.C. Catholic League—in 1956. Wootten's first four teams went 22-10, 17-11, 23-10 and 23-10. It would be thirty-three years until another DeMatha team finished with as many as 10 losses again.

In 1960–61, the Stags won their first conference championship, going 27-1. Over the next twenty-four years, DeMatha wouldn't lose more than five games in any season. The Stags would win twenty-two of twenty-four Catholic League championships.[68] Wootten had learned from Coach Joe Gallagher at St. John's in D.C. to build the program around fundamentals—and a summer camp. Gallagher and Wootten set up their camp together in 1961 and used it to attract talented players. Today, Morgan's son Joe

1962 DeMatha Stags: Gary Ward, John Carroll, John Austin, Bill McDermott, Johnny Jones—"the Fabulous Five." *Courtesy of DeMatha Catholic.*

Wootten, head coach at Bishop O'Connell High in Virginia, runs the camp at Frostburg State University in Maryland. Throughout the summer, he packs the dorms with players who come for the coaching, the competition and the comedy that Joe Wootten provides. The University of Maryland alumnus pantomimes arrogant blue-chippers hot-dogging it for hypothetical college coaches in a well-crafted skit. Wootten deftly pretends to be that too-cool, full-of-himself teenager who short-circuits his own college opportunities with a poor attitude.[69] It's a lesson in how *not* to act, and it resonates with boys. The camp website proudly calls it the "World's #1 Instructional Basketball Camp: Teaching Fundamentals and Values to Young Men and Women since 1961." Hundreds of kids compete each week all summer, some unknowingly playing for a spot on an elite high school roster.

In the 1960s, after experiencing successful but certainly not dominant campaigns in the 1950s, Morgan Wootten also began going to watch the middle school basketball games to see who might be persuaded to enroll at DeMatha. In the D.C. Catholic League, every team recruits players, which is why it's one of the most successful talent-producing leagues in America. Once Morgan Wootten figured out how to supercharge his program, he kept it humming all the way to the Hall of Fame.

DeMatha driving nearly four hours in a caravan to play a basketball tournament in the mountains of central Pennsylvania was Wootten's way of barnstorming his program, expanding its regional appeal. He would build on that step in 1964 and 1965 when he arranged for Lew Alcindor's Power Memorial team to travel from New York to College Park, Maryland, for two of the biggest high school games in history. Just as the Johnstown Tournament needed to grow, so did Wootten's program, as well as high school basketball in general. You can't help but believe that Wootten's and Johnstown's goals mutually benefited each other. To be the best, Wootten knew, you had to beat the best. Wasn't that the premise Charles Kunkle Jr. started with when he conceived this tournament? Neither Kunk nor Wootten ever shied away from facing elite athletes or teams.

And those DeMatha–Power Memorial showcase games not only sold out Maryland's Cole Field House, but they also attracted and inspired other basketball builders. Sonny Vaccaro used the post–Power Memorial game reception at DeMatha High to begin recruiting players and coaches for his mega-concept—a national all-star game pitting Pennsylvania all-stars against all-stars from all over America. The Dapper Dan Roundball Classic went from an idea he mulled over with Trafford, Pennsylvania childhood friend and music promoter Pat DiCesare to an action plan in Hyattsville, Maryland, where Vaccaro would try to recruit Lew Alcindor and his coach from Power Memorial, as well as players from DeMatha, to participate in the first event. Overhearing Vaccaro's pitches to Alcindor and Power coach Jack Donohue, Wootten offered that he would be interested in coaching the American All-Stars in the first game. When you put yourself in Morgan Wootten and DeMatha's sphere, when you surround yourself with big-idea people unafraid to fail, the blades of progress spin mightily.[70]

For Wootten to get what he wanted out of agreeing to play in the 1961 Johnstown Tournament, however, his team needed to be pushed. The tournament tussles needed to be worth the trip. Ironically, most coaches in search of stiff tests for their basketball teams drive *toward* the D.C. Metro area, not away from it. On opening night in 1961, DeMatha's John Austin lit up Altoona High in a ten-point win. Austin scored thirty-one points in a physical battle that left him exhausted. "I have never been so sore," he told a *Washington Daily News* writer. Altoona committed twenty-six fouls.[71] That year, John Austin and Johnny Jones became the first African American basketball players on scholarship at DeMatha. Austin had transferred in from Archbishop Carroll, Jones from Dunbar of D.C. Jones said he had planned to transfer to Carroll to join Austin after those great Carroll teams of the late 1950s, but Coach Bob Dwyer left his post there. Austin and Jones met with a priest at Austin's house, as Jones recalls, and the priest suggested the boys transfer to DeMatha Catholic. Jones said his new daily commute,

The Morgan Wootten Legend

Morgan Wootten's Basketball Record

1956-57: 22-10	1966-67: 26-5	1976-77: 29-4	1986-87: 28-6 *	1996-97: 27-7
1957-58: 17-11	1967-68: 27-1 *	1977-78: 28-0 *	1987-88: 30-3 *	1997-98: 34-1 *
1958-59: 23-10	1968-69: 27-3 *	1978-79: 28-3 *	1988-89: 27-5	1998-99: 28-4
1959-60: 23-10	1969-70: 28-3 *	1979-80: 27-4 *	1989-90>26-8 *	1999-2000: 28-5
1960-61: 27-1*	1970-71: 29-2 *	1980-81: 28-2 *	1990-91: 30-0 *	2000-2001: 29-6*
1961-62: 29-4 *	1971-72: 30-1 *	1981-82: 28-3 *	1991-92: 31-2 *	2001-2002: 32-3*
1962-63: 36-2 *	1972-73: 30-1 *	1982-83: 27-4 *	1992-93: 20-10	At DeMatha: 1,274-192
1963-64: 27-2 *	1973-74: 27-5 *	1983-84: 29-2 *	1993-94: 28-4 *	(.868 win percentage)
1964-65: 28-1 *	1974-75: 26-5 *	1984-85: 26-7 *	1994-95: 26-7	*Conf. Champions
1965-66: 28-1 *	1975-76: 28-5 *	1985-86: 28-6	1995-96: 31-5 *	

Basketball Rankings

The Washington Post and Nationally

1959: #6	1974: #3	1989: #6
1960: #2	1975: #2	1990: #6
1961: #1	1976: #3	1991: #1, #11 USA
1962: #1, #1 USA	1977: #4	1992: #2, #13 USA
1963: #1	1978: #1, #1 USA	1993: #9
1964: #1	1979: #1	1994: #1, #10 USA
1965: #1, #1 USA	1980: #3	1995: #10
1966: #1	1981: #1	1996: #4
1967: #2	1982: #1	1997: #6
1968: #1, #1 USA	1983: #1	1998: #1, #4 USA
1969: #2	1984: #1, #1 USA	1999: #4, #6 USA
1970: #1	1985: #2, #17 USA	2000: #7
1971: #1	1986: #9	2001: #2, #14 USA
1972: #1	1987: #3	2002: #1, #8 USA
1973: #1	1988: #1, #9 USA	

Morgan Wootten's Football Record

1956: 4-4	1961: 4-5	1966: 7-3*
1957: 6-3	1962: 6-3	1967: 10-1*
1958: 4-5-1	1963: 9-0* (Top 10 USA)	1968: 5-4
1959: 6-3-1	1964: 8-2	TOTAL: 79-40-2
1960: 6-3	1965: 4-4	*Catholic League Champs

The Morgan Wootten Legend. *Courtesy of DeMatha Catholic.*

one way, took ninety minutes. Austin and Jones greatly elevated the Stags' talent and put a giant bull's eye across their uniforms as standout players.[72]

The Altoona Lions played for keeps in Johnstown in 1961. "Twenty-six personals and one technical foul were called against Altoona," the *Washington Daily News* reported, "as the Lions threw elbows, fists, hips, and knees at DeMatha." The reward for whoever survived the opening game was a championship matchup against Norristown and six-foot-eight Jim Williams, whom one writer labeled "another Chamberlain." Williams had scored twenty points in the other semifinal game, an easy win over Charleroi.

His coach supplied the motivation to win the championship. "In the locker room speech before we went up against DeMatha Catholic, the No. 1 team in the entire country, Coach Gene Kauler was able to get to us all," said Jim Williams.[73] "He said, 'If you win this game, you'll have something to tell your grandchildren about.' We didn't understand the full significance of it in the moment, but Kauler said, 'Go out and play like you never played before.' He motivated us to the point that I believe we were up at the half. Gene Kauler had as much to do with us beating the No. 1 team as any of the players."

Bruce Young hit a jumper to give Norristown a 51–50 lead late, and then Williams added a free throw. Austin drove the lane for the tying basket, but Williams stepped out and swatted the shot to half court.

Norristown earned its greatest basketball victory other than its state championship victory in 1948. The Eagles would make four state finals from 1962 to 2008, losing to Uniontown, Schenley, Fifth Avenue and Chester, respectively—a panoply of Pennsylvania power programs. DeMatha would finish that season 29-4 and mythical national champions.

Beating DeMatha Catholic was a Bucket List achievement, a lofty goal that you hope to attain but can't be certain you ever will. "I ended up being a high school All-American because of that game," said Williams. "A Parade All-American. Last guy picked. No. 20 on a 20-man roster. Among the Parade 1962 high school All-Americans, I'm the last guy mentioned."

Williams's younger brother, Henry, a six-foot-five player who was the first sophomore to make first-team All-State, played in the Johnstown Tournament in 1969 and 1970. In 1969, he faced six-foot-ten Tom McMillen of Mansfield High. Norristown was in the middle of an era when they'd dominate the Suburban One League on the outskirts of Philadelphia. It's a town rich with sports, producing Hall of Fame coaches Tommy Lasorda and Geno Auriemma.

Henry Williams scored 25 points against McMillen, but McMillen was one better and Mansfield was four better, 71–67. In the consolation against Bishop McCort, Williams scored 27 points in a 67–59 win.

As a senior, Henry Williams would be forced to play inside as the Eagles lacked the height of previous teams. He would face an intimidating St. Anthony's of D.C. team that was taller than Williams, from six-foot-ten coach John Thompson on down. The former Boston Celtic was the coach of a team that would win the next two Johnstown Tournaments with ease. Don Washington was six-foot-seven and one of the nation's most desired recruits. Both Washington and Williams were touted as first-team All-Americans. Thompson's team was ranked No. 1 in the nation in one poll.

St. Anthony's won by 16. In the consolation against nearby Richland High, Williams scored 17 in a 55–42 win. By that point, Henry's elder brother, Jim, had completed a stellar career at Temple University. He would play professionally overseas, but winning the Johnstown Tournament remained special to him.

"I don't think I ever knew how good I really was," he said. "I was raised in a household where you left all of that stuff on the court and at school or on the street, but you didn't bring it into Mrs. Williams' house. There was no room in our house for big heads. 'You don't wear your ass on your shoulders,' as my mother said." Mrs. Williams didn't want her boys self-promoting. "As Wilt would say, 'That's for others to say and not me.'"

Against the elder Williams and Norristown, Wooten got the push—if not the result—that he wanted for his team in Johnstown. Anybody who knew Morgan and his competitiveness knew he would vow to return to win the tournament, which he did in 1963. And 1964. And 1965. DeMatha took a seven-year hiatus from Johnstown before returning in 1973 and 1974 and 1975. Overall, DeMatha would compete in ten Johnstown Tournaments, winning eight.

Morgan's commitment to Johnstown spanned from 1961 to 1988, resulting in eighteen wins, two defeats and a collection of memories. As DeMatha and the classy Wooten became the "it" program in high school basketball, Washington, D.C. agent David Falk became the trusted representative for Stag players who made their way to the NBA. Starting with John Austin and John Jones in 1962, DeMatha has sent twenty players to the league, fourteen under Wooten's tutelage.

"All of the DeMatha guys, we had," said Falk, "Adrian Dantley, Kenny Carr, Danny Ferry, Sidney Lowe, Dereck Whittenburg, Jerrod Mustaf…we had them all because of Morgan. We didn't do anything to get those guys.

The coaches picked us not because of the relationship but because of our track record."[74] Conversely, agents wanted DeMatha guys because of their track record and because of Wootten's. By then, Morgan had become great friends with professional basketball and Washington, D.C. icon Red Auerbach.

WOOTTEN ESTABLISHED A ROUTINE for the Johnstown Tournament visits. He would celebrate Christmas with his family, exchange presents and hugs and then gas up the vehicles for the road trip north, something between a school field trip and a men's getaway. Stag player Joe Kennedy remembers the process from the 1960s.

"We didn't have a bus," he said. "Parents and coaches would drive the team in vans and cars. Any time we would go on the road we'd start out at DeMatha. One of the priests would say the rosary, and then everybody jumped into cars. The guys who were driving would make bets who would get to the hotel bar first. It was like the Cannonball Run."[75]

By the 1980s, after Mike Brey had helped DeMatha to a 55-9 record in his two seasons playing sporadically for Wootten, he returned to coach under Wootten from 1982 to 1987. That new role exposed him to the coaches' side of the Johnstown trip. As an assistant coach, Brey would drive one of the vans to Pennsylvania, a state not unfamiliar to him, and enter into the coaching staff's inner circle. Brey had grown up in Lehighton, Pennsylvania, three and a half hours east of Johnstown. His mother, Betty, became an Olympic swimmer, a statue in the borough of Weissport testifying to her success.

"Last time I was in Carbon County, we put up my mom's statue in Weissport," said Brey, whose uncles were also standout basketball players at places like Duke University. "I looked around that little town. For my mom to fight her way out of Weissport, to be an Olympian, a physical therapist in the Army. Wow!"[76]

Mike's uncle Jack Mullen was a guard on Duke's first Atlantic Coast Conference championship team in 1960. Mullen teamed up with Radnor (Pennsylvania) High's former six-foot-nine center Doug Kistler to beat Wake Forest's squad, led by former Johnstown Tournament player Len Chappell (Portage High) and Billy Packer (Bethlehem High).

When Brey's mother, Betty, moved to Washington, D.C., Mike's basketball future opened to a world of following the great teams at DeMatha and then enrolling there himself. He found his way to Wootten's basketball camp and program.

"Pete Strickland and I would drive the team to Johnstown," he said in 2024 while working for the Atlanta Hawks of the NBA after a successful college coaching career at Duke, the University of Delaware and Notre Dame. "Morgan would have his drivers, and they would play cards the whole way. He'd have his hotel room. Vinny Scalco was in charge of setting up the buffet. The other guy was in charge of Miller Lite. The four of them would play until all hours. It was a guy's trip for him. They would play the PITCH poker games. They would travel together, to Johnstown and to the Alhambra Tournament later in March. In Johnstown, we were in a Holiday Inn. The doors opened to the outside. He had the meatballs stewing in the corner.…That was the routine."

Johnstown Tournament organizers treated Wootten especially well. Morgan was always looking for a good time—and a bargain. He was notoriously frugal. The more Johnstown could do to show their admiration and appreciation for DeMatha, the more likely Wootten would return and lend that marquee high school basketball brand to the tournament nestled in the Pennsylvania woodlands.

"When Coach started going up there, he gave them such credibility," said Brey, "and they took care of him. It almost became a DeMatha Tournament. The town loved him. He had five beautiful children, Christmas is crazy and the next day he's out of there on the way to Johnstown."

After winning the Johnstown Tournaments in December 1964 and 1965, DeMatha would play Lew Alcindor's Power Memorial teams one month later at Cole Field House on the campus of the University of Maryland. Wootten always fixed one eye on the next rung up the ladder. DeMatha lost to Power and Alcindor the first year. They won the second year. Just like how they began their Johnstown Tournaments—losing the first year, learning from defeat and coming back to claim the trophy.

In the 1965 Johnstown Tournament, Wootten brought a team in transition. Five new starters. The field included Mackin Catholic of D.C., which had uber-talented guard Austin Carr and Tom Little. After beating Schenley High from Pittsburgh and Kenny Durrett in the opener, Mackin probably felt like the favorite.

"They had Austin Carr and Tom Little," said DeMatha's Bob Petrini. "This is gonna determine the whole season for us. I think we were losing by twelve or fifteen points at the half. We were getting our ass kicked. I just remember running my ass off, stealing balls and getting layups when we pressed them the entire second half. They couldn't get the ball over halfcourt."[77]

Austin Carr poster. *Photo by Thomas Slusser,* Johnstown Tribune-Democrat.

Mackin Catholic was the D.C. rival ever chasing DeMatha. Carr was the unstoppable guard who would average nearly thirty-five points per game when he played at Notre Dame. He was also the player who had inquired about attending DeMatha, but a secretary did not adequately relay his name to Wootten, potentially costing Wootten one of the greatest players in D.C. prep history.

After pulling off the improbable comeback victory, Petrini remembers looking at Carr and company and thinking, "*We own you.* We beat them two more times that year."

In Petrini's time at DeMatha, the Stags went 78-4. They lost to Power Memorial and Dean Meminger's Rice High team from New York. Petrini remembers losing to the University of Maryland freshman team that included future Terrapins coach Gary Williams.

"I guarantee you someone got to the refs and said, 'You can't let a high school team beat the University of Maryland freshmen,'" reasoned Petrini. "They fouled out four of our players."

After the game, Gary Williams told Petrini, "You guys are really good!"

When you play for a coach who goes 1,274-192 in forty-six seasons, winning five mythical national titles, you expect to win somehow every night. Imagine coaching forty-six years and only losing 192 basketball games!

"On offense we ran the wheel," said Petrini. "We scored so many points in transition at DeMatha. Guys would cut, and off that you could call a corner shot. Running three players off the high post and seeing if they can get open off of that. First cutter would go to the corner and swing the ball to him to shoot the jump shot."

The only time Petrini can remember Morgan putting in a play for a specific player was when he did that for Ernie Austin. Otherwise, it was all team ball. Unquestionably, it worked.

"In my first 25 years there," Wootten wrote in his book *A Coach for All Seasons*, "our basketball teams won ninety percent of their games while playing the toughest schedule in the country.…To be the best, you have to beat the best. And you can't do that if you don't play them. It's not unusual for our basketball schedule to include four or five state champions."[78]

Playing powerhouse opponents in showcase games in expansive venues had another effect that Wootten biographer Bill Gilbert charted: "In one special period of over thirty straight years, every one of his DeMatha seniors—one hundred and seventy-five students, from his biggest stars to the lowest substitute on the far end of the bench, even the manager in some years—won a full four-year scholarship to college. Since 1960, over 95 percent of DeMatha's basketball players have won full college scholarships."

As expected, college athletic directors tried to lure Wootten to the next level. He considered the University of Maryland job when Lefty Driesell applied. Wootten even declared that he would take it if Lefty didn't want it. Then his DeMatha team played brilliantly in a big game, and Wootten said that he prayed Lefty would take the Maryland job, which he did. Georgetown considered Wootten when it hired John Thompson. The Hoyas administration was looking to add more African Americans at that time to better represent the D.C. community. They hired Thompson, and he revolutionized their basketball fortunes.

And North Carolina State came calling in 1980. Wootten's national championship guards Dereck Whittenburg and Sidney Lowe were already freshmen at N.C. State at the time. Wootten mulled an offer of $700,000 for five years. He chose to stay in Hyattsville to remain a legendary high school coach. Iona College coach Jim Valvano took the N.C. State job. He won the national title when Wootten guards Whittenburg and Lowe were seniors in 1983—nine years after their previous one with Whittenburg cousin David Thompson on the team.

MEN OF TROY

Ask Joe Nastasi how tall he is, and his response will fluctuate. "I'm 6 foot now," he says. "I was listed at 5-8 in high school. I'm probably 5-10 today."[79] When you grow up in rural Northern Cambria in central Pennsylvania—where the woodsy terrain consists of tree-covered slopes, hills and mountains—you learn to ignore size the same way David did in the Bible. In 1965, Northern Cambria basketball players focused more on the size of their determination and the depth of their commitment. Not those other quantifiers:

- the size of the town (three square miles)
- the town's population (about 3,000)
- the graduating class (140 students)
- the backcourt players' height (all under six feet)
- the frontcourt (six-foot-one and six-two)

If you intend to do anything huge in life, the size of your effort and will are the metrics that matter.

And if a December basketball tournament in remote Johnstown, a mere thirty miles from Northern Cambria, purports to offer anything, it's the opportunity for teams from all locales to test themselves against mighty elites. Northern Cambria was one of the smallest schools by enrollment ever invited to compete in Johnstown. Wee-sized Wampum High and baseball legend Dick Allen played in Johnstown in 1958 and 1959, losing to powerhouse Overbrook but defeating North Catholic and then losing to larger New Castle and Altoona, despite being perhaps the school with the tiniest enrollment in Pennsylvania.

In 1965, DeMatha Catholic returned to Johnstown, where it would open against LaSalle Catholic from Philadelphia. The Explorers were coached by thirty-year veteran Charles "Obie" O'Brien, who was within two strong seasons of reaching the five-hundred-win plateau. They would oppose DeMatha a month before the Stags would take on Lew Alcindor's Power Memorial team and its seventy-one-game winning streak at a sold-out Cole Field House. At War Memorial, DeMatha dusted LaSalle by 28. In the other Johnstown semifinal, little Northern Cambria pounded host Johnstown 70–45 in a central Pennsylvania shocker. That set up a championship matchup of one of the premier high school programs in America and its Hall of Fame coach against an undersized Colts team raised on hunting, fishing and competition of every kind. It pitted the inner-city private school that was permitted to recruit against a small-town public program that suited up whoever appeared in the hallways—sons of miners.

"Our coach, Ted Keenan, wasn't even a basketball guy," said Northern Cambria leading scorer Greg Kuhn. "He had played professional football once upon a time. He was our gym teacher, and he coached basketball and he always had winning teams. Even though he was not what I could call the Wizard of X's and O's, you worked really, really hard."[80]

Keenan's system was easy to scout. His boys were going to play exclusively man-to-man defense and bump you all night. Even against DeMatha—who started six-foot-eight Sid Catlett and six-foot-seven Bob Whitmore—Keenan had his players defending one-on-one in the low post despite giving away half a foot. Never mind that Catlett and Whitmore would both play at Notre Dame and be drafted into the NBA. Keenan stuck to a system built on pride and machismo, as well as perhaps a pinch of false bravado.

On offense, Northern Cambria would race the ball up court in transition. The players would pass the ball on offense until one of the five players had the open look. Northern Cambria games must have resembled the town on St. Patrick's Day, because everybody had a green light.

"There was an ongoing thing on our team," said Joe Nastasi. "There was always somewhat of a debate who was going to take the ball out of bounds. If you took the ball out, you passed it in and probably never saw it again."

The twin Nastasi brothers, Joe and Tony, symbolized that must-do, attacking mentality. With a graduating class of 140 students, a few boys needed to do much. They'd grown up playing pickup basketball in a mining hall with black dust on the floor and baskets at each end. Nastasi's grandparents had been coal miners. The borough of Barnesboro sat between Johnstown and Altoona, two mid-sized cities, but Barnesboro felt far more remote. When the boys hit eighth grade, the boroughs of Barnesboro and Spangler merged into Northern Cambria. When they were sophomores, they moved into a new high school. Four starters were from Barnesboro, one from Spangler. Four of the five had played youth baseball together. Playing in the Johnstown Tournament was a step up in every way.

"It was a big deal to go to such a prestigious tournament," said Nastasi. "Johnstown had a very talented team also that year. They had a very good team. A lot of the people in bigger towns—Johnstown, Altoona—felt we didn't belong in that tournament because of the other schools that were there."

Against Johnstown, Northern Cambria played half court man-to-man instead of pressing. The Colts had to adjust to a court placed over ice, a huge crowd and being the runt in the tournament litter. "They came out and sort of bullied us," said Nastasi. "They were dunking the ball and everything else. That somewhat fired us up."

Plus, the game was the second of the doubleheader, the featured top billing against Johnstown in Johnstown. Davidson University assistant coach Terry Holland was there recruiting for Coach Lefty Driesell. Northern Cambria had a handful of reasons to buckle. At halftime, the Colts led 42–18. They rolled 70–45. The score certainly indicated that these Colts belonged.

And that victory brought DeMatha, a 23-2 team the year before with ten of thirteen players, back. Coach Morgan Wootten's career record was a cartoonish 197-39.[81]

"At the time," said Nastasi, "every one of their players had gotten D-I basketball scholarships. There were a couple who played at Notre Dame.... We stayed in Johnstown in one of the hotels there. We carried on a little bit after beating Johnstown. We toyed around with DeMatha the night before our game."

It seemed like after earning at least one victory in the tournament over a local big school power, the Colts had nothing to lose against DeMatha. They understood that they could get embarrassed. A Shamokin newspaper misprint reported the halftime score as 46–2 DeMatha. It wasn't as historically awful as that. Northern Cambria trailed 46–22 at the break. A team that typically played in a local pond was drowning in the Atlantic Ocean. The Stags would outrebound the smaller Colts 65–17. DeMatha rolled 94–48 with a team of tall and quick future college stars. Greg Kuhn scored 18 for Northern Cambria, whose undefeated season was obliterated.

"I guarded Sid Catlett," said Joe Nastasi. "It was OK. He did his thing. I did what I could do. Maybe this is our naivete, but we never played one second of zone in our high school career. We played man to man come hell or high water. We never had or practiced playing a zone."

Mickey Wiles scored eighteen for the winners, followed by Catlett, Whitmore and Ernie Austin with fifteen apiece. Austin, considered the top player in America despite being a junior, would play on Syracuse's undefeated freshman team in 1966–67 and average thirty points per game.

Had the Colts played a zone, they might have kept the score down and even forced DeMatha to take more outside shots in an era before the three-point line, but the outcome wouldn't have changed. Nonetheless, the best of Northern Cambria basketball history was still ahead. For DeMatha, in January 1965, the Stags would even the score and defeat the great Lew Alcindor and Power Memorial in a game pitting basketball titans against each other in Maryland's Cole Field House.

Northern Cambria returned to its normal schedule, winning every game heading into the March postseason. After winning the District 6 title, the Colts went into the state tournament and won consecutive high-scoring games by twelve points. They avenged the prior season's loss to Coraopolis in one contest.

"You can talk about [Greg] Kuhn all you want," said Coraopolis coach Vic Bianchi. "Sure, he's a great boy. But they have four other good ones to go with him. They shoot and they really work those boards."[82] Apparently, the rebounding lesson DeMatha gave the Colts left an imprint.

In the Class B eastern final, Northern Cambria beat Cambridge Springs 69–64. Kuhn scored 21 points. The Colts stayed in front despite seeing their 14-point halftime lead whittled to 3 in the second half. The western champions were the defending state champions, the unbeaten Montrose Meteors on a 52-game winning streak. Montrose had beaten Darby-Colwyn 77–66 in the western final to move to within two games of D-C's state record 54-game winning streak. Darby-Colwyn had won state titles in 1962 and 1963 when the Rams went a combined 50-0.

In 26-0 Montrose, 28-1 Northern Cambria would face a mirror image of itself—a smallish team filled with shooters and scorers. Montrose star Burt Crawford had scored thirty-one points in the quarterfinal win but injured himself in the semifinal, although he continued to play the rest of the game. The state final matchup figured to be a high-scoring racehorse contest between similar small towns. Perhaps due to Montrose's streak and unbeaten record, and Northern Cambria having lost once to DeMatha, the pressure was mostly on the Meteors.

That didn't show through one half, as Montrose led 46–42 at the Pittsburgh Field House. The Colts continued to score, and when Montrose missed its shots, the Colts pounced on the rebounds.

"They beat us under the boards," said Montrose coach Si Bernosky. "This kid [Ken] Anderson was terrific and never allowed us to get a second shot. Northern Cambria was by the far best team we have faced."[83]

The Colts prevailed 78–69 as Ken Anderson scored 14 points and snatched a herculean 23 rebounds. The burley Anderson would be recruited to play linebacker at Penn State. Greg Kuhn scored 24 and Frank Frontino 22. Not only did Northern Cambria justify its selection in Johnstown as state champions, but they also became one of the rare District 6 teams to win a state title.

"I played college football and college basketball at Brown University," said Kuhn, "and I didn't find anyone as competitive as our Northern Cambria guys."

After a stint at prep school, Kuhn enrolled at Brown to play multiple sports. Johnstown basketball tournament organizer Clayt Dovey Jr. had a son who had attended Westmont Hilltop High adjacent to Johnstown. Kuhn knew Dovey from when Dovey took a chance on Class B Northern Cambria for his elite tournament. Kuhn remembered Dovey from his writings in the *Johnstown Democrat* newspaper, including his fishing and outdoors column that drew a wide audience. Kuhn described Dovey as "a peach. He was called the old angler. He had all these different fishing stories. Just a gentleman extraordinaire."

The angler's son would also be attending Brown. Dovey III and Kuhn pledged the same fraternity and played basketball together as freshmen. As sophomores, they decided to room together. Both would conclude their basketball careers prematurely. Kuhn focused on football thereafter on meager teams. The night before Kuhn got married years later, his buddies from Brown and from Cambria County all played basketball at Clayt Dovey's basketball court in Westmont. Local football star Jack Ham from Bishop McCort was there too.

"We played basketball until 3:00 a.m.," said Kuhn. "All my guys and all the Clayt guys and guys from Brown. Jack was a very nice guy. Great athlete. Maybe the best outside linebacker to ever play the game....We had a never-give-up atmosphere every night at Northern Cambria. It was fun."

Dovey III went on to become a successful Wall Street trader. He died tragically before his time at age fifty-four. "I was devastated by that," said Kuhn. "He was smart as hell, doing extremely well on Wall Street. He moved to Chicago and was getting married. He's my friend for life and eternity. He would make me laugh, and I would make him laugh."

One of the tournament organizers, Bob Gardill, was part of a group that would hold—what else?—a sports event with the trophy named in Clayton Dovey III's honor. They have reunited for Thanksgiving Turkey Day football games every year since 1967. The Bulls play the Bears, with proceeds benefiting Easter Seals for Cambria/Somerset. It's just how the people from Johnstown's glory days function—sports as the community bonding and healing vehicle.

THE FORWARD WHO AVERAGED about sixteen points per game on the 1965 Northern Cambria state championship team, Frank Frontino, went into professional baseball. He briefly flamed out as a third baseman in the Dodgers organization, but he reestablished himself as a spot starter and relief pitcher in the Pittsburgh Pirates organization.

"I ended up going to Forbes Field on a tryout as a pitcher," he said, "which I did become. They signed me. All I was hoping for was that they give me one year."[84]

Like Kuhn, Frontino happened upon a Johnstown connection to propel him through his career. His manager in Class A was Frank Oceak, who had played in Johnstown in two minor-league stints. Oceak had developed a tight bond with Pirates manager Danny Murtaugh from Chester, best known for being the Pirates third base coach when Bill Mazeroski belted his Game 7, ninth-inning home run to win the World Series over the Yankees in 1960. Oceak guided Frontino's pitching career. Frontino developed into a starter whose early success had him pitching into the ninth and even tenth innings of games.

In one game, Frontino pitched a ten-inning shutout. He followed that with a nine-inning shutout. In the next outing, he pitched the final three innings against the Pirates' AAA team. After giving up a three-run double to tie the score, Frontino blanked the Triple-A lineup from there. The game went into extra innings—six of them! Frontino wound up pitching nine innings that day too.

The next game, predictably, his arm flat-lined. Warming up, he couldn't get the ball to home plate. It began an eighteen-month rehabilitation.

Roving pitching instructor Billy Short pulled Frontino aside a few weeks after the injury. "Frank," Short said, "I don't know if I should tell you this, but I'm gonna tell you anyway. That game there was your last game. They were calling you up to Pittsburgh."

That kind of news was on par with your best buddy telling you that Marilyn Monroe wanted to date you but that she had to leave the country for a few years.

"The Pirates needed a pitcher, and nobody was doing it at Triple-A," said Frontino, a right-hander who says he never knew how fast he could throw a fastball because there weren't many radar guns back then. "And I was kind of doing it. Who did they bring up then? Bruce Kison, and he's a very good friend of mine. He ended up being the World Series hero that year for the Pirates in 1971. I never came back to where I was as a pitcher."

The second-generation basketball story that came out of that 1965 Northern Cambria squad is complete Hollywood. After college at Indiana University of Pennsylvania, Joe Nastasi would move to Altoona, Pennsylvania, and coach basketball with legendary boss John Swogger, who had coached his Mercer High teams to state finals five out of seven seasons, winning two. After Mercer, Swogger came to Altoona, where he took Nastasi on as an assistant when Nastasi was a student teacher. Nastasi would have sons four years apart. He coached them hard in Swogger style in football and in basketball during their formative years, demanding maximum effort and commitment. His son A.J. couldn't help but learn the critical importance of attacking every drill with military intensity:

> *I had a crazy trainer—my dad was all over us. He was our head football coach in high school for both of us. It was the old Italian iron fist, do it one way or you're not doing it. I guess he got everything out of everybody regardless of skill level. To me that's coaching. He kind of did…I don't know…if it was out of fear. The coaching has changed so much now. Now coaches are scared to do anything. My dad was as intense as they came. You rode home with him, you didn't want to ride home with him. He was harder on my brother. Just the screaming and the absolute—you ever do that again!—but it was for the right reason. We have great a relationship now.*

The eldest Nastasi son, Joe Jr., put up pinball scoring numbers in basketball for Northern Bedford High, an hour southeast of Northern Cambria.

Northern Bedford, unlike coal-centric Northern Cambria, is a rural farming community that graduates fewer than one hundred seniors. Joe scored 2,961 career points, missing out on a career 3,000 when his team lost games to inclement weather.

A.J. Nastasi, four years younger, would set the Pennsylvania all-time scoring record with 3,833 points. He eclipsed career scoring leader Tom McMillen of Mansfield High, who sent a congratulatory video message to A.J. the night he broke the record of 3,608 points. A.J. became the fourth Pennsylvanian to surpass 3,000 career points, his 3,833 points elevating him above McMillen (3,608 in 1970), Carlisle's Billy Owens (3,299 in 1988) and West Reading's Ronnie Krick (3,174 in 1961). In 2023, Aquinas Academy's Vinny Cugini finished with 3,189 career points, sliding him ahead of Krick's total. Cugini averaged a Maravichian 43.7 points per game for his career.

A.J. Nastasi averaged more than thirty points per game in each of his four years. Opponents double- and triple-teamed him, with minimal success. "I think I scored 1,100 points from the 3-point line," he said. A.J. became a mega-legend despite being packaged in a medium-sized frame at six feet tall. His basketball exploits made him legendary. Nastasi noted of his record-setting night:

> *On February 7, 1998, against Everett at Hollidaysburg Junior High/Sr. High, I broke the record. We were trying to get a bigger venue. They tried to get it up to the Bryce Jordan Center* [at Penn State University], *but they didn't have room; they had games either for the men or the women. The Hollidaysburg High gym was sold out within a minute. They were doing it like a telecall. It would have been interesting to see how big a venue it could have filled, because they turned tons of people away. They had so many reserved for family and friends and dignitaries. It would have been a lot of fun to see how big a place you could fill up.*[85]

By 1998, both Nastasi boys had become legendary athletes in Pennsylvania, although their exploits were largely relegated to overflowing but modest gyms in the countryside. Neither boy would play in a showcase tournament like their father had in Johnstown. Neither would win a state title. Joe Jr. would go on to play wide receiver at Penn State and A.J. the same position at West Virginia University. They had basketball options out of Northern Bedford High, but having grown up attending summer football camps in State College, they wanted to pursue football, a more realistic pathway to professional sports.

And yet, drive to the Naismith Memorial Basketball Hall of Fame in Springfield, Massachusetts, and you'll find A.J. Nastasi's memorabilia. For years, fans could only locate high school basketball mementos in the Hall with a Sherlock Holmes hat and a magnifying glass, but that is changing. For a sub-six-foot shooting guard from rural Pennsylvania to be represented is astronomically unlikely.

"The hall of fame called me and asked me if all this was available," he said. "They gave me a list of stuff to send up to them. My shorts, my jersey that I wore when I set the state scoring record and my shoes—signed. They have all of them in Springfield. I've never been up to see it. I've had people go up there and take pictures. They have pro, college and high school there."

Those familiar with the Nastasi brothers might have expected to see their wares in Canton, Ohio. But they made the most enduring memories in their father and uncle's high school sport: basketball.

"Even to this day," Joe Sr. says, "people come up to me and want to talk about the state championship. And that was almost sixty years ago." And when they look at the name of the Northern Cambria gym, they'll see Ted Keenan's name.

WE THERE, DURRETT?

How electric was Kenny Durrett of Schenley High? And just how great would the Spartans be in 1965–66?

They'd finished the previous season one rung from the state final, losing to eventual champion Midland, which starred Simmie Hill and Norm Van Lier. Four Schenley starters returned, including twenty-one-point-per-game scorer Kenny Durrett. Ed "Petey" Gibson, the grandson of Negro League slugger Josh Gibson, was back to run the point. Season preview articles broached a subject Schenley coach Willard Fisher found too spicy, too early, in December: Can Schenley win the state championship? Fisher parried those queries.[86]

The Spartans arrived in Johnstown still trying to mesh the pieces. They'd barely beaten Jeannette, 79–76. They would enter Johnstown as the first Pittsburgh city public school team to play here. The field included two Washington, D.C. heavyweights, DeMatha Catholic and the Stags' rival, Mackin Catholic. Oh, and local parochial power Bishop McCort.

How good was Schenley? We'd find out. How good was the six-foot-six Durrett? Well, he was already spending summers working out with Connie Hawkins, the precursor to "Dr. J," Julius Erving. At least one Western Pennsylvania program was trying to entice Durrett's parents to move into their district and work and live within the boundary so Kenny might play for them. The house and jobs were already secured. Waiting for Schenley in Johnstown was a Mackin Catholic team that featured Austin Carr and Tom Little. Carr was a junior about to average twenty points per game for the second straight season.

Ken Durrett poster. *Photo by Thomas Slusser,* Johnstown Tribune-Democrat.

Mackin grabbed the lead early and then endured Schenley's pressing defense well enough to hang on for an 80–73 victory. Mackin rival DeMatha, loaded with a roster that included guard Ernie Austin and six-foot-eight Sid Catlett, downed Bishop McCort by 17.

STEVE SMEAR WAS A tough but undersized player for Bishop McCort. Before his first birthday, his father passed away. His mother remarried when Steve was eleven; his stepfather died when Steve was twelve. Smear's mother continued to run their bar, the Old Toll Gate Inn, giving Smear a transitional supply of townsmen to help raise him. Local firemen signed Smear up for baseball. Mike Kosco drove him around to see sporting events, from the local St. Francis University basketball games to the Harlem Globetrotters, even driving Smear to Pittsburgh a few times each year to see the Pirates and Steelers. Men like Kosco showed Smear a wide world of sports beyond the one-channel black-and-white television set in Smear's mother's bar.[87]

"The first game that I ever saw on a color TV was at the GBU Club in Johnstown with my stepfather," said Smear. "He took me to see when Notre Dame played Oklahoma in football. It was a color TV, but it bleeded out from the colors that it was supposed to be. Oklahoma still had the streak going [forty-seven straight victories]."

Oklahoma, under Coach Bud Wilkinson, would beat Notre Dame that day. The Irish weren't too strong then. But they would ultimately break the Sooners' streak in 1957 with a 7–0 shutout. Smear got introduced to all the major sports.

"Frank Oceak, the third base coach of the Pirates, each year after the baseball season for three to four years when I was a kid, he would come and sit in our kitchen next to the bar," Smear remembered, "and he would bring me a bag of baseballs. I would hit them into the woods and not even go after them because I was afraid of snakes."

The men of Johnstown stepped up for the local boys, over and over. "I always tell people that I couldn't have been born in a better city than Johnstown, Pennsylvania, and played sports," Smear said. "The Catholic Athletic Association that was there was just unbelievable. They had all kinds of fairs to raise money for basketball and football for the kids to go to tournaments."

Every block, it seemed, had a Catholic church, a Catholic elementary school…and a bar. The churches all had teams, and the town was filled with eager boys like Smear and his buddies Mike Patcher and Jack Ham looking for positive outlets. In 1965, the outlet was the Johnstown Tournament.

Bishop McCort's Mike Patcher, at six-foot-five, would guard Durrett and keep him somewhat under control with 26 points. Patcher himself scored 19 and snared 16 rebounds. Teammate Stan Rok also had 19 points. McCort led by 16 late in the third quarter when the Schenley pressure started to force turnovers. Petey Gibson harassed McCort's point guard. Momentum shifted and Schenley made a game of it late. McCort held on, 68–66. Schenley finished 0-2 in Johnstown. How good would Schenley become? Still too early to tell, but the Spartans were surrendering a ton of points.

PATCHER WAS TALENTED ENOUGH to eventually choose Pitt for his college, where he would become captain of the basketball team. And being in Pittsburgh, Pitt would be a local reminder of the night Patcher helped McCort beat nearby Schenley at War Memorial Arena. McCort would finish 28-2 and win the parochial state title. Schenley would win the public school state title in Class A, beating Punxsutawney, Uniontown and finally Chester en route to the public state championship. In the state final, three Spartans seniors scored in double figures, but that fifth starter, Montel Brundage, led them with twenty-two points, a huge improvement over his two prior scoreless state playoff games. Schenley grew up after its tepid performance in Johnstown.

"We had let the coach down two nights in a row," point guard Petey Gibson told the *Post-Gazette*'s Marino Parascenzo after the state final victory. "We couldn't let him down again."[88]

After topping Mackin 71–70 for the Johnstown Tournament title in December, DeMatha went on to win its sixth straight Washington, D.C. Catholic League title, earning Morgan Wootten Coach of the Year honors. Despite having graduated Bernard Williams, Terry Wiles and Bob Whitmore from a 24-1 team, the Stags went 28-1. Whitmore was named third-team Parade All-American. Mackin's Tom Little—MVP of the Johnstown Tournament—made the sixth team. Little would be suspended from Mackin's team in February, a move that placed the scoring onus onto Austin Carr, who led the Trojans to the finals of the vaunted Alhambra Catholic Invitational Tournament final, where Mackin lost to St. Agnes Cathedral of New York.

Three of the four Johnstown Tournament representatives from December 1965 won major titles in the spring of 1966—two state, one Catholic league, one Knights of Columbus and nearly the Alhambra title. Hard to beat that!

IN DECEMBER 1966, SCHENLEY returned to Johnstown hoping for better results. Durrett was now six-foot-seven and considered the nation's No. 1 recruit after averaging 25 points per game on a state title team. In the *Somerset Daily American* preview story, the writer settled on one word to describe Durrett: "frightening!"[89] And with Gibson back too, Schenley was loaded again. But so was Mackin, who was back again with Austin Carr, a senior who'd already scored more than 1,100 career points. Camden High from New Jersey, like Schenley, had gone 19-2 the year before. The Panthers had posted a record of 197-30 in the past decade and featured six-foot-nine Jeff Smith.

Ken Durrett poster. *Photo by Thomas Slusser,* Johnstown Tribune-Democrat.

Johnstown's 342-83 mark under Coach Paul Abele was scintillating too. The *Tyrone Daily Herald* reported that in the tournament's seventeen years, it had produced sixteen state champions, twenty-one champions of other kinds and thirty-eight first-team All-Staters.

In the opener, Schenley hammered Johnstown 92–63. Durrett scored 29 despite briefly injuring his knee. Gibson added a tournament-record 17 assists. Camden nosed Mackin 76–73, as Smith scored 28 points and dominated the rebounds. The Purple Avalanche (now Panthers) advanced to the final, where they would try to repeat as tournament champions and match their 1959 team. That team had Sonny Sunkett. This one had Glen Sunkett (18 points).

Durrett was fabulous again, scoring 29 points. Gibson added 13. Camden would take another three-point victory, however, as Glen Sunkett scored 21 points to atone for Jeff Smith's foul troubles. Tournament director Clayt Dovey Jr. declared it the greatest tournament game yet. Camden jumped ahead 22–13 after one quarter. Schenley, in typical fashion, rallied back, falling just short. Another Sunkett may have won a Johnstown title, but Durrett claimed MVP honors. In the consolation game, Carr and Mackin held off the hosts 76–72 to avoid going 1-3 over two years, as Schenley had.

THE MIDDLE 1960s WERE great years for Johnstown and great launching points for several athletes. Bishop McCort's Steve Smear would visit Notre Dame, Michigan State and Penn State in search of his college football future. He didn't want to follow Bubba Smith at MSU, where Duffy Daugherty had built a national power that had earned a share in two straight national titles. Smear had grown up rooting for Notre Dame, but too often the Irish disappointed him.

"My choice of colleges came down to two schools, Notre Dame and Penn State," said Smear. "I went to Penn State because Pete Duranko [from Bishop McCort] was at Notre Dame, and I knew it would be tough to be compared to Pete. He was one of the best high school players ever from Johnstown. His college career was incredible, and I think he was drafted in the second round by both the NFL [fourth round] and the AFL. On my visit to Notre Dame, I was hosted by Pete."

Duranko developed into an All-American defensive lineman on Notre Dame's 1966 national championship team, the year the Irish had tied Michigan State, 10–10. "After college Pete and I would become friends," said Smear. "When I would come home to visit my mom, I would visit Pete. He had ALS [commonly known as Lou Gehrig's disease] the last 15–20 years of his life. He was an inspiration, as he always had a positive attitude. Pete was one of a kind."[90]

Smear chose Penn State, where he would play with McCort product Jack Ham, one year behind Smear. Coach Joe Paterno would register consecutive 11-0 seasons in 1968 and 1969, yet the eastern power wasn't recognized as national champions either time. Smear would become an All-American defensive lineman, just like Duranko.

In basketball, Kenny Durrett would become three-time Big Five player of the year at LaSalle University before a knee injury shortened a would-be brilliant career.

"Durrett was the man," Gibson said. "And that's how we rolled."[91] The teammates had planned to enroll together at Niagara University, where Calvin Murphy was a three-time All-American, but when it fell through, Durrett chose LaSalle and Gibson veered to the University of New Mexico for Coach Bob King, who never had a losing season there. Like the bigwigs had in Johnstown, King helped the university build a new basketball arena, known as "The Pit," site of the 1983 national championship game.

In 1971, Schenley would have a team that included three superstars—Rickey Coleman, Robert "Jeep" Kelley and Maurice Lucas—that would win another state championship.

Mackin's Austin Carr would continue his ascent, twice earning All-American honors at Notre Dame. At Mackin, he scored more than 2,000 points. At Notre Dame, in three seasons, he scored 2,560, averaging 34.5 points for his career. His 60 points against Ohio University is still the high mark for an NCAA tournament game.

With Camden High having so much fun and success in Johnstown, it was time to expand an invite to another New Jersey squad.

JERSEY? SURE!

Policemen removed little Ed Salmon from his home in York, Pennsylvania, when he was six, relocating him to the home of an older couple in a quiet neighborhood near Harrisburg. At his new home, the sudden semi-orphan was permitted to ride his tricycle down the street to the end of the block, which worked for him since a pretty girl lived at the cutoff. He would pass Marilyn Groninger every day and force conversation, cupping his hand to holler up to her porch.

"I was her grandmother's lawn boy and paper boy," said Salmon. "She blew me off repeatedly. She said I was too outgoing. She was really strong-minded."[92]

Unlucky in love and embroiled in an unstable childhood, Salmon remained chatty among strangers, optimistic without cause. His new caretakers, he'd learn, were blood relatives, his great-aunt and great-uncle. The nineteen-year-old girl he'd call his "sister" Betty had been adopted too. She would counter Ed's tribulations by leading him to a life of faith. In time, after trials that would test his resolve, the breaks would begin to bend to Ed's passions.

At his new home in LeMoyne, Salmon would follow his sister's lead, earning solid grades. He stayed active playing basketball, running long distances and setting a course toward college. His prowess in cross-country and basketball would get him recruited to Gettysburg College.

After sitting the bench for the basketball team and then graduating with a degree, Salmon moved to New Jersey, near the love of his life, that young girl from down the street in LeMoyne. He earned master's degrees at Glassboro

Ed Salmon at his new home as a boy with his caretaker in LeMoyne, Pennsylvania. *Courtesy of Ed Salmon.*

State University (now Rowan University) as he began a teaching career at Millville School District at age twenty-one.

Marilyn would teach there, too, not far from where her parents had relocated. Eventually, Ed would propose to Marilyn at the Peace Light Inn (no longer there) by the renowned Gettysburg Battlefield.

Salmon would coach Millville's freshmen basketball team in a school district elevated by football. Marilyn would coach the cheerleaders. "My first year coaching they fired the head varsity basketball coach," said Salmon. "My second year coaching they fired the head basketball coach."

In coaching, too, bad breaks would shadow Ed Salmon. But blessings would follow. He coached rising giant Alan Shaw on his second freshman team, but then Shaw got injured. "Al brings his arm down and hits me on the head," remembered teammate Bill Hughes. Broken arm. "He would wrap it in foam."[93] The freshman team finished 12-0 anyway.

Salmon was promoted to varsity coach in his third year. Coaching basketball at Millville High had all the stability of his childhood, and yet he shuffled through the fragile program.

Hughes described playing for Salmon as its own, more difficult boot camp, beyond what he'd experience at West Point Military Academy. Salmon, more than Uncle Sam, got him in the best shape of his life. Salmon, like his childhood, was tough; his exacting ways as a basketball coach alienated many potential ballers.

Undaunted, Salmon's first year as head coach the Thunderbolts went 14-9, then 17-4 in 1967–68, when the 'Bolts won the Southern New Jersey Group IV championship, drawing attention from the famed Johnstown Tournament organizers. With blue-chip six-foot-eleven prospect Alan Shaw on the roster, Millville received an invite to a tournament that included Mansfield High and future all-American Tom McMillen, a six-eleven left-handed sophomore averaging thirty-one points per game. This was a full year before *Sports Illustrated* would posterize McMillen on its cover with the heading "The Best High School Player in America."[94] First, the young McMillen would have to face Shaw. Salmon would need permission from his school district to participate in the Johnstown Tournament.

"The superintendent was against us going," said Salmon. "He thought it was too much competition, and we would embarrass Millville. The Thunderbolt Club got up and fought for us to go. I never got involved in it....One member said, *I agree with the superintendent. We're going to get embarrassed and dishonor the school district.*"

Millville ventured to Johnstown in December 1968 with only nine players. Disgruntled potential squad members who might have played on Millville's varsity had formed an intramural squad and called themselves "Ed's Rejects."

Ed's Survivors at Millville High drew McMillen and Mansfield High right away, of course. Mansfield had won 43 of 47 games under Coach Richard Miller. The prior year's JVs had gone 16-2. And against Mansfield, Shaw, who averaged twenty-three points and twenty-three rebounds for the 'Bolts, fouled out in the third quarter with Millville trailing.

"Ed sent in Bob Abbott, who was a linebacker on the football team," said Hughes. "About 200 pounds. I think I was about 180 or so. He said, 'Park your butt right behind McMillen.' Bob kept him away from the basket in a zone. Anytime the ball was around us, and McMillen was there, I would be standing in front of him. Most of the time I was holding his shorts. They called a foul one time, but I kept doing it. McMillen was classy and didn't get frustrated."

Hughes scored 11 points in the final quarter. Cliff Johnson scored 15. Millville's press forced turnovers, and the 'Bolts rallied for a 59–57 victory. "We were far from home, and the weather was wintery, so we didn't have many fans there," Shaw remembered, "but by the last few minutes of the game we'd won over a lot of the fans from other schools, and they helped cheer us to victory.…Winning the Mansfield game was huge for us. It was early in my senior season, and it showed everyone that, even with me on the bench, this was a very good team, and that this was going to be a very special season for Millville basketball."[95]

In the other opening-night game, Laurel Highlands dusted Johnstown 76–59 behind six-foot-four scorer Jim Hobgood (19 ppg). Coach Harold "Horse" Taylor was 91-11 in his tenure at the suburban Pittsburgh school to that point.

By winning at least one game in Johnstown, Millville and Salmon had justified making the trip. In the championship game the next night, Shaw (33) and Johnson (29) combined for 62 points in a 77–74 victory over Laurel Highlands. The school that had fired its last two coaches after one season was champion of the biggest tournament around. Shaw recalls how it had evolved:

I've often said that the stars were aligned for that '69 team. In 1965, several key players on that '68–'69 team—Bob Hutchings, Bill Hughes, Bob Abbott and Bobby Gant—were already in the Millville schools. I'd started school in Millville but then moved away in the second grade and moved back to Millville in 1965 to start the eighth grade. At that same time, Ed Salmon, a recent Gettysburg college graduate, moved to Millville to take a teaching position at the junior high school. In 1967, Cliff Johnson, a star in the Johnstown game, would move down from New York City to live with his grandmother near Millville. All the pieces fell into place for a great senior season. My family moving back to Millville and me coming under the wing of Ed Salmon was a huge turning point in my life.

The 'Bolts finished the dream season 26-1. That after a 9-1 football season the previous fall. But in Ed Salmon's life, good fortune was fleeting. The superintendent, according to Salmon, believed that the coach had lobbied discreetly to gain favor to participate in Johnstown. Despite the team winning the tournament, that suspicion and perceived betrayal remained. At the end of the school year, "I was called into the principal's office. They wanted to fire me," said Salmon. "It all happened because of the Johnstown situation."

Salmon could become the third coach to feel the axe in three years. "The school board voted unanimously to keep me," he said. "Whatever the Lord does, it's gonna happen. You accept it and go on to the next thing."

Salmon decided then that he'd only coach six seasons, which he did, posting a record of 80-18 in his four varsity seasons, good enough, as it turns out, to get him into the school's athletic Hall of Fame. The town elected him mayor when he was thirty. In that role, Salmon would oversee the election of school board members, ironically enough.

Salmon didn't believe in holding grudges. He wouldn't retaliate against administrators who had tried to fire him. But he also wouldn't forget. For years when he'd worked as a physical education teacher, he had ordered supplies for his classes, but he said they never arrived. "I never got what I asked for when I taught there," he said. "One month after being elected mayor, all the stuff I had ordered showed up at the gym."

Salmon, it turns out, has everything he ever needed. He was going on sixty years of marriage with the girl at the end of the block in LeMoyne. That and the Johnstown title were enough.

Instead of a key to the city, Millville School District gave Salmon a key to the gymnasium upon retirement. Every day he meets other men for pickup games with whoever wants to show up. He remains active in basketball while making his life's work in politics and business. Shaw went on to earn his doctorate in English, following his coach, who'd earned his in educational leadership.

DESPITE THE MARQUEE NAMES of the 1969 tournament being intimidating giants, the Johnstown Most Valuable Player was Laurel Highland's Jim Hobgood, a six-foot-four shooter who scored twenty-five points against Millville.

The previous March, Hobgood had lit up Johnstown High in the same War Memorial Arena for thirty-seven points in a playoff win over the Trojans. The Mustangs rode that performance and went to the state championship. They met Cheltenham, coached by Paul Westhead, the future "Guru of Go" fast break wizard. Craig Littlepage, a future University of Virginia player, was Cheltenham's star. Highlands won in overtime in a rare state final played at the Pittsburgh Civic Center.

Johnstown Tournament organizers brought Hobgood and the Mustangs back to War Memorial Arena in December and pitted them against the inspired host Johnstown team. "They may have had me earmarked for the tournament," admitted Hobgood.[96]

At one point in the rematch, Hobgood drove in for a layup and was undercut. He went after the player who had knocked him off his feet. The benches emptied before calm could be restored. "I was a skinny little kid," said Hobgood. "I'm lucky I didn't get hurt."

Nobody was going to intimidate Hobgood. He grew up in a tough Pennsylvania coal town where Uniontown High made regular runs at state titles. Hobgood played nearby at North Union High, which merged with South Union High to make Laurel Highlands in 1965. Laurel Highlands faced off against Uniontown, with both teams undefeated midway through the 1965 season. When Highlands prevailed, the new school toppling the established powerhouse, anything was possible. In 1968, Laurel Highlands went to the state final.

Lost to graduation after that 1968 championship season was scintillating guard Will Robinson, who would head to West Virginia University to become the Mountaineers' third all-time leading scorer (now fourth). As a senior at Laurel Highlands, Hobgood had to fill in where Robinson had excelled. The Mustangs couldn't match the success of the first two seasons, when the basketball team had won fifty of fifty-three games.

They limped into Johnstown. Power forward Buzzy Harrison was still recovering from injuring his leg after he had tried to play football for the first time as a senior. Once again, Hobgood shot lasers from the outside, two decades before the advent of the three-point line in high school basketball. He scored twenty-four points to move the Mustangs into the final against upstart Millville.

Johnstown pin from Alan Shaw. *Courtesy of Alan Shaw.*

Hobgood would post 25 more points. The Mustangs led by three entering the fourth quarter, but Millville prevailed 77–74. Hobgood would go on to play in the Atlantic Coast Conference at Virginia. He'd face Johnstown Tournament alumni like Shaw at Duke and McMillen at Maryland.

POWER SURGE

In 1964, Coach Morgan Wootten scheduled a game against New York City's Power Memorial Academy, led by seven-foot-one center Lew Alcindor, the best player in America. Recognizing that the game simply could not be held in a typical high school gym and meet the demand for tickets, Wootten gambled and rented Cole Field House on the University of Maryland campus for the February 1 contest. The tilt sold more than twelve thousand seats. Alcindor's 35 points led Power to a 65–62 victory. The Panthers extended their win streak, which would eventually balloon to seventy-one games.

In so many ways, that game has resonated in basketball history. A clash of schoolboy titans from different states. The commercialization of the high school basketball genre.

FORMER MCKEESPORT HIGH STAR athlete Lanny Van Eman was a rare multi-sport athlete who donned the Yankees pinstripes as a minor leaguer, was drafted into the National Basketball Association and also coached on the Boston Celtics staff when the likes of Larry Bird, Kevin McHale, Robert Parrish and Johnstown Tournament alumnus Reggie Lewis played.

After playing college basketball and baseball at Wichita State University, where he was a two-time MVP of the Missouri Valley Conference—where Van Eman was one of over a dozen former McKeesport High ballers to matriculate on the recommendation of legendary McKeesport coach

Neenie Campbell—Van Eman became an assistant coach at Wichita State under the great Ralph Miller, who then took Van Eman with him to coach at the University of Iowa. Eventually, Van Eman became the head basketball coach at Arkansas before Eddie Sutton and Nolan Richardson.

Perhaps his most fortuitous experience on campus—other than connecting with Coach Miller—came from getting to know Western Pennsylvania sports fanatic Sonny Vaccaro, a student getting his master's degree at Wichita State at the time. The young Western Pennsylvanians became fast friends half a country away from Pennsylvania.

In 1965, Van Eman told Vaccaro that he'd be driving from the Pittsburgh area to Washington, D.C., to see a high school basketball showdown between the great Lew Alcindor and DeMatha Catholic at Cole Field House. A gap in Van Eman's recruiting schedule permitted the trip.

"Sonny was a schoolteacher at Trafford Middle School at the time," said Van Eman. "He was thinking about starting his first roundball classic all-star basketball game. When I told him I was going to see this particular game, he said, 'Can I go, too?' He brought a particular friend too. We stayed at a Holiday Inn overnight. As a coach I was acquainted with Morgan Wootten, the DeMatha coach."

The men witnessed perhaps the most famous high school basketball game in history. "After the game we went over to DeMatha to a priest's home," Van Eman said. "The rectory or something. We went for milk and coffee and donuts, and the two teams were there, too. The game was sold out with twelve thousand tickets when Maryland was still getting three thousand for its games."

Van Eman was eager to leave the postgame gathering to get on the road back to Pittsburgh. Vaccaro, however, pounced on the sudden networking opportunity. "Sonny was the one who was persistent," Van Eman recalled. "He wanted to talk to Alcindor and Power Memorial Coach [Jack] Donohue. When we got to the reception Sonny really went to work with the coaches and the players. That's where he got close to Alcindor. Morgan Wootten more or less saw that Sonny couldn't get a firm commitment from Alcindor. Sonny told Donohue he could coach the first Dapper Dan All-Star game. Morgan heard that and said he'd be interested in coaching the first Roundball Classic. I don't think Donohue or Lew made a decision at first."

Vaccaro's grand plan fell into place. Since Vaccaro had teaching duties during the day, it fell on his buddy Pat DiCesare to chase talent for the Pennsylvania versus America All-Star game. All DiCesare had done to that point was mortgage his family home and his future to bring an up-and-coming British band to Pittsburgh's Civic Arena for a landmark concert.

The Beatles sold out the venue. DiCesare was a music promoter, but those talents expanded to luring basketball talent to Pittsburgh.[97]

The first Dapper Dan Roundball Classic game in 1965 drew more than ten thousand fans as Pennsylvania downed the national stars 89–76. Midland High's Simmie Hill was named the star for the Pennsylvania team, DeMatha's Bernie Williams for the national team. The second year, Farrell High's Sam Iacino and Connecticut's Calvin Murphy dueled in a battle of hot-shooting diminutive guards. The national stars won that game.

Sonny Vaccaro's Dapper Dan showcase event—the precursor to the McDonald's All-American game—lasted until 2007. Growing up in Pennsylvania, Vaccaro had seen the formula work for the Big 33 football game that pitted Pennsylvania stars against all-stars from Texas (and later from other states like Ohio and Maryland). He and Van Eman brainstormed how to make it work for basketball during conversations when both were at Wichita State.

ONE YEAR AFTER POWER Memorial downed DeMatha in the first Cole Field House showcase, the teams returned to play the rematch at Cole. Alcindor was now a senior, and DeMatha knew not to treat him like just another talented center. The Stags surrounded Alcindor and got revenge with a 46–43 victory, limiting the giant to 13 points and ending Power Memorial's win streak at seventy-one games.

More than anything, these two games elevated high school basketball nationally. Rather than local high schools competing in modest gymnasiums, Wootten booked a game where two superpowers competed in a sold-out college field house. Ironically enough, DeMatha's only loss that season came against the University of Maryland freshman team.

The University of Maryland would later add nearly three thousand more seats to Cole for a greater home court advantage. If they were going to become the UCLA of the East, as Coach Lefty Driesell prophesied when he was hired in 1969, the arena would be packed for showcase games. Before Driesell even arrived, Cole Field House would host three of the biggest games in the sport's history—the two Power-DeMatha games and the 1966 NCAA national championship game between Texas Western and Kentucky. Texas Western University coach Don Haskins's all-Black starting five toppled Adolph Rupp's all-white Kentucky squad 72–65 in what unofficially became the "Civil Rights game."

In the span of almost twenty-six months, Cole Field House had become the epicenter of basketball history. The 1964 Power Memorial team would

From left to right: Neal Murphy, Morgan Wootten's longest tenured assistant; Pete Strickland ('75); Toney Ellis ('76 and University of Colorado); and Bill Ruback ('75 and Niagara University). *Courtesy of Pete Strickland.*

be designated the best high school team of the twentieth century by some outlets. In the same spirit that Johnstown Tournament organizers sought to expand their reach and test themselves against the best teams in the East starting in 1949, Wootten and Power coach Jack Donohue had done the same in the middle 1960s.

Lefty Driesell recruited extremely well at Maryland—maybe too well. Toney Ellis played at DeMatha and then went to the University of

Colorado. In time, Washington, D.C. phenom JoJo Hunter would transfer from Maryland to Colorado and join Ellis. "When you stack All-Americans on top of All-Americans," Ellis said, "somebody's not gonna be happy. Then it was a semi-exodus."

Back in Johnstown, however, locals wondered how tournament organizers had failed to attract the great Lew Alcindor and Power Memorial to compete in War Memorial. Rest assured, the Dapper Dan folks couldn't secure Alcindor for their event either. Wootten, above all, appreciated the value of competing in Johnstown. He brought his DeMatha teams to town in December 1961, 1963, 1964 and 1965, losing only the first year in the championship game to Norristown, Pennsylvania, by two. DeMatha was 7-1 at Johnstown, Power Memorial 0-0.

In 1969, Johnstown organizers finally landed Power Memorial Academy as well as the nation's No. 1 recruit in Mansfield High center Tom McMillen, a skinny and smooth six-foot-eleven center with a deadly accurate jump shot. McMillen was two months away from becoming the second high school basketball player (after Lebanon, Indiana's Rick Mount) to grace the cover of national *Sports Illustrated* magazine. The photo taken from behind the backboard shows McMillen ready to slam a two-fisted dunk next to the headline: "THE BEST HIGH SCHOOL PLAYER IN AMERICA."

Power Memorial players had heard about McMillen and wanted to show what they could do against the phenom whose six-foot-seven brother, Jay, already had completed his college playing career at the University of Maryland, averaging seventeen points per game over his three seasons. Mansfield High was a small-town team that would win the state title in the middle classification in 1969 and reach the eastern final in 1970. McMillen was the local boy with the pointy elbows deadlifting the town to glory. He was so good that Lefty Driesell declared whichever college team recruited him would win a national title.[98]

Power Memorial was just the opposite of rural Mansfield. The Panthers were the city school on the upper west side of mid-Manhattan—one block from Lincoln Center—that attracted players from all over the Big Apple, often with the promise that they could play elite basketball at the school made famous by Lew Alcindor, whose UCLA college teams would go 88-2 and win three national titles.

Both Power and Mansfield needed to win on opening night in Johnstown to set the championship matchup. In a battle of the two top-rated teams in Pennsylvania in Mansfield and Norristown, Mansfield was the defending Class B state champion, winning 4 state games by a combined 104 points.

They had finished 25-3, with one of the losses coming on opening night in the Johnstown Tournament against eventual champion Millville High. In his first three seasons of high school ball, McMillen (2,320) had outscored the great Wilt Chamberlain in his three seasons at Overbrook (2,252). As a junior McMillen had averaged 39 points per game. As a senior he was averaging 56. On opening night in his senior season, McMillen scored 64 points in a 100–46 rout of Canton.

Mansfield High opponent Norristown was a favorite to reach the larger Class A state final behind six-foot-four widebody Henry Williams. Norristown quickly forced McMillen into four fouls as the Eagles took a lead to halftime. Norristown must have felt confident. Williams's elder brother, Jim, had scored the winning basket in the 1961 Johnstown final to bounce national No. 1 DeMatha.

McMillen would face the longest second half of his high school career in 1969. He played the rest of the game against Norristown and Henry Williams without drawing a fifth foul, scoring 26 points, one more than Henry Williams, in a 71–67 decision for the Tigers. Johnstown's hoped-for finals matchup was set after Power Memorial drilled Bishop McCort by 16.

LEN ELMORE HAD BEEN a tall kid shooting baskets in gym class in New York growing up when a physical education teacher noticed him. "Wouldn't you rather play against kids your size?" the teacher asked.[99]

Elmore was passionate about baseball at that point, not basketball. When he jumped center in gym class, he was flummoxed as to which way he should run after the tap, which basket he should shoot at and which basket he should defend. Elmore attended public school through ninth grade.

As eighth graders in parochial school, Jap Trimble and buddy Ed Searcy would reach the finals of the city CYO tournament with Our Lady Queen of Angels but lose in three overtimes. Power Memorial coach Jack Kuhnert saw the game and recruited both players to his high school. Now they were playing for a Johnstown Tournament title with Len Elmore on their team, a collection of three Division I prospects and future All-Americans going against the much-ballyhooed and smooth-shooting Tom McMillen.

Elmore, at six-foot-nine, matched up with McMillen but quickly had to leave the game due to foul trouble. "We were accustomed to a little bumping and jostling, playing a little more physical brand of basketball in New York," Elmore explained. "My teammate Ed Searcy decided he was going to avenge my victimhood, and I think he goaltended five or six of Tom's shots. Whether they were going to go in or not, I can't say."

The triumvirate of the six-foot-five Searcy, the six-foot-three Jap Trimble and Elmore was overwhelming for the Mansfield squad, but McMillen scored 40 points and grabbed 20 rebounds anyway. Power Memorial won 79–62 (newspapers published different final scores) for the Johnstown title. McMillen was named tournament MVP. "Tom basically gave us credit for having a monster team," said Trimble, who scored 28 points for Power that game. "There was no animosity or true ill will from the game that we played."[100]

One effusive scribe wrote that the game was attended by 8,500 fans, double the capacity of War Memorial Arena.[101] "Tom and I got to be friends afterwards," Elmore remembers. "We're all staying at the same hotel in Johnstown. We compared notes on being recruited to Maryland. It kind of started our friendship. A lot of road games in college we alternated roommates, so Tom was mine periodically. We developed a good friendship that's lasted 55 years."

Maryland coach Lefty Driesell convinced McMillen, Elmore *and* Trimble to enroll at Maryland, while Searcy started at Duquesne before transferring to St. John's. As freshmen, the Terrapin players went 16-0, unable to compete for the varsity at that time until sophomore year due to NCAA rules. McMillen averaged twenty-nine points per game for the freshman team, with Trimble averaging twenty.

But the nucleus of that Maryland freshman team began at Power Memorial. Trimble earned Player of the Year for New York Catholic schools. Elmore established himself as an inside force and dominant rebounder. And Searcy handled the rest. They won Power's first city title since Alcindor's team had done it. "I led the team in scoring, averaging about 21 points per game," said Trimble. "Ed averaged about 19. Lennie probably averaged around 13 points and 20 rebounds."

Power Memorial finished 22-0, New York City champions and consensus national champions in 1970. The Panthers returned the school to the glory it had known in the mid-'60s. "If you look at headlines during that time, early spring of 1970, you could see people were saying we're the best high school team they've ever seen," said Elmore, "and that would include Power's teams that had Alcindor. They would get into lighthearted debates. Certainly Alcindor would have dominated [in a head-to-head matchup], but with us it was the totality of the team. We had three guys— me, Trimble and Searcy—that received a lot of attention, but it was the sum of our parts that carried us."

Brendan Malone was a teacher and assistant coach at Power back then under Jack Kuhnert. Malone would eventually become head coach, winning two city championships. He moved on to coach in college for ten years and then the NBA for twenty. His son Michael coached the Denver Nuggets to the 2023 NBA title.

Before deciding on the University of Maryland, Len Elmore received serious attention from UCLA and Head Coach John Wooden, no doubt with a little help from Kareem Abdul-Jabbar, the former Lew Alcindor. Elmore had a ready response for UCLA: "I followed that guy once; no way am I going to do it again!"

At Maryland, the Terps battled North Carolina State for the ACC's one NCAA bid. Two of the greatest teams in the entire NCAA played for one spot. Elmore, Searcy and Trimble were high school national champions and champions of the famous Johnstown Tournament. They would not be NCAA tournament champions. However, teaming up with Tom McMillen, Maryland would win the 1972 National Invitational Tournament, making them national champions nonetheless. McMillen earned the MVP award as Maryland topped Niagara 100–69 in the championship game. Six Terrapins scored between 16 and 20 points. McMillen had 19, Elmore 18 and Trimble 2. One newspaper headline read, "Maryland Wins with 5 Sophs."[102] Lefty Driesell called it the greatest win he's ever had.

"I've never won a national championship," he said, "and, in a sense, this is a national championship." Maryland finished 27-5, champions of the

Maryland's unbeaten freshman team. *Courtesy of Len Elmore.*

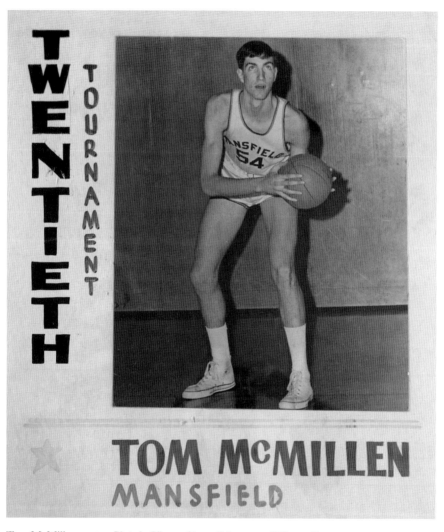

Tom McMillen poster. *Photo by Thomas Slusser,* Johnstown Tribune-Democrat.

NIT, Atlantic Coast Conference runners-up, but not quite the UCLA of the East. Niagara, oddly enough, had won a game on February 7 against St. Francis in a game played at Johnstown's War Memorial Arena, where the Maryland stars first met.

In 1973, Maryland made the NCAA field, advancing to the Elite 8, where they lost to Providence by 14. In 1974, Maryland played North Carolina State in the Atlantic Coast Conference championship game. The Wolfpack won 103–100 in overtime in one of the greatest college games

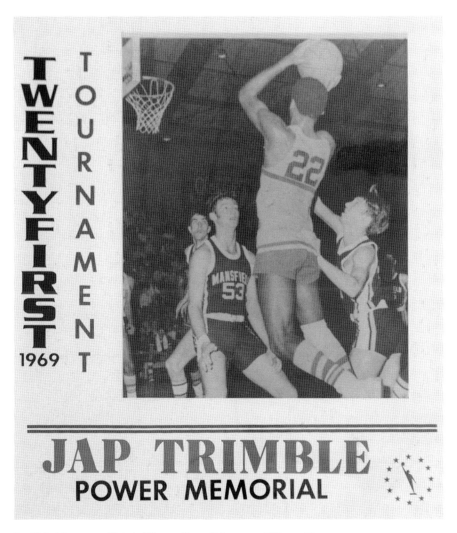

Jap Trimble poster. *Photo by Thomas Slusser,* Johnstown Tribune-Democrat.

ever played between perhaps the two best teams in America. N.C. State went on to win the national title with a 30-1 record, breaking UCLA's run of seven straight championships. Maryland didn't even make the NCAA tournament, as back then conferences only sent one team—the conference champion—a questionable policy that soon was amended the next year presumably because of the snub to Maryland, which finished 23-5 with six future NBA players. Maryland declined an invitation to the NIT.

B EFORE SHUTTING DOWN, THE Power Memorial Panthers were set up for one last run at glory. Rising stars Mario Elie and Chris Mullin competed on an undefeated junior varsity team. Chris Mullin would soon transfer to Xaverian, however, where he would win the New York state title in 1981.

When the rent for the valuable and rare New York City land increased exponentially, Power Memorial was forced to close in 1984. The building has since been torn down so apartments could be erected in its place. Those prominent basketball teams might be Power Memorial Academy's greatest legacy. And the fact that Johnstown drew DeMatha Catholic and Power Memorial—the two heavyweight high school programs in the United States—to their quaint town for a basketball tournament says everything.

PART III

THE 1970s

From Big John to Tinkerbell
to the Big Apple

BIG JOHN

Before he landed a Division I coaching job at Georgetown University, big John Thompson made his name in coaching at St. Anthony's High in Washington, D.C.

The school was small, the enrollment tiny—around fifty students per class. It sat symbolically downhill from Thompson's renowned alma mater, Archbishop Carroll High, which overlooked the St. Anthony's neighborhood from a more prominent vantage point. Catholic University bisected the schools, a constant reminder of the next stage in a successful academic life. But the six-foot-ten Thompson soon landed a few key players who changed the fortunes of the Tonies, starting in 1966. Johnstown noticed as Thompson lifted St. Anthony's toward becoming one of the best teams not only in Washington, D.C., but also in America one season after a 28-3 campaign in 1969. In 1970 and 1971, War Memorial Arena hosted talented St. Anthony's squads in consecutive seasons.

In 1970, the Tonies pounded a strong Norristown team with All-American forward Henry Williams by 16 and then outscored Rice of New York, who featured standout six-foot-nine center Bill Campion, 68–49. John Thompson's star was six-foot-eight All-American Don Washington, who scored 22 points each night to earn Most Valuable Player honors. When Washington's mother died in 1970, Coach Thompson stepped up to become Don's legal guardian, moving him into the Thompson house with his sons, John III and Ronnie, and the rest of the family.[103]

As St. Anthony's of D.C. rose to become a national power, Johnstown continued tinkering with its now-famous tournament. When the calendar was transitioning from 1969 to 1970, it seemed the perfect time to experiment with using an ABA basketball, as the field delivered several future professionals from Donald Washington to teammate Merlin Wilson to New York Rice High's Bill Campion. Campion would go on to play for Harlem Globetrotters' foil the Washington Generals for seven years, but not before lighting up nearby Richland High with twenty-six points and nineteen rebounds in Johnstown.

"The high school I went to, Dean Meminger went there," said Campion. "Those guys graduated when I was coming in. I used to see Meminger playing a lot in the summer down at Rice. Rice was an old YWCA, built in 1936; the gym was on the sixth floor in the place. It was a little bandbox."[104]

Like Power Memorial, Rice High in Harlem closed its doors in the early 2000s. Campion eventually settled in Altoona and gets back to War Memorial on occasion when the Globies perform there.

IN 1971, COACH JOHN Thompson returned to Johnstown with his Tonies looking to repeat. They faced more pushback than expected on the first night from Pittsburgh-area Upper St. Clair High and center Jonathan Dye. The six-foot-nine Dye scored twenty-three points and snatched seventeen rebounds. St. Anthony's countered with twenty points from Jonathan Smith, a zippy six-foot-one guard.[105]

Another Western Pennsylvania team, Hopewell High, made a strong showing too, led by a hobbled six-foot-seven Stan Sligh. He would average twenty and twenty at the Johnstown Tournament, losing by six to Dewitt Clinton High from the Bronx, New York, and then rebounding to beat Upper St. Clair by two in the consolation game. In games during his senior year, the All-American Sligh would post a fifty-point night and another thirty-thirty performance.[106] So dominant was Sligh that fans barely noticed the contributions of a smallish guard who scored five points for the Vikings in the Johnstown opener. The junior might not have been the best basketball player at that Johnstown Tournament, but he was easily the best football player. Tony Dorsett would go on to win a national title and Heisman Trophy as a running back at Pitt. Hopewell High sits in Aliquippa, Pennsylvania, a town that has produced a football assembly line of NFL players like Mike Ditka, Sean Gilbert, Ty Law and Darrelle Revis. The football stadium at Aliquippa is called Heinz Field after the sponsor of the historic stadium's renovations. Over at Hopewell High, the football field is adorned with the name Tony Dorsett Stadium, for obvious reasons.

On Sligh's big scoring night of fifty points for Hopewell, Dorsett added twenty.

DEWITT CLINTON HIGH WAS an interesting team to bring to Johnstown. The school was the largest in the world in the 1930s with twelve thousand students. The list of accomplished alumni reads like a who's who of entertainers, artists, politicians, scientists, scholars and athletes. Director Gary Marshall; playwright Neil Simon; actors Burt Lancaster, Don Adams and Judd Hirsch; author James Baldwin; designer Ralph Lauren; boxer Sugar Ray Robinson; publisher M. Lincoln Schuster; screenwriter Sherwood Schwartz; and many others attended Dewitt Clinton.[107]

Dewitt Clinton produced its share of basketball greats too. Actor Burt Lancaster was good enough as a basketball player to earn an athletic scholarship to New York University. Dolph Schayes and Nate "Tiny" Archibald rank among the NBA's all-time greats. Tom Henderson was co-captain of the 1972 Olympic basketball team that lost to the Soviet Union in the controversial gold-medal game. The quote attributed to Henderson on that game was, "The game ended, and we won. Then it ended again, and we won again." Unfortunately, the Soviets were given a third chance to score the winning basket, and they completed a full-court pass and layup to win. The Americans never accepted their silver medals. Dewitt Clinton sent Tom Henderson, Steve "The Bear" Sheppard and Puerto Rico native Butch Lee to play Olympic basketball in 1972 and 1976. Three players from one high school in two Olympics!

You might have heard a few other dramatic NBA play calls during Boston Celtics games by announcer Johnny Most, another Dewitt Clinton alumnus. "Havlicek stole the ball" captured the last-second victory over the 76ers. "Now there's a steal by Bird…underneath to D.J.…He lays it in!" as Boston beat Detroit. Most described Celtics games in his raspy, cigarette-stained voice from 1953 to 1990, after his high school days at Dewitt Clinton. Of course, not all alumni are Hall of Famers. Ed Warner would go from Dewitt Clinton to the City College of New York, where he would become the Most Valuable Player of the National Invitational Tournament and then help CCNY to a second national title in the NCAA tournament. Warner also became part of the point-shaving scandal of 1951 that saw players assist gamblers to fix games for money.

Bob Piano taught physical education at Dewitt Clinton for thirty years and was an assistant coach under Johnny Wyles on the 1971 basketball team that came to Johnstown. "We had 6,500 students—all boys—in grades 9 to 12 when I started teaching there," he said. "And it was on double sessions. Certain kids started at 7:00 a.m. and other kids started at 10:00. It was an open school, not a district school. You didn't have to live in the district. They offered programs that a lot of other schools didn't. The alumni of Dewitt Clinton are a who's who in entertainment, politics, sports....Forget it!"[108]

The star player in 1971 was Steve "The Bear" Sheppard, a six-foot-six forward who would play at the University of Maryland, on the 1976 United States Olympic team and in the NBA.

"St. Anthony's, they had a very good team," Sheppard said. "It was a very close

The statue of former Georgetown basketball coach John Thompson inside McDonough Arena. *Photo by Bradley A. Huebner.*

game between us and them 'til the last half of the last quarter. I couldn't believe we were in a hockey stadium. It was cold up there. It was on those real cold portable floors. The Pittsburgh Pipers used to play on those with Connie Hawks. It was cold until the arena got warmed up. It was like that in the old Chicago Stadium when I was playing with the Bulls."[109]

St. Anthony's topped the Governors by eleven to halt their eighteen-game winning streak. Merlin Wilson scored twenty points and grabbed eleven rebounds for the Tonies to earn MVP honors. Steve "The Bear" Sheppard scored twelve points in the championship game for Dewitt Clinton.[110]

JOHN THOMPSON HAD WITNESSED and experienced how to build a national basketball powerhouse during his high school days in Washington, D.C. His 1960 Archbishop Carroll Lions team is considered perhaps the greatest ever produced in the District of Columbia. His senior year, they went undefeated, winning the national Knights of Columbus Tournament over a squad from Wisconsin. Thompson posted a double-double that game.

He would go on to coach the St. Anthony's Tonies to their own Knights of Columbus Tournament title. Asked if he would take recruit Merlin Wilson with him to Georgetown University when Thompson was hired as the Georgetown Hoyas coach, Thompson had the perfect response for *Washington Daily News* reporter Charlie Rayman: "Would I like to bring Wilson here [to Georgetown]? I'd like to have the whole team. I'm starting to work now on recruiting."[111]

Thompson would share stories from his playing days for Archbishop Carroll and with Providence College and then the Boston Celtics to instruct his players. "He would talk about being with the Celtics more than with Carroll," said Tonies guard Aaron Long. "Thompson's former teammate at Carroll, George Leftwich, would eventually return to Archbishop Carroll as basketball coach. George was the coach there when Big John was at St. Anthony's, and we would play them every year."[112]

During Thompson's playing career at Archbishop Carroll, the Lions featured an all-icon roster: Edward "Monk" Malloy (Notre Dame), George Leftwich (Villanova), Thompson (Providence), Tom Hoover (Villanova) and defensive specialist Walt Skinner were stars for the Lions, which in one stretch won fifty-five straight games. Malloy would rise to become the Notre Dame University president. Thompson and Leftwich became successful coaches, Leftwich after taking Villanova to an NIT title as a player. Thompson eventually coached a national champion at Georgetown University and nearly won two other national titles with Patrick Ewing as his center.

In his two visits to Johnstown, Thompson led the Tonies to a 4-0 record with two titles. Nearby Georgetown University hired him to resuscitate its basketball program, which had fallen to 3-23 in 1971–72. Thompson probably had more talent on his St. Anthony's High team than Georgetown had returning for the next season. So Thompson brought four Tonies players with him to bolster the Hoyas roster: Aaron Long, Merlin Wilson, Jonathan Smith and Greg Brooks competed for starting positions. The next year, St. Anthony's guard Alonzo "Cheese" Holloway would join them.

In Thompson's first game as a college head coach at McDonough Arena, three of the six players who scored were freshmen from St. Anthony's. Another occasional starter with Pennsylvania ties for Georgetown was point guard Tim Lambour, who scored six. Despite growing up near Johnstown and playing for Bishop Guilfoyle in Altoona, Lambour didn't remember going to the tournament as a kid. His father had contracted polio in 1955. "I never knew him to be able to walk," said Lambour.[113]

St. Anthony's High gymnasium, where John Thompson was head coach. *Photo by Bradley A. Huebner.*

Outside of St. Anthony's gym in Washington, D.C. *Photo by Bradley A. Huebner.*

As a freshman at Georgetown, Lambour could remember playing against Maryland's unbeaten freshman team before first-year players were eligible for varsity competition. That meant Lambour went against a loaded squad of Johnstown veterans that included Tom McMillen, Len Elmore and Jap Trimble.

Lambour was a junior playing point guard for the Hoyas when Thompson was hired. Georgetown went 12-14 that first season, with Thompson's old Archbishop Carroll High teammate George Leftwich serving as one of his assistant coaches. "We had at least two players from DeMatha on our team when I got there," Lambour recalled. "We never got another player from DeMatha once Thompson got there."

Thompson and Morgan Wootten had been quiet rivals as D.C. prep coaches. They never played each other during the winter, leaving locals to argue about who had the better team. When they were slated to finally face off in a summer-league game, local fans crammed around the court for the big showdown. Thompson, in an underhanded yet typically sly maneuver, sent his second and third stringers. The game was a blowout in DeMatha's favor. Then Thompson and Wootten were both considered for the Georgetown job. Thompson was hired, and DeMatha players stopped showing up on Georgetown's rosters. Former DeMatha player Mark Edwards was a senior on Thompson's first Georgetown squad; former Stag Don Willis was a junior.

There may have already been an unspoken rivalry between 1950s Archbishop Carroll coach Bob Dwyer and Wootten. Dwyer would often proclaim that he had never lost to Morgan Wootten in his coaching career. Talented Archbishop Carroll guard John Austin would transfer to DeMatha to play for Wootten after Dwyer left Carroll.

A NEARLY CATASTROPHIC GAME that first season at Georgetown came on another trip to Pennsylvania, about half the distance of the trips from Washington, D.C., to Johnstown. On February 10, 1973, the Hoyas traveled to Carlisle to play Dickinson College in its Alumni Gym on the two hundreth anniversary of the school's founding.[114]

Central Pennsylvania product Jeff Thompson was a senior on that Dickinson squad. Years later, he wrote an essay about the game that spanned sixteen typed, double-spaced pages. It reveals that his basket early in the second half gave Dickinson a 41–32 lead. Today, Georgetown competes in the vaunted Big East in Division I college basketball. Dickinson competes in

Above: Georgetown's on-campus McDonough Arena. *Photo by Bradley A. Huebner.*

Opposite: Johnstown Tournament queens from the *Tribune-Democrat.*

the Division III Centennial Conference with academic—not basketball—superpowers like Johns Hopkins, Swarthmore and Haverford. For Dickinson to be leading Georgetown at all was a major story in 1973. The two thousand delirious fans watched as a squad of nine uniformed Dickinson Red Devils tried to pull the upset.

After taking a 45–35 lead, according to Jeff Thompson, Dickinson didn't score for the next four minutes. The teams exchanged leads until Dickinson grabbed a 65–62 lead in the final minute. Before the advent of the 3-point line, a 3-point lead was relatively safe. A reliable free-throw shooter for the Indians missed the front end of a 1-and-1 opportunity. Down the stretch, Vince Fletcher of Georgetown made a steal and canned a jump shot, and then he added another—the last in the final seconds—as the Hoyas escaped with a 66–65 victory.

Fletcher had been recruited by former Georgetown coach Jack Magee out of New York's Dewitt Clinton High. Coach John Thompson later said that a loss that Saturday night might have cost him his job, which was a huge exaggeration but speaks to how shocking a loss at Dickinson would have been. And the manner he won it spoke volumes too.

23ᴿᴰ ANNUAL INVITATIONAL BASKETBALL TOURNAMENT

TOURNAMENT QUEEN AND HER COURT

Celebrating the twenty-third birthday of Pennsylvania's first and the nation's finest Scholastic Invitational Basketball Tournament, is the tournament queen of the twenty-third event and her court of eleven high school hostesses representing the ten senior high schools in the Greater Johnstown area. Pictured here from left to right: Debbie Helsel, Richland; Marlane Strafka, Greater Johnstown; Terrie Ferguson, Greater Johnstown Vo-Tech; Sue Courier, Ferndale; Brenda Wirick, Richland; Donna Reis, Maid of Honor, Bishop McCort; Kim Syman, Tournament Queen, Greater Johnstown; Susan Olenik, Windber; Kathy Strank, Conemaugh Valley; Debbie Villa, Conemaugh Twp. Area; Terry Coder, Westmont; and Mary Chance, Westmont.

AT THE CAMBRIA COUNTY WAR MEMORIAL ARENA
"Pennsylvania's First and The Nation's Finest"

WEDNESDAY, DECEMBER 29th	GENERAL ADMISSION	THURSDAY, DECEMBER 30th
	Students $1⁰⁰ Adults $1⁵⁰	
	RESERVED SEATS ....$2⁰⁰ & $2⁵⁰	

★ **HOPEWELL** VIKINGS
● 1970-71 Record .... 20 Wins 4 Losses

★ **DEWITT CLINTON** GOVERNORS
● 1970-71 Record .... 16 Wins 6 Losses

★ **ST. ANTHONY'S** TONIES
● 1970-71 Record .... 25 Wins 4 Losses

★ **UPPER ST. CLAIR** PANTHERS
● 1970-71 Record .... 14 Wins 7 Losses

Stan Sligh
6'7"
THIRD TEAM ALL-AMERICAN
HOPEWELL

Merlin Wilson
6'8"
SECOND TEAM ALL-AMERICAN
ST. ANTHONY'S

Dwanne Goodman
6'1"
DeWITT CLINTON

John Dye
6'9"
UPPER ST. CLAIR

TOURNAMENT SCHEDULE

WEDNESDAY -- 7:30 P.M.
HOPEWELL vs. DEWITT CLINTON

WEDNESDAY -- 9:00 P.M.
ST. ANTHONY'S vs. UPPER ST. CLAIR

THURSDAY -- 7:30 P.M.
CONSOLATION GAME
(TUESDAY'S LOSERS)

THURSDAY -- 9:00 P.M.
CHAMPIONSHIP GAME
(TUESDAY'S WINNERS)

WE WISH YOU GOOD LUCK -- AND MAY THE BEST TEAM WIN

"Basically, he was going to play his guys from St. Anthony's when he came to Georgetown," said Hoya veteran Edwards from DeMatha. "He didn't care about us. Until he was losing. I remember that Dickinson game like it was yesterday. He had to put other guys in to win it."[115]

Edwards, junior Vince Fletcher and others—the veteran players for Georgetown—rallied the Hoyas back. "If Vince Fletcher was playing, that means he took out the guys from St. Anthony's to help us win," said Edwards. "The fact that Vince Fletcher was playing tells you everything."

Edwards remembers, a few years prior, back in high school, when John Thompson had asked him to come to St. Anthony's gym to offer tutelage to St. Anthony's guard Jonathan Smith. "I helped him," Edwards said. "I used to go over to practice with him to help him out." By the time Smith made it to Georgetown, he was taking minutes away from Edwards. The old St. Anthony's–DeMatha rivalry became inflamed in 1968, as Edwards recalls, when the teams squared off in an early summer league game before the Tonies had reached elite status.

"We played St. Anthony's the summer going into my senior year, at Jelleff Boys Club," he said. "We played them and beat them badly. Everybody who started that game normally played. We beat them up bad. That is when the feud started. That's when John told me he wasn't going to forgive the 1968 summer.…We played them, and they were talking a bunch of shit to us that game. We were the No. 1 team in the country that year. They just took their ass-whooping."

Edwards said coaches who wanted to play DeMatha knew the deal. "If you called Morgan to play a game, I don't care who you were," Edwards said. "This is what Morgan would say: *We'll play if it's 60-40 after expenses. End of story.* Morgan would get the greater share of expenses. You don't dominate [like Morgan had] and then they tell Morgan what to do. You don't tell Morgan you're going to play at Morgan State University or Howard. You're probably going to play in a Catholic gym."

WELCOME HOME

From the early 1960s to 1972, Johnstown High lost six straight tournament games. They weren't in the field at all from 1969 to 1971. In 1972, however, the Trojans once again had a team that could compete. They were tall, built around six-foot-nine Pat Chambers. The most productive player, however, was six-foot-five senior Don Maser, who had averaged nearly twenty points per game as a junior. Already in 1972 he had set and reset the school's single-game scoring mark with outputs of thirty-nine and forty-two points. Maser was averaging thirty-five points per game.[116]

The Trojans' dire need for a point guard was filled when Ken Horoho transferred in from nearby Bishop McCort. New head coach Paul Litwalk had ramped up expectations in his second season after taking over for the highly successful Paul Abele. Everything was trending positively, including Johnstown receiving recognition for being one of eleven cities nationally awarded All-American City status. Places like Erie, Pennsylvania; Wilmington, Delaware; and Hampton, Virginia, were also recognized.[117] In hindsight, the list didn't age too well.

The 1972 Johnstown Tournament field included nemesis Chester, St. John's of Washington, D.C., and the first team from Ohio, Cleveland's John F. Kennedy. With three teams commuting considerable distances, tournament organizers feared a light gate. But the Trojans were enough of a draw, with more than four thousand fans watching them light up the scoreboard in a 73–68 victory over St. John's. They sank 32 of 50 shots, with Maser netting a game-high 29 points. Chester downed JFK by four with Herman "Helicopter" Harris scoring 21. Harris was a preseason All-

DON MASER JOHNSTOWN

OUTSTANDING PLAYER

1972

JOHNSTOWN

CHESTER
JOHN F. KENNEDY (OH)
ST. JOHN'S (D.C.)

Don Maser poster. *Photo by Thomas Slusser,* Johnstown Tribune-Democrat.

American who had set the Delaware County single-game scoring record with a 64-point night of his own as a sophomore.[118]

Chester had last won the tournament in 1955, when the Clippers downed Johnstown; Johnstown hadn't won it since beating Chester by two in 1953. The gym would be packed again as the hometown fans recognized a rare opportunity for a tournament title.

Maser's family members were lifelong Johnstown natives. He had relatives killed in the 1889 flood. His parents survived the 1936 flood. And in a few years from the 1972 tournament, in the 1977 flood, Maser would be out of town. He had to call home to see who had survived this natural disaster:

We lost our home in that flood in Kernville, which was one of the low points. I was in California at the time. My brother said they were on the second floor of the house and water was up to the second floor. He said, "I watched my car flood down the street." You couldn't get through to anybody. All the telephones were down. Couldn't get into the town because the roads were impassable. I didn't know what was going on for three, four, five days. My uncle called me and said, "Everybody's OK, you just don't have a house anymore." My father had a friend who lived in Tanneryville. He lost his whole family in that flood. People died. Lost his whole family. He was at work, his family was at home, the house was swept away, and that was it.[119]

The mere formation of dark clouds means something different here, and because of that, so do sunny skies. Playing Chester in the hometown tournament championship had the natives inspired and ready to be jubilant. This was a Johnstown team that had scrimmaged well earlier in the season against a Ringgold High group featuring Ulice Payne and future Hall of Fame quarterback Joe Montana, an athlete worthy of a basketball scholarship offer to North Carolina State.

Against Chester, with the arena bustling and people standing behind the chairs laid out on the gym floor behind the baskets, Johnstown took an early lead and stayed ahead by just enough to post a 79–73 victory. Everything clicked. Maser scored 24, Horoho 22 and Cummings 21. Coach Litwalk remembers one play that symbolized the sharing of the basketball. "Pat Cummings got a rebound and threw it out to the wing to Gary Shaw," he said, "who threw it into Kenny Horoho, who threw it to his left. Then he threw it back to Shaw and he laid it in. Not one dribble from one end to the other. Six passes and not one dribble. We worked hard at it."[120]

Still unbeaten following their hometown tournament that was attended over two nights by more than eight thousand fans, Johnstown kept winning after the calendar hit 1973. School and arena higher-ups decided to move the rest of Johnstown's home games to War Memorial. The Trojans registered their third unbeaten regular season in the seventy-eight-year program's history, the only unbeaten team left in the state tournament that year. It was playing out like the perfect season. In the PIAA playoffs, they round-housed Punxsutawney High 73–41 to advance to the second round. They met Sharon, the No. 4 seed from the talented WPIAL suburban Pittsburgh area, in a game slated for War Memorial Arena. The *Latrobe Bulletin* reported that Sharon hadn't played one good game in the postseason so far. Sharon stifled the Johnstown fast break and found rebounds in abundance against the Johnstown 1-3-1 zone for a blistering 77–41 rout.[121] It was all too familiar. Johnstown's 1952–53 squad had started 27-0 before losing in the state playoffs to…Sharon. That 1953 game was a 42–40 squeaker. Which was worse, getting housed by 36 points or losing by 2? Both stung. At least Coach Litwalk had one prestigious title to celebrate in 1972–73.

"The best thing about that game against Chester for the tournament title was that both teams played to the best of their abilities," said Litwalk, who would win 441 games in twenty-seven seasons. "We had three guys score in double digits. That game went down to the wire. That was a big win. Back then that was almost like winning a state championship."

Maser would go on to star at Duquesne University. In 2024, Maser became the subject of feature articles when the Dukes reached the NCAA tournament for the first time since Maser's playing days in the '70s. Both Maser and Cummings played big-time college basketball, with Cummings setting records at Cincinnati then playing in the NBA for twelve years. Horoho also played at St. Francis.

"Johnstown was always a high school football town," Maser said. "Basketball was something you did between football and baseball season. They never really won anything. None of the schools. I would never say that Johnstown was a hotbed for high school basketball. I think we only ever had one pro: Pat Cummings. He played on that team that won that tournament. When they were in—whatever conference they were in [the Metro]—he was the conference player of the year [in 1978–79]." In 1977–78, Cummings shot a school-record .642 percent from the field and remains atop Cincinnati's all-time rankings. Only Oscar Robertson made more field goals as a Bearcat than Cummings.

Chester's Herman "Helicopter" Harris and two teammates would be recruited to play at the University of Arizona in Tucson. Harris was recruited out of triage at a summer-league game.

"We were playing somewhere during the summer, but I had a cast on my foot," said Harris. "The Arizona assistant coach, Jerry Holmes, was at this tournament. He was watching Phil Mann and Lenny Gordy play. Me being antsy, I didn't know no better, I'm out there shooting with a cast on my foot. I guess Jerry Holmes became curious and talked to the coach about me and Lenny taking a recruiting visit out there. They wanted all three of us: me, Lenny and Phil."[122]

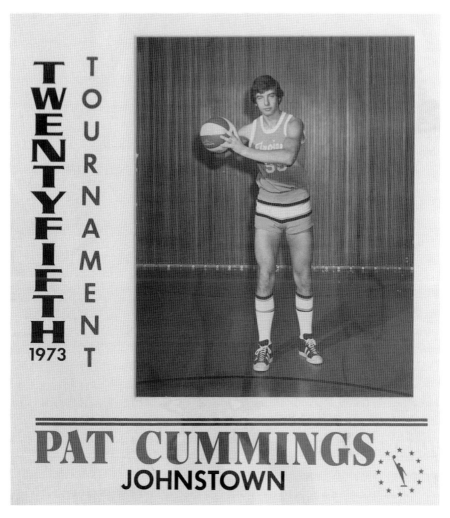

Pat Cummings poster. *Photo by Thomas Slusser,* Johnstown Tribune-Democrat.

All three made plans to enroll at Arizona and play for Fred Snowden, the first African American head coach at a major university. The six-foot-five Helicopter Harris would commit, score 1,158 career points and be drafted by the 76ers in the second round of the 1977 draft. Gordy would score 504 points. Mann started out in junior college but never made it to play for the Wildcats.

It would take a lot to top the 1972 Johnstown Tournament and that tall and talented hometown Trojans team, but the best game local fans witnessed in the tournament in forty-six years would take place in 1976.

GREATEST GAME

Epic games etch into our brains with permanence. Notre Dame ending UCLA's eighty-eight-game winning streak. A young Michael Jordan scoring sixty-three points against the Celtics in the NBA playoffs. Duke beating Kentucky on Christian Laettner's turnaround at the buzzer, giving him a perfect shooting night and a comeback victory on the way to the 1992 national title. And if only Gordon Hayward's half-court bank shot would have fallen, hometown upstart Butler would have shocked Duke for the national title in Indianapolis. We remember where we were, how we felt, what damage the drama did to our stomachs…burning butterflies in our bellies.

What goes into elevating one historic game over others? Championship stakes? Marquee players? A scintillating, late climax? Some inconceivable context?

In the Johnstown Tournament's twenty-eighth year, which coincided with the United States' bicentennial celebration, the finalists delivered the epic game. Ask the people of Johnstown which game they remember, and two sets of names come to mind: Gene Banks and Sam Clancy…and West Philadelphia and Brashear. For all the aforementioned reasons.

West Philly High entered the game ranked No. 1 in the nation, Brashear No. 3 after an early loss to Beaver Falls. Pennsylvanians billed it as the state's east versus west unofficial state championship—in December! Gene Banks was widely considered the No. 1 player in America following his do-everything performance on Long Island months earlier. And partially because of that context, the 1976 tournament final had everything.

FOR THE FULL PICTURE, travel back eleven months to January 1976. In another elite tournament, at Long Island Lutheran High School, West Philly traveled to face the host team. Long Island Lutheran had been No. 1 nationally the year before behind six-foot-eight Wayne McKoy, who was becoming an All-American for the second time. West Philly's six-foot-six All-American Clarence Tillman—a likely matchup against McKoy—was injured and unable to play. On the bus ride to Long Island, West Philly Speedboys coach Joe Goldenberg laid out the challenge for star forward Gene Banks with Tillman out: "You're gonna have to pick it up this game."[123] That after Banks's forty-one-point, twenty-eight-rebound effort against Dobbins Tech, but this was different. McKoy was different. He and Lutheran guard Reggie Carter would both go to St. John's University, followed by brief NBA stints. In one prior Lutheran game, McKoy had tallied seventy points by himself.

A throng of professional and college scouts would be on hand in a gym with a capacity of 2,400. In the Philadelphia *Daily News*, 76ers general manager Pat Williams called the Lutheran tournament the "one with three of the best high school players in it" (McKoy, Banks and Mackin Catholic's JoJo Hunter, averaging twenty-five points per game).[124] The Sixers were considering drafting Hunter right out of high school, a first for a guard. Banks, who shattered multiple backboards on dunks in high school, more than delivered.[125] "It was," said Goldenberg, "the performance of all performances."[126]

So impressive was the talent in that tournament—including the burgeoning Banks—that during the action a reporter phoned Howard Garfinkle, who ran the famed Five-Star Basketball Camp that attracted the nation's best prep players, and said, "You gotta get here and see this Banks kid! He's something special!" Garf somehow made it for the second half of the game and was dutifully flummoxed.

Banks posted a stat line that dwarfed his Dobbins totals: 46 points, 15 rebounds, 7 assists and 6 blocks. McKoy scored 18 and hauled 15 rebounds. Spectating Mackin Catholic coach Harry Rest was as effusive in his praise of Banks as Goldenberg, calling Banks "head-and-shoulders above [former DeMatha High star] Adrian Dantley." Long Island Lutheran coach Reverend Ed Visscher called Banks the "greatest big man I've seen since Lew Alcindor was at Power Memorial."[127] Then he called it the greatest game he'd ever seen by a high school player.[128] Banks rose from prep sensation to the quasi-mythical. "That was the game," Banks said, "that really shot me up to the top of the rankings for No. 1 high school player."[129]

Gene Banks poster. *Photo by Thomas Slusser,* Johnstown Tribune-Democrat.

Banks was not only the boss in that tournament. He was also being hailed as Pennsylvania's best, the nation's best and even the best player Pennsylvania had *ever* produced. Banks was blossoming into a living legend. Call it lofty praise or blasphemous hyperbole in a city and state that had already produced the great Wilt Chamberlain.

Future Davidson College coach Bob McKillop, who would famously coach perhaps the greatest shooter in the history of basketball in Steph Curry, was a high school coach attending that game in Long Island.

"Gene was a man among boys," he recalled. "As was Wayne McKoy. What was most impressive about Gene was that he had a highly-touted teammate who did not play because of an injury, so Gene had to take complete control of the game, which he did. He scored in every way possible, bringing fans to their feet with a spectacular array of shots, moves, passes. Remember, there was no three-point shot nor a shot clock, but the action was fast and furious in every game. Teams went after each other and held nothing back. For a high school tournament at that time, it was a remarkable display of terrific talent. While McKoy was a center, Gene played every position on the court and excelled in every role. Every game in the tournament was played in front of a packed house at Long Island Lutheran, which was considered by many people on the East Coast, at that time, as the Madison Square Garden of high school basketball."

That was the backdrop heading into the December 1976 Johnstown Tournament. Gene Banks and West Philly were national names, even if Long Island Lutheran had won the matchup the prior January. Even before the 1976–77 season began, Banks's precocious talent and drive heralded extra media attention. Basketball writer and legend Dick "Hoops" Weiss had helped convince his editors at the *Philadelphia Daily News* to commit young reporter Gary Smith to follow Banks and West Philadelphia the entire season, making West Philly High basketball an actual beat, something that hadn't been done before nor since for one high school basketball team at the *Daily News*.[130]

Gary Smith, fresh out of LaSalle University, would pull a John Dillinger and align his laser focus on Banks. "Mike Rathet, the sports editor, quickly realized that Banks was kind of a national story," recalled Smith in 2023. "Since Wilt Chamberlain, there hadn't been a Philly prospect that had this kind of attention and magnetism. You had a dynamic individual who was the No. 1 player in America, the biggest Philly player since Chamberlain, playing on a team that could be the No. 1 team in the nation. I was to follow that team rather than spend my Tuesdays and Fridays going to different gyms."

Brashear High School from Western Pennsylvania brought its own superstar to Johnstown's War Memorial Arena that December. Sam Clancy was a six-foot-six Hercules in the low post, gifted with "the most amazing strength that I ever saw on the basketball floor," according to national sportswriter Mike DeCourcy, a native of the Pittsburgh area writing for the *Post-Gazette*. "This was before guys lifted, before strength training was a thing. He just had that incredible natural strength."

Gene Banks was no wispy pushover. When Banks was sixteen, local scribe Hoops Weiss described him as a "muscular Colossus, a Greek statue." But Clancy's bulk and strength were greater than a Greek god's, on par with the most imposing Titans of lore.

Brashear brought several motivations for showing out in Johnstown. Due to a teacher's strike during the 1975–76 season, the school—then called Fifth Avenue High—missed some early games. Fifth Avenue may have started late, but the Archers put together a 16-0 state championship run. Fifth Avenue handled state standard-bearer Farrell High by twelve

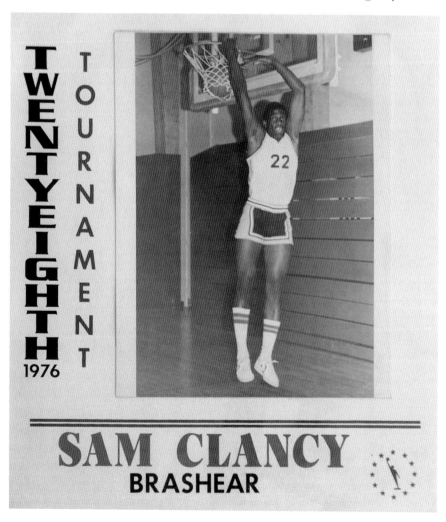

Sam Clancy poster. *Photo by Thomas Slusser,* Johnstown Tribune-Democrat.

in the semifinals and then bounced Norristown by eleven for the banner. Legendary Farrell coach Ed McCluskey, who would win seven state titles from 1952 to 1972, deemed Fifth Avenue "one of the most talented teams ever to play in the state final." The next school year, all that pride from a Fifth Avenue state title was nominally scrubbed when the city school was renamed Brashear following the merger.

The new Brashear School District "was created to help with segregation issues in the Pittsburgh Public Schools. The Pittsburgh Board of Education closed Fifth Avenue High School, Gladstone High School in Hazelwood and South Hills High School and merged the students in the building with 5,000 or more students attending," according to Wikipedia. "School security and local police were on hand the first week of school in 1976. The school colors are black and gold, and the original school mascot were Bullets, depicted by two large bullets with mean faces and fists clenched. They were replaced in the mid-1990s with a new mascot."

Despite that influx of additional basketball bodies from schools merging with Fifth Avenue, the resultant team essentially comprised Fifth Avenue players. Brashear's basketball team, more than anything else, could unite the swollen student body. It could also, potentially, bring about the kind of positive press the district desperately needed. Three key players had graduated from the unbeaten state title team. Back were Clancy, point guard Warner Macklin, wing David "Puffy" Kennedy and a host of players used to winning.

"We were undersized. We didn't have the team that we won state with," said Kennedy. "Plus, the name change. We only had Sam, one big guy. The other big guy Coach cut because he couldn't run laps. He was 6-foot-8, 270 pounds."

As WEST PHILADELPHIA'S PROFILE ballooned, players became used to traveling to tournaments, but that wasn't yet the case in 1976. Out-of-town forays were damn near extraterrestrial voyages for city kids. When West Philly coach Joe Goldenberg loaded the team for the trip to Johnstown, he noticed that one of his players had packed a bulky portable television set. "You don't have to bring that," Goldenberg told the player. "'All the hotel rooms have colored TVs. And they have rugs on the floors.' You might have thought I gave them a million dollars." When the Speedboys reached Johnstown, Goldenberg met with them amid frigid, snowy conditions.

In his Sheraton Hotel room in Johnstown, Banks hung out with an admiring eleven-year-old boy whose father had coached most of the Speedboys growing up at Philly's Sherwood Recreational Center. James Flint's son must have felt like he was touring with Michael Jordan during his Bulls run as Banks became a national figure. Before the championship game in Johnstown, the boy—James "Bruiser" Flint—would tie Banks's leather Converse sneakers tight for him. In 1976, many players had transitioned from canvas Chuck Taylors to the leather Converse made fashionable by Dr. J in the NBA. Flint tied a strong knot and sent Banks out to face Brashear before nearly four thousand fans.

"I tried to emulate those guys," said Bruiser, a Philly guy and coach who had assisted Pittsburgh guy John Calipari with the University of Kentucky's basketball program. "My dad would go on the trip. I would stay with him and hang out with those guys. They used to take care of me a little bit."[131]

Bruiser would grow up to become the head basketball coach at UMass and Drexel, taking the game uber-serious after being around it all his life. Banks would eventually see him in a different, adult light. "We used to call him the Black Bobby Knight," Banks joked, referring to both Flint men's commitment to coaching disciplined teams.

The opening night of the Johnstown Tournament played out like a formality, an obligatory green show of sorts. West Philly thumped John F. Kennedy High of Cleveland, Ohio, 68–37. Banks scored 16, 9 below his career average. Clarence Tillman tallied 13, point guard Darryl Warwick 14. In the other opening game, Brashear flirted with the century mark in a 99–76 romp over local Johnstown High. Warner Macklin scored 30, David Kennedy 20 and Clancy 14 (with 23 rebounds). A pair of talented five-foot-nine point guards would square off in the championship game in Macklin and Warwick, diminutive co-stars on stacked rosters.

Blending in with the sellout crowd at War Memorial Arena that night was another Pittsburgh legend. Eddie Beidenbach had starred at Edgewood High near Pittsburgh before heading south to play college basketball at North Carolina State. Beidenbach and Kutztown High product Dick Braucher expected to be sharing court time with Coach Press Maravich's precocious son, Pistol Pete, in college, but Pete did not qualify academically to play for the Wolfpack. At State, Beidenbach would play for three Hall of Fame coaches: Everett Case, Press Maravich and Norm Sloan. By 1976, Beidenbach was coaching at N.C. State and recruiting blue-chippers for his alma mater. He'd already reached back into his Pennsylvania roots to entice Clancy and Banks to visit the Raleigh campus.

"I was close to Clancy," Beidenbach said. "I liked Clancy better. I can't say he was a better player, but I liked him better for us. He was a better rebounder, strong."[132]

BRASHEAR HIGH COACH ELMER Guckert schemed to slow Banks, assigning Kennedy to guard him while the other four players set up in a zone, a box-and-one defense to limit the superstar. The game remained close in the first half. Two-point margins after the first and second quarter testified to these titans being equals, two of the top three teams in America. Banks was playing at his best after Goldenberg implored him to become more selfish, which went against Banks's team-first, pass-first nature.

"I asked him politely if he would mind taking at least 20 shots," Goldenberg told Gary Smith, who would become the greatest magazine feature writer in America at *Sports Illustrated*. "And if he didn't, I'd punch him in the chest."

Banks scored 22 of the Speedboys' 36 first-half points on his way to a 32-point, 18-rebound, 5-block night. All that would be wasted, however, if he didn't deliver in the final minutes. The teams exchanged the lead twenty times, according to one reporter. With the game tied at 65 in the final two minutes, Banks converted a mid-range jumper to give his team the lead. Brashear turned to Puffy Kennedy to tie the game. "I took a shot from the baseline," he said. "I missed it, Sam grabbed it....He forgot he was allowed to dunk."[133]

Clancy gently laid the ball back up toward the rim. "I went up and got the rebound and put it back up and finger-rolled it. I could have dunked it," he said. "I didn't think I was that high, plus I was rushing, and that's how they won the game."

Clancy's miss rebounded out to Banks, who fired a full-court pass to Darryl Warwick for the culminating layup and a 69–65 final. Banks was named tournament MVP. Four of the five Speedboys starters scored in double digits. When Mike Nichols didn't get a trophy for being on the all-tournament team, Banks gave him his, always preferring the assist.

Not that the showdown needed it, but a thunderous, exclamatory, tying dunk by Clancy before the buzzer would have elevated the already epic game even higher. Instead, the West Philly bench erupted onto the court around Banks, dogpiling all around him, and the postgame superlatives dropped like party confetti. "It was one of the best games I've seen in years and years and years," Beidenbach told Gary Smith. "I see so many high school games, and it's seldom I REALLY enjoy one, but I REALLY enjoyed this game."

Goldenberg called Clancy "the strongest thing since Dino De Laurentiis invented King Kong" in Smith's game story. Clancy totaled fourteen points and sixteen rebounds, but he left with an eternal regret for not punctuating the night with a putback slam that would have put him in the pantheon of such powerful finals finishers like future N.C. State hero Lorenzo Charles seven years later. Kennedy paced Brashear with eighteen points. Edwin Peoples added sixteen.

FUTURE NBA REFEREE JOE Crawford has probably witnessed tens of thousands of basketball games at all levels. He got his start in Philadelphia working public and Catholic league games, many of them raucous playoff tilts in the hallowed Penn Palestra. To evolve into an NBA referee, Crawford needed to get accustomed to calling games that involved dynamic stars like Gene Banks.

"Gene was the best high school player that I had ever seen," he said. "He and Lewis Lloyd from Overbrook High. They were part of that great Overbrook and West Philly rivalry, which was huge. When I was a kid doing high school games, I actually worked some pretty cool games."[134]

Crawford saved just three box scores from high school games he worked. One was the showdown between Overbrook and West Philly, when Lloyd and Banks squared off. At the end of the season, Banks and Lloyd were once more pitted against each other in the Public League championship game. The day before the game, West Philadelphia had moved its practice to the famed Penn Palestra, where the championship game would be held. Goldenberg put his team through drills and reviewed how they would defend Lloyd. Banks was not there for any of it.

"I missed a practice and that was Coach Goldenberg's rule—if you don't practice, you don't play," said Banks. "At the last minute he got a chance to use the court at the Palestra. That was word of mouth at school. When I came to practice at our gym, they weren't there. It was a big to-do."

An hour into practice, Goldenberg addressed the elephant not in the room: "Anybody know where Gene is?" Nobody did.

"If Gene had called me and given me an excuse, he might have played," Goldenberg said years later. "We go to the Palestra the next night.

Everybody's changing in the locker room. Gene's already in there putting his uniform on. 'Put your street clothes on. You'll sit next to me on the bench,'" Goldenberg said.

"But Coach…."

When Goldenberg informed his athletic director, Doug Connelly, about the idea of possibly sitting his superstar the night before the big game, Connelly invited Goldenberg to his house for Manhattans. Connelly anticipated potential problems Goldenberg hadn't even considered. "If you don't mind, I'd like to sit next to you on the bench," Connelly said.

"He had never interfered or offered any suggestions unless I asked him," said Goldenberg.

"This could be dangerous," Connelly explained. "There's gonna be a lot of money bet on this game." Connelly had been the coach when Goldenberg played for West Philly in the 1950s, back when the Speedboys lost only nine games in three years, but seven of them were against Wilt Chamberlain and Overbrook.

"I was a little naïve," said Goldenberg. "I did know that there was point-shaving. I didn't really pay much attention."

Connelly warned that the crowd might turn ugly against Goldenberg when they saw he was sitting Banks. Connelly would be there for moral, emotional and physical support.

"When Gene walked out behind me in street clothes for the game," Goldenberg said, "the place became a hush, like a morgue. The assistant coach said, 'Coach, let him play.' Maybe I would change my rule for a game this big. Well, I'm not changing it."

Goldenberg risked a league title, a city championship, an undefeated season and a mythical national championship by sitting Banks. Nevertheless, he stuck to his convictions knowing that Overbrook wanted to pay back his team for ending its unbeaten season in 1975. In late February 1977, heading into this showdown, West Philly was undefeated; Overbrook had one loss.

Goldenberg assigned Mike Nichols to shadow Lewis Lloyd on the court. Lloyd had been expecting a one-on-one showdown against Banks in the February 22 tilt. Players on both rosters had to adjust their mindsets with Banks in street clothes.

"I was in 10th grade. We had maybe 30 plays for Gene, and Gene didn't play," said Overbrook's rising star Ricky Tucker. "We had all our plays for Gene. Darryl Warrick had a good game for them. We had practiced different [defenses] to try to contain Gene. To me, their most valuable player was

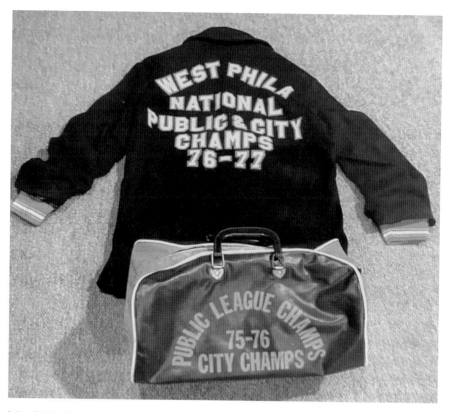

West Philly High champs warmup. *Courtesy of Gene Banks.*

Darryl at point guard. Then they had one of the best shooters in the country in Clarence Tillman. Tyrell Biggs, the future heavyweight boxer, was on that West Philly team too. We called him Bird."[135]

Biggs wouldn't start until the following season. In seven years, he'd be the gold medal–winning super heavyweight in the Olympics. In a decade, he'd be fighting Mike Tyson for the heavyweight championship of the world. Tyson would knock him out in the seventh round.

West Philadelphia proved itself a great all-around team before more than nine thousand fans, toppling Overbrook and Lewis Lloyd without Banks, 61–51, for a fourth straight league title. Lloyd scored 19 points for Overbrook (23-4), but that was only six more than Banks's replacement. And the Speedboys' six-foot-eight Joe Garrett, who had played at Roman Catholic before transferring into West Philadelphia, now had a Public League title to go with his Catholic League title.

The Speedboys finished the season 30-0, No. 1 in America.

AFTER THE 1976 JOHNSTOWN Tournament, Banks and Clancy struck up a friendship that would endure. They'd team up on the Pennsylvania squad in Sonny Vaccaro's Dapper Dan Roundball Classic All-Star game in Pittsburgh. Banks earned MVP honors there too, although he felt undeserving. The Pittsburgh audience booed Banks because he earned the award over local favorite Sam Clancy, who had been fabulous that night too.

Vaccaro remembers Banks walking to the middle of the court, grabbing the microphone and telling the audience that Clancy deserved to be the MVP. Banks gave away that trophy too. Local Pittsburgh scribe Mike DeCourcy, now a national sports media figure, recalled the scene.

"Sam was the best player on the floor for Pennsylvania," he said. "Wes Matthews for the United States was really great that night. It was Sam that made the difference. When they announced Gene as the MVP, people were booing. They hosed Sam. Gene took the trophy, took the microphone, and said, 'This isn't right. Sam deserves the trophy.' Then everybody went nuts! I always thought highly of Gene after that."[136]

THE JOHNSTOWN FINAL, IN hindsight, was a springboard for so many great careers. Goldenberg would post a 410-84 record. That Speedboys team would finish 30-0 amid a 68-game winning streak. Banks lost just two of 81 games in high school—one to Long Island Lutheran and one to LaSalle College High, led by a fabulous point guard named Fran McCaffrey (current Iowa coach) whom Banks dubbed a "mini-Maravich." Overbrook defeated West Philly on both sides of the long winning streak, but Banks wasn't there for either loss. He would sign with Duke University and play for Pennsylvania native/head coach Bill Foster, reaching the NCAA national championship game in 1978. Clarence Tillman (Kentucky), Nichols (Delaware), Warwick (Hampton) and Joe Garrett (UTEP) all played basketball in college. Johnstown was a springboard, for sure.

"That was the game that put us over the top, made us No. 1 in the nation," said Banks. "That's how big that Johnstown tournament was."

For Brashear, Macklin (Point Park), Kennedy (Cincinnati) and Clancy (Pitt) played basketball in college. Clancy's career highlight at Pitt came against Duke—and Gene Banks. In 1979, the Panthers upset No. 3 Duke at Cameron Indoor Stadium. Clancy scored 23 points and grabbed 11 rebounds. Banks had 17, including a field goal that tied the game 69–69 with three minutes remaining. It was playing out just like the Johnstown finish had. Duke stalled from there in the era before the shot clock. By then former

DeMatha Catholic standout Pete Strickland—another former Johnstown Tournament participant who had become Clancy's teammate at Pitt—was on the floor in crunch time.

"I was being posted up by Duke's Jim Spanarkel," he said. "They inverted their offense. Spanarkel screens down for [center Mike] Gminski to pop out. Spanarkel has me on the block; I can't get around him. Spanarkel has me under his armpit. If you don't know who the fish is, it's probably you! Spanarkel's 6-5. I'm 6-foot. I can't get around him. They try to throw the ball in. Sam shoots the passing lane, knocks it down, gets it. I look up and Sam has stolen the ball."[137]

Clancy dribbled down the left side of the court and pulled up for a shot six feet out. The ball hit the rim and bounded up and back toward Clancy. Gminski had inside position on him and jumped with two arms extended. The ball seemed to hit his hands and pop away, right to Clancy. And here Clancy was, back in time. The scene played out like a do-over, an interminable replay from the Johnstown ending. This time, Clancy took his time, grabbed the rebound and banked it in without ever coming back to earth. This time, Sam was the undisputed hero. Gminski did get a chance at redemption. Duke sent a three-quarters court pass to him, but Gminski's open seventeen-footer to tie the game hit the back of the rim.

"There's fifteen guys in blue and yellow screaming. Everything else is silent in Cameron Indoor Stadium," said Strickland, who would become a D-I head coach. "I get the ball and just throw it into the Duke student section."

Two years after Johnstown, Clancy made good. As delirious as Pitt's players were, that's how furious Duke coach Bill Foster was in the locker room after the game. "That's when Bill Foster lost it," said Strickland. "A rare February nonconference game. He lost it in the locker room after that, and they never got it back. High expectations."

Clancy would eventually be drafted into the NBA *and* the NFL. He averaged a double-double in college at Pitt and nearly did the same in the Continental Basketball Association. Despite not playing football in college after sustaining an injury in the spring of his freshman year, and being admonished by Pitt basketball coach Tim Grgurich to play only basketball, Clancy still played a decade of professional football as a physical defensive end. His herculean body would do greater damage on a football field. In 2023, his hometown named a street after him.

Clancy's Brashear High teammate Puffy Kennedy would have a son named D.J. When Schenley High won its own state title over mighty Chester in 2007, D.J. matched his father's accomplishment with his own state title.

Gene Banks, Dan Baker, Dick Allen and Clarence Tillman at a Phillies game. *Courtesy of Gene Banks.*

After playing for St. John's University and then overseas in professional basketball, D.J. Kennedy returned to the States and won five titles in the Basketball Tournament comprising former college players, which netted him close to $500,000 in prize money.[138]

Gene Banks played six years in the NBA. Among his career mementos, he keeps a box score from when he played for the Chicago Bulls against the Boston Celtics in the 1986 playoffs. Banks had eight points, three rebounds and three assists in twenty-five minutes. But that's not why he kept the box score. Three lines above Banks was Michael Jordan, who used the game as a springboard to superstar status. Jordan scored sixty-three points in fifty-three minutes against a Celtics team with Larry Bird, Kevin McHale, Robert Parrish, Danny Ainge, Dennis Johnson and Bill Walton. Boston won in two overtimes.

In his six NBA seasons, Banks scored more than thirty points five times, with a personal best of forty-four in a close win over the Lakers in 1983. He recorded one triple double, which had been a common achievement for him at West Philly High. Banks could occasionally be great, but not consistently at the highest level.

Back in 1977, he'd been regaled as one of the greatest high school players in the country along with Albert King, Jo Jo Hunter and Earvin "Magic" Johnson. He joined them on the first McDonald's All-American team and then became Duke's first McDonald's All-American recruit.

And still, the fond memories of those December nights in Johnstown persist. "Life couldn't get any better back then," he said. "Those were great times." To commemorate them, Banks is raising money to start a West Philly High Hall of Fame. He knows about honoring heroes and taking West Philly to the big-time. Back when he played, the school hosted a showdown with rival Overbrook in West Philly's gym, capacity 150. Goldenberg later moved the Speedboys' games out of what *Inquirer* writer Don McKee called "a cubbyhole" to the larger Sayre Junior High. To be big-time, you must think big-time. The men who played in Johnstown's greatest tournament game understand it better than most.

And America's top magazine feature writer was there to chronicle the great Gene Banks. "The intensity with which he played," Gary Smith remembered. "There'd be times you'd see the dried spittle on his lips after games. Just a ferocious will to succeed. I remember after his last game at the Palestra he took roses and handed them out to all four sides of the arena. He had that political sense to play to the crowd."

SOAKED

But of that day and hour knoweth no man, no, not the angels of Heaven, but my Father only. But as the days of Noe were, so shall also the coming of the Son of man be. For as in the days that were before the flood they were eating and drinking, marrying and giving in marriage, until the day that Noe entered the ark, and knew not until the flood came, and took them all away; so shall also the coming of the Son of man be.
—Matthew 24: 36–39 (King James Version)

The summer following the greatest game ever played in the Johnstown Tournament, a storm blew into town on July 19 and settled right over the city. Nearly a foot of rain fell in a day, which resulted in streets being flooded and six dams being compromised, sending more water into towns than the infrastructure could handle.

After rural Johnstown had endured the big flood of 1889 and another in 1936, the flood of 1977 brought destruction of its own. Residents had felt secure. After the 1936 flood, the U.S. Army Corps of Engineers dug concrete river walls twenty feet deep to handle future water spillover. The river walls spanned ten miles.[139] If you're at the high school, you can see them. If you're downtown, you can see them, probably even drove over them on a bridge.

In 1977, Clarence Robson was a boy living in Cambria County. After the thunderstorm parked over the town, rain poured and poured and poured relentlessly. Water accumulated in Robson's house, forcing the family to evacuate. The water destroyed most of their possessions.

"We had five feet of water in my basement," he said. "The water ran into the creek, filled up the creek and the road was the creek. There was a gully, and it washed out bridges. I slept in a fire truck because we had five feet of water in my dining room. Then they put us in a flood trailer with other people who got flooded. There were HUD trailers for two years before we got back into our house."[140]

On top of all that, Robson said his family got scammed. "The people who renovated our house got the check and took off."

Some Johnstown residents who'd survived the first flood stayed, probably convinced that it couldn't possibly happen again. When the second flood hit in 1936, townspeople had to feel jinxed or targeted by a higher power. And in 1977, seven months after the greatest game ever played in the War Memorial Tournament, the third flood slammed the town.

Mr. Robson's 1963 Cadillac—which he'd just paid off—was carried by the water until it wrapped around a telephone pole. Chad Fetzer, who owns Fetz's Sports Pub in town near Point Stadium, saw his father's life change after the flood. His father worked in town hauling garbage, owning two trucks. "Back then there wasn't waste management like today," he said. "My dad worked two months cleaning up after the 1977 flood. Seven days a week. He had three others working for him. I would ride in the trucks with him."[141]

Others said it took two weeks just to shovel the water, mud and sediment out of the local bank. Reports claimed that eighty-four people died in the flood, fewer than the two thousand in 1889 but more than the two dozen from 1936.[142]

By December, the mess was mostly cleaned up. Greg "Dutch" Morley was the starting point guard for DeMatha. More than any games, he remembered the remnants of the flood that year when the Stags hit Johnstown in December. "I remember looking at the buildings and looking at the water lines that were still on the buildings," he said. "That must not have been any fun. That's what I remember about the time."[143]

Morley's family had roots in Pennsylvania, twenty-five miles outside Johnstown in Barnesboro, where Northern Cambria High hailed. They moved to Maryland before he was born, but Morley returned to Pennsylvania during the summers to visit family. "I wore No. 21 in my career because I watched Roberto Clemente play from my aunt's couch every day," he said. "We went to the all-star game when it was in Three Rivers Stadium one year. Went to Games 6 and 7 in 1979 when the Pirates won the World Series. They were trailing 3-2 and they won both games. I got some tickets from friends at [the University of Maryland, where Dutch played college basketball]. We sat right behind the Pirates dugout."

Trojans basketball coach Paul Litwalk remembers dealing with the water, during and after the storm. "I lived down in the west end of Johnstown," he said. "It hit my place along with my family. Our basement was loaded with flood water, and it almost got up into the first floor. I sat and watched it. I thought for a second that I better start taking some doors off of rooms just in case if they turn our house over. Our main street on Fairfield Avenue, cars were just going down, down, down. It was terrible. The next day when people got up, it was just a mess. I don't know how many people we lost. This hit in July. We didn't open the school up until the middle of September. The students came back. Our football team, we moved our schedule back a little bit. Point Stadium where they play the AAABA tournament in summer time, they had to clean that up too."[144]

War Memorial Arena wasn't spared from the flood either. "They got hit, too," said local broadcaster Tim Rigby. "In fact, that's what prompted the Johnstown Jets hockey team to leave. That was the death knell for them."[145]

With tragedy comes solace—and even sunshine.

OVER THE SUMMER OF '77 in Washington, D.C., DeMatha's basketball fortunes could not have looked any better. The Stags had plenty of motivation, coming off a 29-4 season that saw the program fail to win the Catholic league championship for just the second time since 1961. Eleven players with experience returned, including all five starters. That summer, the Stags' freshman, junior varsity and varsity teams all went undefeated in their leagues. The launch for that perfect 1977–78 season began that same summer when DeMatha and the Howard University basketball program traveled to Brazil to see the sites and play a packed schedule of games.

"Howard played Brazil's national team," Dutch Morley said. "[Hall of Famer] Oscar Schmidt was on Brazil's national team. We actually played 12 games in 15 days and went 12-0. They added more sites because they were selling out the arenas, and they were shipping us around. They had a couple of junior national teams that we played, and we also played some local teams they put together just to play us. Rio. San Paulo. A long way from Johnstown. That was the only time I know of DeMatha going that far away."

The senior-led 1977–78 team brought junior guards Sidney Lowe and Dereck Whittenburg off the bench. These were guys who would be named McDonald's All-Americans in a year. And since 1961, when DeMatha lost by

2 points in the Johnstown championship game, the Stags had won fourteen straight games here—seven tournament championships without a loss.[146] In December 1977, they swept their Johnstown games against Nazareth of New York (63–57) and Norwin (62–54), which was led by six-foot-nine center Doug Arnold.

That 1977–78 DeMatha squad became Wootten's first unbeaten team, national champions again! Prior to that, DeMatha had finished six seasons with just one loss (1960–61, 1964–65, 1965–66, 1967–68, 1971–72 and 1972–73).

ENTERING DECEMBER 1978, DEMATHA boasted a 15-1 record against elite competition in War Memorial Arena. Beaver Falls High was making its Johnstown Tournament debut. "The guys for us were all-section," Tiger starter Dwight Collins remembers. "The other guys for them were All-American. You get a chip on your shoulder."

The pretournament luncheon showcased DeMatha players dressed in formal sport coats and ties. They looked polished, professional. "We were wearing our regular clothes," said Collins. "Blue jeans. Sweatpants. It made a mockery of us, though not intentionally."[147]

Adding further insult was that the Beaver Falls players, as well as most people involved in the tournament, believed that the tournament was aligned to funnel the semifinals toward a classic DeMatha-Overbrook championship matchup, since they were ranked Nos. 1 and 3 nationally, respectively. In the spring of 1978, Overbrook defeated West Philadelphia to end the Speedboys' sixty-eight-game winning streak. They, too, were loaded.

In December 1978, DeMatha's backcourt of Whittenburg and Lowe weren't starters as juniors, although they finished most games. They would win a national title at DeMatha and would later do the same at North Carolina State. But in December 1978, Whittenburg was out with a broken bone, his fifth metatarsal.[148] That omission and the absence of starting six-foot-six center Percy White (blood clot issues) sort of opened a window for Beaver Falls to believe that it could chance an upset.

Then again, Morgan Wootten's twenty-three-year record to that point was 605-85, according to scribe Ted Silary. Morgan didn't lose often—and not at all in the 1977–78 season.[149]

The Beaver Falls Tigers were famously the alma mater to New York Jets football icon Joe Namath. And yet, DeMatha's winning streak hit 34 games by the time they made it to Johnstown in December. Some newspaper accounts had the streak at 42 and 44 straight wins, but DeMatha officials verified that 34 was the accurate count. DeMatha's greatest streak was its 125 straight wins in its on-campus gym from 1961 to 1976. That streak does not include home games that had been relocated to larger arenas like the loss to Power Memorial at Cole Field House.

For those criticizing DeMatha for never generating a consecutive wins streak like Overbrook or West Philly or Power Memorial, well, in many of the years DeMatha posted great records with a few losses, the defeats came against college freshmen teams. DeMatha also played streak snapper on occasion. When Baltimore Dunbar won fifty-nine straight games from 1981 to 1983, DeMatha broke the streak. It wasn't quite breaking Alcindor's seventy-one-game streak as DeMatha had done in the 1960s, but it was still significant.

The end of long streaks can be prolific, or painful, as DeMatha would learn.

BEAVER BROOK

The town of Beaver Falls—which rings oh so similar to the fictional Bedford Falls from the classic black-and-white Christmas movie *It's a Wonderful Life*—is a homespun hamlet where sports dreams get manufactured into storybook American moments. Joe Namath grew up here, throwing passes for the Tiger football team from the late 1950s into the 1960s. Because of Namath, the tendency is to think of Beaver Falls as a football town. And it is, and was. The Tiger program, however, didn't post its first football state title until 2016. But as you drive up Route 18 toward the Beaver Falls campus, the first building you notice in the distance is beige with a stark-white, curved roof: Beaver Falls Middle School—the former high school where Joe Namath played high school basketball, where the Tigers have toiled on the way to reaching six PIAA basketball state finals since 1970, winning four. During that 1970s title run, Beaver Falls played its state quarterfinal and semifinal at War Memorial Arena. Guard Oscar Jackson remembers playing from behind, including being down nine in the final 2:24 against Altoona High in the quarterfinals. The Tigers' trapping press brought them back.

"The one thing about the Altoona game, there was a very bad snowstorm," he said. "All of our fans were on the buses headed back home toward the end of the game. They left the game after the third quarter heading back to Beaver Falls. We were down. They didn't find out that we won until the next day." In the semifinals, Beaver Falls returned to War Memorial Arena and defeated a stacked Schenley team 87–83 despite trailing much of that game. Schenley had future NBA player Maurice Lucas, Jeep Kelly and

Beaver Falls gymnasium at Beaver Falls Middle School. *Photo by Bradley A. Huebner.*

Ricky Coleman. Coleman was considered the best junior in the state, and Kelly had averaged 30 points per game in junior high.[150]

Doug Biega, a two-time championship coach at Beaver Falls (2005 and 2013), still teaches at Beaver Falls Middle. He's raising a son and coaching the next batch of players in another district known for a football legend—Tony Dorsett's Hopewell High. His Hopewell junior high teams have gone 30-1 the past two seasons. The championship cycle repeats, right down the road—in basketball.

Behind the Beaver Falls Middle School gym, spatially and symbolically, you'll find the high school football and baseball fields. Athletes play all three major sports in this town, but it's clear that the basketball gym can claim as much sports history as either football or baseball. Honoring that history, the Tiger varsity basketball squad still plays in the sunken black-and-orange pit whose upper-level seats are rimmed by team photos of past ballers.

Talented all-around athletes graduate from Beaver Falls every year. Heck, professional baseball franchises even tried to sign Namath to a contract right out of high school when he played just down the road from Wampum High star athlete Dick Allen. Like Allen, Joe could do it all.

With its considerable basketball history, starting with the 1970 state championship under Coach Frank Chan, one of Beaver Falls' greatest hoops moments came in the first round of the 1978 Johnstown Tournament. The Tigers got matched up against a DeMatha squad on that 34-game winning streak. Chan was in the middle of a twenty-one-year career that would see him post a record of 367-115. Stars Damon Bryant (23 points per game as a junior) and Dwight Collins (16.5 points per game as a sophomore) were returning six-foot-three athletes with considerable résumés. And after ending the 1977–78 season with an upset loss to a Butler High team missing two stars, Beaver Falls had plenty to prove.

Before playing in Johnstown, however, the Tigers had to compete in Farrell High's Ralph E. Dresch Memorial Tournament. They opened with an 82–66 victory over Mercer as Collins scored 30 points and snared 18 rebounds. Collins earned co-MVP after the Tigers nosed Farrell 61–58 for the title. Without any rest time in between, Beaver Falls headed to the Johnstown Tournament to open up against the DeMatha machine.

Beaver Falls held the Stags to their lowest point total under Wootten. The Tigers won 55–45 as Damon Bryant scored 17 and Collins 14. Beating Mercer, Farrell and DeMatha in consecutive days has to go down as one of the greatest achievements in Pennsylvania basketball history.

DeMatha was led by John Carroll's 13 points. In the other semifinal, Overbrook squeezed past Altoona 62–54 to earn the right to face the steaming-hot Tigers, who wouldn't be criticized if their legs betrayed them in their fourth straight game against strong competition. Beaver Falls was 10-0, Overbrook perfect as well.

The Tigers charged to an 11–1 lead. Collins, a lithe athlete on the Division I football radar with comparisons already being made to Johnstown Tournament alumnus Tony Dorsett, pounded home a dunk during the run. Just how good was this Beaver Falls team? They beat Farrell, then the nation's top team, and now they were up big on the nation's No. 3 team, an Overbrook program with a tradition of Chamberlain and Hightower, both former Johnstown Tournament MVPs. The Overbrook team without a loss yet this season. And Beaver Falls was embarrassing them.

Overbrook star guard Ricky Tucker was incredulous. His free throws had ended West Philly's sixty-eight-game winning streak in February 1978, 62–61. This wrong-sided dominance against his Overbrook squad was something altogether unfamiliar. The Panthers were shell-shocked. But they started chipping back into the game and led 22–21 in the second quarter en route to a 68–60 championship victory. Had Beaver Falls worn down? Or was Overbrook that talented with guys like Joe Washington (28 points), Tucker (14) and six-foot-ten All-American center Tony Costner (14)? Collins scored a team-high 15 for the Tigers, and Bryant added 14.

Overbrook polished off a 34-1 season in 1978–79, the year Tucker claimed MVP honors in Johnstown. The next year, they would go 34-0 behind Costner, making them 68-1 over two seasons. DeMatha still wanted to test itself against Overbrook during the 1978–79 season, even though the matchup hadn't materialized in Johnstown. A four-team doubleheader in Maryland was scheduled for March, with two Philly teams busing south to play two Baltimore/D.C. teams. DeMatha (25-2) would finally play Philadelphia city champion Overbrook (30-1). Call it the Johnstown Tournament makeup.

Overbrook coach Max Levin had taken a team to Maryland before for a similar event. He remembers that his best player, Lewis Lloyd, was saddled with three quick fouls that time. The only way he'd go back down, he said, was if he could bring his own referee, which he did.[151]

In the other matchup, West Philadelphia—the only team to beat Overbrook—would face Baltimore power Cardinal Gibbons at the Capital Centre in Landover, Maryland. Overbrook was the new national No. 1, DeMatha No. 4. Washington scored 15 points, Ricky Tucker 12 and Jeff Tucker (no relation) 10 as Overbrook downed DeMatha 52–50 before more than six thousand fans. Richard Congo hit the game-winning shot with four seconds remaining. His heroics brought the crowd to its feet, the noise booming to all but Congo's parents, who were deaf.[152]

"Richard was the nicest, 6-foot-6 gentle giant you could meet," said Levin. "I worked in a summer camp for kids. He used to ride his bicycle over to my house, and I would take him to work every day. Everybody loved Richard."

Carroll scored 17 for DeMatha, which got 10 points apiece from sophomore wings Bob Ferry Jr. and Tommy Branch, future All-American Adrian Branch's brother. Sidney Lowe scored 8, a healthier Dereck Whittenburg 4. Quentin Daily lit up the other game for Cardinal Gibbons (25-4), scoring 36 points and grabbing 17 rebounds in a 73–62 win over West Philly (20-2). Overbrook and West Philly shared the bus down and back, so the neighborhood buddies were able to connect even more during the commute.

"We were all friends," said Ricky Tucker. "Even when we played each other we would go out and party together after the game."

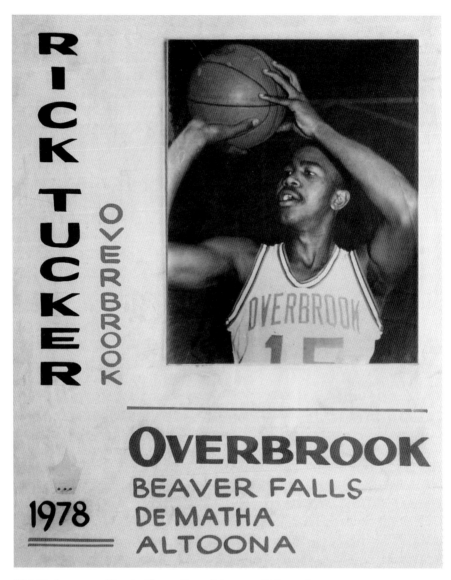

Rick Tucker poster. *Photo by Thomas Slusser,* Johnstown Tribune-Democrat.

Ricky Tucker and Joe Washington would enroll at Providence College. Tucker would enjoy a solid career after being recruited by Dave Gavitt, who would go on to create the Big East Conference that revolutionized college basketball. After college, Tucker would return to his Philadelphia roots and give back to his sport and his neighborhood. Tucker runs the Ricky Tucker Summer League right near Overbrook High School. Kobe

Bryant's Mamba Foundation, along with Nancy Leiberman Charities, paid to put a brand-new surface over two neighborhood basketball courts in 2022. They also painted murals on surrounding walls. "That's my neighborhood," Tucker boasted.

The court is purple with a yellow paint area, reminiscent of Kobe's Lakers colors. On a wall just off the court is a mural of Kobe with his daughter Gianna, or Gigi. Kobe and Gianna's names are also encircled to honor them further after their untimely deaths in a helicopter crash. On a wall behind one glass backboard are Kobe's Mamba eyes keeping watch over games with his usual intensity. Kobe's No. 24 is displayed prominently around the court as well, including being encircled by a heart near the free-throw stripes.

"The Mamba Foundation usually only does one court at a time," said Tucker. "They partnered with Nancy Lieberman Charities and did both courts at the same time."

Two courts and four glass backboards at Tustin Playground, where Tucker grew up playing basketball, where Kobe's uncle John "Chubby" Cox and his boys had played. Where basketball history continues.

BEAVER FALLS RETURNED TO Johnstown in December 1979, the closest team to the Flood City that year with Johnstown and Altoona and Bishop McCort absent. Stars abounded in 1979. The Tigers' first opponent was W.T. Woodson from Fairfax, Virginia, which featured six-foot-seven, two-hundred-pound forward Pete Holbert, who was averaging 41 points per game. This Beaver Falls group had added six-foot-five shooter Ron Rowan. He would play at Notre Dame and then become a starter at St. John's with players like Walter Berry and Chris Mullin, winning sixty-two games in his final two seasons. The starting lineup for Beaver Falls High in 1979 had a six-foot-eight center and two six-foot-five wings. Holbert scored 38 against them the first night, but the Tigers won 81–61. Holbert remembers a key play early that cost his team, then ranked No. 30 in the nation. "Our point guard Steve Haas got a season-ending injury," he said. The backup was a 110-pound freshman, new to the high school and the program. "That forced Tommy Amaker to grow up real quick."[153]

Red Jenkins was Woodson's legendary coach. He would post a career record of 615-290 playing Washington Catholic Athletic Conference titans, as many as half a dozen ranked nationally in a given year. He hadn't planned on handing the keys to the offense to a freshman, but it worked.[154] "They threw a long pass down court," said Jenkins. "They collided and my point guard went to the ground and got hurt. Beaver Falls had five great athletes. Peter scored 38 points. That's the only reason we were in the game."

Collins led the Tigers with 23, followed by Noble Miles (20), Forest Grant (16) and Ron Rowan (15). Collins would average 22 points per game his final two years of high school in basketball and then excel as a receiver and wingback at Pitt, catching passes from Dan Marino, running behind linemen Bill Fralic, Jimbo Covert and Mark May. The Panthers were in their glory years under Coach Johnny Majors, then Jackie Sherrill, then Foge Fazio, having won the national title at 12-0 with Tony Dorsett in 1976 under Majors. The Panthers posted records of 11-1 in 1979, 1980 and 1981. They were ranked No. 1 at some point in the season in 1981 and 1982. Collins, one of the greatest athletes in Beaver Falls history, would grow from being an All-State basketball player and the Associated Press Football Player of the Year in Pennsylvania in 1979 to being drafted by the Minnesota Vikings of the NFL.

FRESHMAN POINT GUARD TOMMY Amaker became "next man up" in Red Jenkins's Woodson High program against elite competition after Haas injured his knee.

"Tommy came in and played the rest of that game and never lost his starting job in four years," said Jenkins. Jenkins coached in Sonny Vaccaro's prestigious Dapper Dan Roundball Classic in 1978 and would win four straight Northern Division titles with Amaker, who would blossom into a McDonald's All-American and—eventually—a John Wooden National High School Defensive Player of the Year award winner. Amaker and former Johnstown MVP Johnny Dawkins from Mackin Catholic teamed up at Duke to reach the 1986 national championship game. They lost to Louisville and Johnstown Tournament alumni and Camden High graduates Billy Thompson and Kevin Walls, as well as former fellow Camden High star Milt Wagner. In the Atlantic Coast Conference, Amaker would face off against Johnstown alumni like Muggsy Bogues at Wake Forest and Jeff Lebo at North Carolina.

Amaker would play at Duke, then coach at Duke, Seton Hall, Michigan and Harvard on the way to 468 career victories and counting.

National No. 9 Ben Franklin High of New York bounced Roman Catholic of Philadelphia in the other semifinal. Gerald Roberts was the high man for Speedy Morris's Cahillites with twenty-three points in defeat. Morris would win more than 1,000 career games between high school and college,

Morgan Wootten kneels in front of his 1976–77 seniors: Mike Brey, Mark Booker, Clarence DesBordes, Joe Lucas and Mark Hammond. *Courtesy of DeMatha.*

coaching men's and women's teams. His LaSalle University team in 1989–90 finished 30-2 behind national Player of the Year Lionel Simmons.

Ben Franklin then topped Beaver Falls 61–48 for the 1979 Johnstown Tournament championship as six-foot-seven sophomore Gary Springer scored 27 points, giving him 50 for the tournament to earn MVP honors. In 2021, his son Jaden was drafted by the Philadelphia 76ers with the twenty-eighth pick in the first round.[155]

Roman Catholic found enough offense to topple Woodson in the consolation game, but Holbert scored thirty-two more for a record two-day total of seventy points, topping Larry Miller's sixty-nine in 1963. Holbert still fondly remembers the players he competed against that year in Johnstown. "Roman Catholic had Lonnie McFarlan. He, Gary Springer, and myself all made the McDonald's All-America team and were friends."

Coach Red Jenkins didn't win any tournament games, but Johnstown still left a mark on his illustrious career. "I've often wondered whether the tournament is still going," he said in 2024. "I would be interested to see if Peter's record still holds up." It does, Red.

After coaching for thirty-five years against powerhouse opponents, Jenkins decided to retire. Finally. No more matching wits with the likes of Hall of Famer Morgan Wootten. But that didn't last. "A priest called me from a Catholic school in Fairfax, Virginia, about a job opening, and I decided to take it," he said. "They had been in that league for thirteen years and never won a game across the river against the big guys. It was a challenge, to stay the least."

But Red Jenkins has always accepted challenges.

PART IV

THE 1980s

Dunbar, Dobbins and Death

NEW YORK

In 1980, the crowd at War Memorial Arena signaled to Mackin High guard Johnny Dawkins before the first game had even begun that even without DeMatha, the field was loaded.

"At that time, Mount Vernon had lost only a game or two in two years," said the former Duke University All-American and current coach at the University of Central Florida. "They were basically a team that didn't lose. We were in the layup line vs. that team. I'll never forget it. It was the first time you could dunk in warmups. Hearing the crowd yell and yell, and they were just going nuts. These guys from Mt. Vernon were doing dunks that I had never even seen before. And we were pretty athletic ourselves."[156]

Mount Vernon coach Tony Fiorentino was a basketball lifer who now announces games for the Miami Heat. The program three miles from Iona College had produced basketball icons like Gus and Ray Williams, Scooter and Rodney McCray and Earl Tatum, aka the "Black Jerry West." Actor Denzel Washington was from Mount Vernon, although his mother sent him away to school to shield her son from the deleterious effects of the streets. Washington went on to play for the junior varsity team at Fordham University under Coach P.J. Carlesimo. For music lovers, the town of Mount Vernon has produced rapper Heavy D and announcer Dick Clark. Oh, and Chester Bickelhaupt, the grandfather of this book's author.

"We all grew up at the Boys and Girls Club in Mt. Vernon," said small forward Curtis "Smiley" Moore, the latest star in a line of siblings and the younger brother of former Knight Lowes Moore. "When we would finish

John Dawkins poster. *Photo by Thomas Slusser,* Johnstown Tribune-Democrat.

high school, we'd come home and play at Fourth Street Park. They had three full courts—regulation size—and two to three baskets on the side. It was real crowded. Mt. Vernon was one of the tournaments people would come to from the city. They had their pros, and we had our pros."[157]

Mount Vernon High drew from a four-square-mile radius. All the talent it needed could be found close to home. "We're ranked as one of the top ten public high schools in the country for producing NBA players," Fiorentino said. "We've had nine drafted or had a cup of coffee. We also had three guys who left [to attend other schools], or we would have had twelve. Al

Skinner was born in Mt. Vernon. Andre Drummond of the Philadelphia 76ers started here but matriculated to a private school in Connecticut."[158]

Nobody felt short-changed by the athletic displays showcased during warmups in Johnstown in 1980. At the beginning of that year, the U.S. Olympic hockey team had produced its "Miracle on Ice" in Lake Placid, New York. By December, Johnstown fans were watching the "Aerial on Ice" at War Memorial Arena.

"We were defense oriented," Fiorentino said. "A lot of what I did at Vernon was from Hubie Brown's playbook. There were so many great athletic players from both teams in that game."

No defense could stop Mackin's Johnny Dawkins the first game. He scored thirty-eight points, canning pull-ups and slip-sliding down the lane for floaters and runners. The score rose quickly for both teams. Smiley Moore dunked five times for Mount Vernon as the Knights executed a series of alley-oops despite playing nobody taller than six-foot-five. Moore would register 105 dunks in his high school career.

Mackin won the game 93–84. Largely based on that thrilling end-to-end classic, Dawkins would earn tournament MVP. In the championship game, Mackin downed Cardinal Gibbons of Baltimore 76–67. Dawkins shot erratically, but he'd already won over the Johnstown fans. Mount Vernon would lose later in the year by one point to another team with a talented left-hander, Xaverian and Chris Mullin, in the New York State Federation championship game.

Dawkins probably needed Mackin to win the Johnstown championship to win the tournament MVP award because Cardinal Gibbons's star Tim Coles had scored 25 points and snatched 16 rebounds in the 55–40 opening-night win over Johnstown. Smiley Moore's career path would endure a few post–high school bumps. He started out at a junior college and then played for Moe Iba at Nebraska. The six-foot-three small forward averaged 9 points, 4 rebounds and 2 assists per game over fifty-three college games. The Portland Trail Blazers drafted him in the sixth round of the 1985 NBA draft.

Moore's high school coach, Fiorentino, rose from being a high school history teacher and basketball coach to a college coach to an NBA assistant coach to a WNBA assistant to a TV broadcaster to a Heat ambassador 1,300 miles from Mount Vernon.

"I'm one of seven originals from the Miami Heat that still work for the franchise, a long way from Mt. Vernon," he said. "I was brought up in the projects of Mount Vernon. Five buildings in a circle, and 100 families in

Bill Thompson poster. *Photo by Thomas Slusser,* Johnstown Tribune-Democrat.

each building—10 flights, 500 families total in 2½ blocks. The basketball court was Fourth Street Playground. Thirty to forty years ago they did a survey. Fourth Street was picked as the second-best playground in the country and second-best talent in the country. Louisville was No. 1. Gus and Ray Williams used to be the NBA guys to play. That was right below my window in the projects."

Johnny Dawkins became part of Duke coach Mike Krzyzewski's 1982 recruiting class that probably saved Coach K's job—not unlike how tournament alumnus Larry Miller probably saved Dean Smith's job at North

Carolina—and set the Blue Devils on a path to national championships. Dawkins joined Mark Alarie, David Henderson, Weldon Williams and a future basketball broadcaster named Jay Bilas in the class. They would lose to Louisville in the 1986 national final.

Louisville's Billy Thompson teamed with fellow Camden High products Milt Wagner and Kevin Walls to win the 1986 NCAA national championship over Duke. Before that, Thompson played on the 1983 Final Four team that lost to Houston in Albuquerque in a game filled with fast breaks and dunks, perhaps the most electrifying and entertaining game in college basketball history. During the 1985–86 season, when Louisville captured the national championship, Thompson made an even more momentous decision. "I gave my life to Christ my senior year at Louisville," he said. To this day, Thompson pastors a church in Florida.

After college, Thompson would win an NBA title with Milt Wagner and the Los Angeles Lakers in 1986–87 and then again in 1987–88, making Thompson one of five players to win NCAA and NBA titles in consecutive seasons.

And to think that the Johnstown natives got to see Billy Thompson in War Memorial Arena in 1981, when Thompson was regarded as the top recruit in America.

CAMDEN HIGH

In December 1981, Johnstown welcomed back New Jersey kingpin Camden High, tournament champions in 1959 and 1966. In 1980–81, the Panthers featured Milt Wagner, an All-American guard who had graduated to attend Louisville. Now Denny Crum and the Cardinals were trying to recruit the next two Camden High greats: the nation's No. 1 player in Billy Thompson and sophomore guard Kevin Walls.

Thompson had been a 24 and 15 double-double machine as a junior for 27-1 Camden. Now he was the standard as a senior, the top-ranked player in America playing on the team ranked second nationally by *Basketball Weekly*. Thompson, listed at six-foot-eight, and Walls made it to Johnstown in December to compete in a field of three national top 20 teams.[159] Camden, Ben Franklin and repeater Mackin Catholic were all ranked in the top 10 nationally. Camden drew the weakest link on opening night. Belle Vernon High from Western Pennsylvania was hoping to have a talented sophomore to showcase, but he had transferred to another school. So, against a team from Western Pennsylvania near Charleroi and Uniontown, Thompson scored 29 points and swatted five shots in a 113–49 rout. Walls sparked the blowout with 15 of his 29 points in the opening quarter.

In the other opening-night game, Ben Franklin High of New York narrowly escaped the latest Mackin squad, 76–73.

In the championship, Camden started fast again, taking a 24–19 lead after one quarter. But the Franklin team from New York with Mr. Smooth, Walter Berry, and sophomore sensation Eric Singleton kept pace for a 65–61

Walter Berry poster. *Photo by Thomas Slusser,* Johnstown Tribune-Democrat.

tournament title. Singleton scored a game-high 23 to earn Most Valuable Player honors. Berry added 13. For the Panthers, Thompson (20) and Walls (17) led a balanced offense.

Johnstown didn't see the best of Walter Berry. At the end of the basketball season, the six-foot-eight forward led Ben Franklin to the Public School Athletic League title over Andrew Jackson High, scoring twenty-one points, grabbing twenty-two rebounds and blocking seven shots in the championship game.[160] More than three thousand fans saw that game at St. John's University, a school trying to recruit Berry.

To capture the underlying dysfunction of Ben Franklin High, however, go back one year. "Franklin was 12-0 when it was disqualified from the Public Schools Athletic League playoffs for having used two ineligible players."[161]

Ben Franklin High would close in 1982. Walter Berry would drop out of Ben Franklin, his third high school. Journalist Jaime Diaz explained what happened in a 1984 *Sports Illustrated* article titled "There's a Berry in the Bushes":

> *Berry was nearly a year behind his class when he left high school, not through lack of effort—he had a C average—but because he had lost a substantial number of credits in transferring from DeWitt Clinton to Morris High and from Morris to Franklin, in search of better basketball opportunities. Walter's mother, Mamie, who works as a maid and raised her son alone, says he fell behind when he helped her find an apartment after a fire destroyed the building in which they had been living.*[162]

This was the Ben Franklin program that had won the 1979 Johnstown Tournament over Beaver Falls behind MVP Gary Springer. The team that won again in 1981 behind Eric Singleton, a five-foot-nine sophomore. A basketball success story turned sour upon closer inspection in the article "Franklin Fades Out":

> *Franklin is the only public academic senior high school in Harlem. Over the years, it has picked up a reputation for poor attendance and lack of academic achievement. Last June only 76 seniors graduated and only nine passed the tests needed for a Regents diploma. As a result, the Board of Education has announced that the school, built in 1941 to hold more than 3,500 students, will close after the academic year next June.*

A new, rebranded school called the Manhattan Center for Science and Mathematics took over the property.

Berry would attend junior college and find his way back to St. John's University, where he'd become the national player of the year and the fourteenth overall pick in the NBA draft by Portland. Singleton would eventually wind up at Martin Luther King along with fellow Ben Franklin product Kenny Hutchinson and Coach Stan Dinner. In 1982, MLK was competing in the Johnstown Tournament.

BALTIMORE DUNBAR

Snowy Johnstown was almost the undoing of the legendary Baltimore Dunbar basketball team in December 1982. Widely considered the greatest high school team of all time, with four future NBA players in the rotation, Bob Wade's boys came to Pennsylvania and left with their perfect season intact. Barely.

Weeks before venturing north to Johnstown, Dunbar had handled DeMatha Catholic by double digits in the Maryland National Beltway Classic before nearly five thousand fans at Towson University. Stags coach Morgan Wootten was so impressed with Dunbar that he declared they could beat any Division III college team and most Division II teams.[163] A week before at the King of the Bluegrass Tournament in Kentucky, the coach of the Carlisle County High team that Dunbar pounded 65–48 felt great that his team hadn't lost by 35 points, like the other teams Dunbar faced.

Bob Wade's Dunbar squad entered Johnstown on a forty-game winning streak, having won every game during the 1981–82 season. To that blue-chip lineup they added a transfer and future pro point guard in Tyrone "Muggsy" Bogues, the five-foot-three ultraquick distributor and defensive nag.

During the summer, Wade's players often went to Howard Garfinkel's Five-Star Basketball Camp. High school superstars climbing the ladder to college and the pros assembled there as elite coaches and scouts provided tutelage. Michael Jordan, Dominique Wilkins, Patrick Ewing, LeBron James and Chris Mullin have all played in this showcase camp.

Mount Vernon High coach Tony Fiorentino worked the camp the year Muggsy Bogues participated. "Funniest story," he remembered, "when we were choosing our teams around midnight on a Sunday night—drinking a beer, having a sandwich—Howard Garfinkel had a chart of point guards, 2's, 3's, 4's, 5's. Dunbar coach Bob Wade had the fifth or sixth pick at PG. He said, 'You can't take Muggsy. You're gonna f--- up the camp.' He winds up taking Muggsy Bogues and wins the championship."

That's how impactful Bogues was despite standing five-foot-three. Dunbar star shooting guard Reggie Williams was already entrenched as the No. 1–ranked player in America, fielding recruiting offers from bluebloods like UCLA, Georgetown and others, with his unstoppable mid-range jumper and six-foot-seven frame.

The opening-night matchup at War Memorial Arena in 1982 pitted the Poets against Bay Village of Ohio. Northeastern University's young coach, Jim Calhoun, flew in to watch his recruit, Dunbar's sixth man, Reggie Lewis, hoping that other coaches wouldn't notice the six-foot-seven forward's potential and try to recruit him for their program. "It was starting to snow. I didn't see anybody else on the plane, and I thought I would," Calhoun said. "I don't remember seeing any other coaches there."[164]

Coaches on hand were more apt to be drawn to Williams or Tim Dawson, another transfer to Dunbar (from Towson Catholic) who was six-foot-six and menacing. Calhoun's target—six-foot-seven Reggie Lewis—was slender like Williams but played inside like Dawson. When players worked on their weaknesses at Dunbar practices, Lewis worked on his triple-threat square-ups and shooting a baby hook shot, but he naturally drifted to shoot perimeter shots. Coach Wade would chastise him that he couldn't shoot, which fueled Lewis to show him that he was, in fact, a deadeye.[165]

"Their team was No. 1 in the country," said Calhoun. "You knew even their tenth man was pretty good. Reggie was probably a mistake in some ways. He looked like a kid who hadn't had a good meal in two years. He still was quick as a cat. He had a praying-mantis jump shot—the ball was above his head, maybe even behind it."

At this time, the stars on Lewis's team were more skilled than he. After going undefeated the previous year, the Poets were 11-0 in 1982. Lewis had benefited from matching up against Williams every day at practice. Or Dawson, whom one reporter observing a practice mistook for the nation's top recruit instead of Williams. Lewis blended into the deep talent pool, quiet and unassuming but surreptitiously ultracompetitive.

"I always remember this conversation," said Herman "Tree" Harried, a junior on that squad and part of Dunbar's second team with Lewis. "We're sitting at the end of the bleachers in the gym. We're committed to

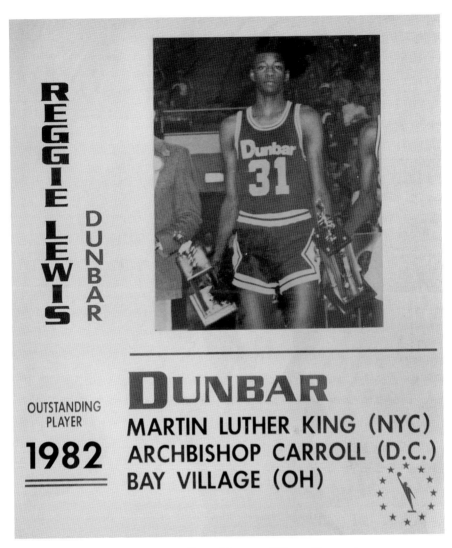

REGGIE LEWIS

DUNBAR

OUTSTANDING
PLAYER

1982

DUNBAR
MARTIN LUTHER KING (NYC)
ARCHBISHOP CARROLL (D.C.)
BAY VILLAGE (OH)

Reggie Lewis poster. *Photo by Thomas Slusser,* Johnstown Tribune-Democrat.

schools like Syracuse, Georgetown, all these big-name schools. Reggie comes up and says, 'I'm going to Northeastern.' We don't know anything about Northeastern. He said clear as day, 'I know what I'm doing.' And he knew what he was doing. We never had that kind of camaraderie. It was more like, *What is Northeastern?* Everybody knew about Georgetown, Syracuse, Wake Forest. We were more like, 'Where is that? What is that?' Him being an eighteen-year-old with a twenty-five-year-old mentality, he knew. And that was the end of the conversation."[166]

These were boys hardened by Baltimore's streets, coached by a former Pittsburgh Steeler defensive back. When a local housing project was torn down near Dunbar, Coach Bob Wade salvaged the bricks. He wrapped them in old baseball uniforms and repurposed them as "ghetto dumbbells." Players carried them during defensive slide drills or on closeouts, or they hoisted them high while running laps or line-touches for conditioning. So while many of the Poets were skinny, their "praying mantis" arms and legs featured sinewy muscle tone.

Dunbar pressed on defense, with Bogues ball-hawking the entire court. That style allowed Wade to play ten people and his deep bench to wear down opponents.

They were cobbling together a basketball powerhouse in a city 183 miles from Johnstown. Wade's boys supplied their community with pride in accomplishment and hope in life's emerging possibilities in a downtrodden city, much like school namesake Paul Dunbar had written in his poem "Sympathy":

> *I know what the caged bird feels, alas!*
> *When the sun is bright on the upland slopes;*
> *When the wind stirs soft through the springing grass,*
> *And the river flows like a stream of glass;*
> *When the first bird sings and the first bud opes,*
> *And the faint perfume from its chalice steals—*
> *I know what the caged bird feels!*[167]

If it were birds and slopes and grass Wade's boys wanted, they'd find it in more abundance in rural Pennsylvania. Against Bay High, an Ohio region known for fugitive Sam Sheppard's Bay View Hospital practice, Dunbar benefited from early intimidation.

"When they did the announcing of players," remembered Bay High power forward Steve Geuther, "we are watching them, going, 'Oh my gosh!' Every player had inches on us. When they turned the house lights down for introductions, we had some players who were all-conference. Ours was a very short introduction—I was 6-foot-3 with no accolades. When they announced their lineup, it took fifteen minutes. First-team of this tournament, MVP of that tournament. McDonald's all-star. We're like, 'Holy crap!'"[168]

Johnstown locals can remember watching Dunbar players in the layup lines. They saw arms and hands well above the rim when Dunbar finished layups and dunks, a height not reached in most high school gyms in

America. Dunbar took an early lead. Then superstar Reggie Williams got into foul trouble. "We were like, 'Sweet! One of their stars is going out,'" said Geuther. "Now we get into their bench."

And that meant Reggie Lewis, a budding Division I recruit but still a bit player for the Poets. Reggie Lewis, who had been cut by the coach at Patterson High years earlier, keeping him from playing alongside his elder brother in high school and necessitating the transfer to Dunbar. There's a fine line between a chip on your shoulder and an inferiority complex. Lewis never lost his motivation, nor his confidence.

Dunbar handled Bay High 55–41 as Lewis filled in admirably, scoring key baskets and pulling rebounds.

In the championship, Dunbar faced Martin Luther King from New York. MLK had taken on some players and the coach from Ben Franklin when that school shut down. Once again, Dunbar's Reggie Williams got into foul trouble, earning three before the first quarter was halfway over. Dawson, too, was whistled repeatedly, eventually fouling out. After sitting over seventeen minutes to start the game, Reggie Lewis came into a tight contest against an MLK team with star Kenny Hutchinson. He'd match up against him, just he like he would match up against Reggie Williams every day in practice.

Late in the fourth quarter, Muggsy Bogues was still guarding MLK's point guard full court, despite playing with four fouls himself. "Coach kept me in because I knew how to play with my fouls," said Bogues. "I was full-court pressing but in a way where I was able not to touch my man, just let him know I was there."[169]

Lewis scored on weak-side putbacks and on feeds from Bogues. He totaled nine points and eleven rebounds, picking up the slack for both Dawson and Williams. In addition to earning tournament MVP, Lewis rescued the perfect season. "I wasn't surprised because he went against us every day in practice," Reggie Williams remembered. "When it was happening, we weren't surprised at all. We were hoping he would do that. We were in a battle, and it was close. We got out of there by the skin of our teeth. Reggie Lewis came on for us when we needed him."[170]

Williams was fine with not winning the MVP at Johnstown. He had won three MVPs at the showcase Five-Star Camps over the years. He'd be winning a national title at Georgetown in a year along with Patrick Ewing and Coach John Thompson. The Johnstown Tournament was Reggie Lewis's coming-out party.

"Reggie got some tough rebounds and put them back," Wade said. "Made a couple shots from the top of the key. Defensively he did a yeoman's job,

Coach Bob Wade and his team. *Courtesy of Bob Wade.*

coming up with big blocks, big rebounds. He was very tough. He did not display it, his demeanor. Didn't say much, but he was quite a player."

Calhoun hoped that his prize recruit, that hidden gem, hadn't been uncovered and exposed to the world of blue-chip recruiters. "Everyone knew his name after that tournament," said Wade. "He was the sixth man that folks couldn't understand why he wasn't a starter after that tournament."

Lewis gave Calhoun a knowing nod after the game. Dunbar would finish the season undefeated for the second straight year, extending the win streak to fifty-nine games. Lewis would join rising coaching star Calhoun in Boston. He'd continue his ascent, scoring 20 points many nights on his way to setting the school's career record with 2,708 points. Said Dunbar teammate Herman Harried, "He made Northeastern known to us."

"He was a very, very beautiful, special kid," Calhoun said. "He reminds me of Kemba Walker. He was cut from his high school team as a freshman. He had the unique ability to love the game....He'd come into the gym and smile like it was his church."

Kenny Hutchinson led MLK with fifteen points. In 1981, he had led Ben Franklin to the Johnstown title with sixteen points.

HEAVY HEARTS

Premature deaths due to heart ailments claimed the lives of some of basketball's best players, including several former Johnstown Tournament players.

After being drafted by the Boston Celtics, Reggie Lewis developed into a star as greats Larry Bird, Kevin McHale and Robert Parrish aged through their twilight years. In six seasons, Lewis averaged 17.6 points. He averaged 20.8 in his final two seasons, earning one All-Star appearance. He succeeded Larry Bird as captain of the heralded franchise.

On July 27, 1993, however, Lewis collapsed while playing basketball at Brandeis University in Massachusetts. He died of a heart attack at age twenty-seven. Lewis's former teammates said that it was a defect of his heart rather than something more sinister like what had befallen Len Bias.

Former 1984 Johnstown MVP Hank Gathers from Philadelphia's Dobbins Tech High was playing college basketball for Loyola Marymount in California during a game in 1990 when he collapsed and died. Both Lewis and Gathers had passed out before their final cardiac event. Both had received warnings of the dangers of playing basketball before their final day. The cause in Gathers's case was hypertrophic cardiomyopathy, where the heart's muscle tissues harden without any obvious cause. Another Dobbins Tech graduate and basketball phenom, Linda Page, would die young of a heart attack too, but she was forty-eight, an age when heart trouble isn't as rare.

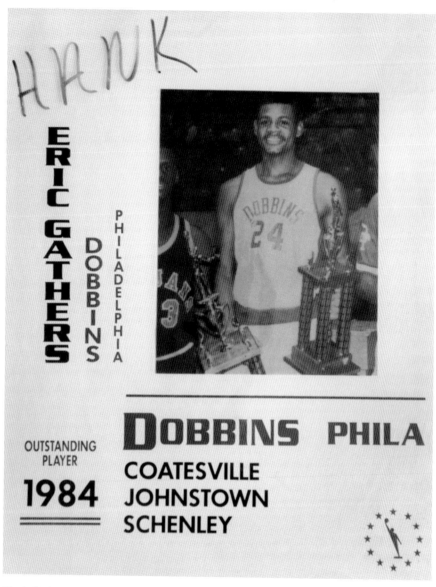

Hank Gathers poster. *Photo by Thomas Slusser,* Johnstown Tribune-Democrat.

"Hank also had a cousin who died early," said Dobbins Tech teammate Darrell "Heat" Gates. "He went to William Penn. That was after Hank died. Derrick [Gathers] got the same problem as Hank."

The cousin who died, Joseph Marable, had transferred to William Penn from Dobbins Tech the year before. When he collapsed during a basketball tryout, he was seventeen. His only prior health condition was childhood asthma. Unlike Gathers and Lewis, Marable apparently hadn't experienced any prior heart issues.[171]

When reflecting on the teams and players who have participated in the Johnstown Tournament, it's clear that basketball and its aerobic demands can tax a young man's heart, especially if there are already inherent problems. At least four heart-related premature deaths took the lives of players who either played in Johnstown or whose high school program played there. In 1968, a former Chester High player named Paul Williams had returned to Mount St. Mary's College for his sophomore season. At an informal pickup game, Williams suffered a fatal heart attack at age nineteen. In high school, the All-State Williams had twice led the Clippers to the state final. Chester hadn't played in Johnstown during Williams's career, but they did before and after his death.

In the early 1980s, Carlisle High coach Dave Lebo was starting to build a strong basketball program. In a January game against Steelton-Highspire, with the Thundering Herd leading 96–71 and under two minutes remaining, Carlisle senior Jay Hodge collapsed. Doctors on hand performed CPR, and Hodge was rushed to Carlisle Hospital. By night's end, he was gone. The cause was attributed to "rheumatic heart disease." By 1983, Carlisle was making a name for itself statewide as a basketball dynasty, led by coach's son Jeff Lebo. Carlisle went on to win four consecutive state titles once six-foot-nine phenom Billy Owens arrived at the high school. But the townspeople still mourn the loss of Hodge, who had predicted the coming basketball dynasty.

Coach Lebo said that the tragedy of losing Jay Hodge—whose younger brother, Shawn, would later win three of the four consecutive big-school state titles with Owens in the mid-1980s—brought the town together in community mourning. Everybody needed one another, and basketball games gave the townspeople an outlet for their grief. The rising dynasty Jay Hodge had predicted materialized as he anticipated.

Coach Dave Lebo experienced another ignominious connection to basketball, heart conditions and premature death:

Press Maravich had a basketball camp at Juniata College alongside a guy who was a teacher at Cedar Cliff High School. Jeff was 5 or 6 years old. I took him along and the guy said, "Let's go out to eat for the last night." A college counselor said, "I'll watch Jeff." I was gone a little bit and came back. Jeff wasn't in the room. Do I have to call my wife and tell her I lost my son? He got away. He's down in Press's room. Press's door was halfway open. There was Press sound asleep on the couch with his arms around Jeff. That story about Press taking care of him and all that, was special. We went to the Raleigh Times Tournament [in North Carolina, where Pete had played high school ball] *years later. Pete Maravich was getting his jersey retired. I sat up in the balcony. And Pistol Pete was there. I introduced myself and we talked. Jeff was playing in the tournament. A short period of time after that Pistol Pete passed away* [from a heart attack at age forty]. *My wife, for Christmas, said that Pistol Pete sent Jeff a note. I told Pete what a fan Jeff was of his. Pete sent a letter to Jeff that said, "Thank you for being a Pistol Pete fan. Maybe one day you'll grow up to be a great basketball player like Pistol Pete." We sent it to Jeff, and he put it up in his office where he was coaching.*[172]

Reggie Lewis's passing ended a life that had been transformed one night in Johnstown, when he became the star among stars—the Celtic captain immediately after Larry Bird was gone, not long after Bias. The grief was overwhelming. Maravich, ironically, also had played for the Celtics before retiring in 1980.

One year before Gathers collapsed and died in a college game for Loyola Marymount, Hank Gathers had led the nation in scoring and rebounding. The Dobbins Tech alumnus was another former Johnstown MVP and six-foot-seven superstar, like Lewis, his best years in the pros seemingly ahead of him.

BO AND HANK

So much athletic talent filled the hallways at Philadelphia's Dobbins Tech High in the 1980s. Was there too much at one time?

When Greg "Bo" Kimble and Eric "Hank" Gathers—Dobbins Tech High, University of Southern California and Loyola Marymount University teammates forever linked by success and tragedy—started rising through high school, they blended among many talented peers. Hank's brother Derrick, like Hank, was a tall, athletic late-bloomer. Darryl "Heat" Gates was a guard who could amass quick points like video game chomper Pac-Man. Doug Overton was a six-foot-three combination guard who would go on to log eleven NBA seasons. Mark Stevenson was a tall and rangy six-foot-six wing who would go on to score about eight hundred points at both Notre Dame and Duquesne universities. Stevenson, however, would transfer out of Dobbins Tech.[173]

On the girls' side, Dobbins Tech's Linda Page broke Wilt Chamberlain's record of ninety points in one game. Page tallied a Chamberlainesque one hundred against Mastbaum in 1981. She chronicled her career in the book *Love, Pain, and Passion*, her logo comprising a basketball, No. 43 and tears of blood.[174] In 1988, Dobbins Tech point guard Dawn Staley was named the girls' national Player of the Year among prep players. She would go on to a Hall of Fame career as a player and coach. Although the Mustangs didn't possess the historical gravitas of Gratz or Roman, they were kings and queens in their day.

Before competing in Johnstown in 1984, the Mustang boys had competed in two other national tournaments. At the National Bank of Washington Tournament at George Washington University, Dobbins played fairly

Bo Kimble poster. *Photo by Thomas Slusser,* Johnstown Tribune-Democrat.

well in a loss to DeMatha Catholic in a game Coach Rich Yankowitz felt was compromised due to biased officiating. Dobbins was given $1,000 for expenses for that tournament, according to Ray Parrillo's article in the *Philly Inquirer,* yet they felt they'd been robbed. Dobbins was promised $1,000 again to compete in the King of the Bluegrass Tournament near Louisville, Kentucky.[175] That amount turned out to be a bargain for the Bluegrass people.

"Dobbins Tech was probably one of the best teams we ever had here," said King of the Bluegrass Tournament director Lloyd Gardner. "Baltimore Dunbar was the best team we ever had here. It was so loud in the gym that you couldn't hear the whistle."[176]

Dobbins impressed locals with its play, earning a championship matchup against highly rated Seneca High, a team locals felt couldn't be beaten. Seneca had future Louisville Cardinals Tony Kimbro—who would be named the state's Mr. Basketball—and Keith Williams. Preseason magazines ranked Seneca anywhere from No. 1 to No. 3 nationally. The tournament was loaded with that kind of talent, as Felton Spencer, Rex Chapman and Kenny Payne were among the stars in the sixteen-team field.

Dobbins didn't care who played for Seneca. They built a 15-point halftime lead and then held on as Kimbro caught fire en route to a game-high 38 points. Bo Kimble's free throws late helped the Mustangs to a 75–70 tournament title. Kimble scored 23, Gates 17, Hank Gathers 16 and Overton 15. Fifth starter Derrick Gathers, the defensive specialist, held Seneca star Keith Williams to 6 points.[177] "There were coaches from all over at that game," said Gates. "We weren't on the radar yet, just in Philly."

A Southern Cal assistant coach named David Spencer, who'd grown up in Philadelphia, was certainly interested in Kimble and Hank Gathers. Gates said that "Spence" wanted all five Dobbins starters to come west and play in Los Angeles. And after their scintillating performance in Kentucky, a local girl also took a liking to one of the Mustangs. Gates said when the team drove eleven hours back home to Philadelphia, the girl was right behind them in her car. When they went to the Johnstown Tournament days later, she followed them there, too, on her way back to Kentucky. Dobbins Tech basketball was becoming quite the attraction.

Johnstown would dole out $1,500 for the Mustangs to come to town in late December. Dobbins would be matched up against Coatesville High, which featured six-foot-ten Marty Eggleston and six-foot-eight Jody McMillan. The Red Raiders were billed as the top team in Pennsylvania. Dobbins Tech players disagreed. They rode Kimble's 23 points and 13 rebounds, followed by Hank Gathers's 17 and 12 to an 83–55 romp. Eggleston and McMillan combined for only 19 points and 12 rebounds. In the other opening game, Johnstown delivered a 51–50 upset of Schenley High.[178]

In the final, tournament MVP Hank Gathers further dominated with 23 points, 7 rebounds and 4 blocks in a 70–44 rout of Johnstown. Kimble and Gates each made the all-tournament team. McMillan and Eggleston each scored 17 points as Coatesville held on against Schenley, 70–68, in the consolation game.

Bo and Hank led Dobbins Tech to its first Public League title in March, 86–62, over a Southern High team led by future LaSalle University great Lionel Simmons. Kimble did it all: 27 points, 12 rebounds, 3 assists, 2 steals and 2 blocks, as charted by scribe Ted Silary. Gathers turned in another impressive line: 27 points, 14 rebounds, 4 assists and 2 blocks. In his book *For You, Hank*, Kimble chronicled how upset Gathers would get if Kimble or Gates wasn't getting him the ball on offense. Heat Gates, as the point guard, understood the dynamic too, and always felt pressure to appease the temperamental big guy. After drubbing Southern, everybody on the Dobbins Tech side showed beaming smiles.[179]

Reflecting on a breakout season in which Dobbins Tech lost only two games—the DeMatha game early in the season and an overtime loss to another great Baltimore Dunbar team that went 30-1 and won the mythical national championship—the Mustangs were nearly perfect. Baltimore Dunbar's only loss was in overtime against Pooh Richardson and Philadelphia's Ben Franklin High in overtime.

Former Dobbins Tech Mustang Mark Stevenson would get all the acclaim and shots he wanted at Roman Catholic following his transfer. He would be named an All-American, be selected for the Dapper Dan Roundball Classic team from Pennsylvania and be recruited to play at Notre Dame. Stevenson's Roman Catholic team, however, would be upset in the Catholic League quarterfinals by Archbishop Carroll.

Coach Ken Hamilton remembers how agreeing to play in big-time events transformed not only his Ben Franklin High program in Philadelphia but Dobbins Tech's program too:

> *Dobbins came along after me too. Joe Goldenberg had something to do with that. They gave Joe two games at the Spectrum that he could play before the Sixers. They expected him to play Camden and Chester. He said, "We're gonna showcase the public league. Is there anyone who wants to play?" Everybody put their head down. Two people raised their hand, me and Rich Yankowitz from Dobbins. Now Joe allows Franklin and Dobbins to play at the Spectrum. We got killed, but nobody remembered that. Now these super kids in north Philly don't go to West Philly anymore. Next thing you know Franklin and Dobbins are on top of the public league. Joe didn't realize it was going to take place like that.*[180]

Hamilton would win 456 games, Yankowitz 486, and develop four NBA players: Horace "Pappy" Owens, Larry Stewart, Doug Overton and Bo Kimble. A fifth—Hank Gathers—would have played in the NBA if he had been healthy. Essentially, three players from the team that competed in Johnstown in 1984 were NBA quality. Stevenson played overseas as a professional. Heat Gates played against pros all the time during the summers when he was attending a junior college.

HURLEY'S FRESHMEN

St. Anthony's High of Jersey City, New Jersey, made its only appearance in Johnstown in December 1985. By then, future Hall of Fame coach Bob Hurley had won ten of his twenty-eight state championships in a program leveraged by inner-city toughness and grit. Hurley wouldn't win his first of four mythical national championships until 1989—when his current freshmen were seniors.[181] The Friars turned out no-excuses teams that might have worn hardhats if the rules permitted. Shoulder pads, at the very least, because they were tough and never backed down.

But in 1985, Hurley brought one of his youngest squads to Johnstown. His inexperienced team, in his assessment, wasn't very good. Seven players had graduated with Division I scholarships, led by David Rivers, Hurley's first All-American who would attend Notre Dame. His next point guard coming into 1985–86 was another tough veteran named Jasper Walker, who would start and run the motion offense in a Friars lineage that included Kenny Wilson (Villanova), David Rivers (Notre Dame) and Charles "Mandy" Johnson (Marquette). Jasper Walker expected to start next to a freshman six-foot-four forward named Jerry Walker, his wild card younger brother. In middle school, Jeremiah "Jerry" Walker was finding trouble throughout Jersey City in a territory rife with gangs. Hurley hoped to fashion those rough edges into smooth curves with his Machiavellian mentoring.

"All these kids were just junkyard dogs," Hurley said. "They would play anyplace—the gyms were bad, the baseball fields were bad, the facilities that they were training in were bad. But these were kids that would do anything to be successful."

The Walkers grew up in a cluster of housing projects next to a basketball court known as "Baby Rucker," an ode to the famous Harlem courts where Walker's idol Julius "Dr. J" Erving lit up the night with an array of dunks.

As an eighth grader, Jerry had averaged thirty points, fifteen rebounds and seven blocks for Assumption All Saints Middle School, but what he did best for the St. Anthony's varsity at first was rebound and pass. He would expand his game to the perimeter and expand his role in short order.

Walker possessed the talent that within a year would put him atop the national recruiting boards for his class. He would benefit from the discipline of Coach Hurley, a full-time probation officer when he wasn't coaching, a widely respected man who had eyes all over the city and a bank vault mind that helped him, according to Walker, "remember every f---ing thing!"[182]

St. Anthony's basketball had already claimed control of Jersey City. Statewide they had chased New Jersey power Camden High, which had won the Johnstown Tournament in 1959 and 1966. Now Hurley was taking his team on the road to tournaments to raise his program's profile, like Camden and Millville had, taking the program national. The year before St. Anthony's invaded Johnstown, the Friars had ventured south to the Beach Ball Classic tournament in Myrtle Beach, South Carolina. They ran into Pennsylvania's emerging public school dynasty at that time—the Carlisle Thundering Herd from suburban Harrisburg—in the semifinals. Carlisle would win four straight state titles.

Hurley remembered two controversial block/charge calls on plays between future North Carolina Tar Heel Jeff Lebo of Carlisle and future Villanova guard Kenny Wilson of St. Anthony's. Hurley recounted two plays that changed the game:

> We were up late in the game and Jeff Lebo drove to the basket. Kenny Wilson steps in for a charge; they call a block. Lebo shoots the free throws. Then Kenny Wilson goes down and Jeff Lebo takes a charge. Same play. Carlisle gets both calls. Kenny gets a technical foul walking off the court. Now it's going to be two shots, a T. We go to the huddle. After he gets the T, my assistant had left and gone down the bench and went to the table. Says, "Back-to-back calls, they get both calls?"
>
> Coach Hurley gets a T because his player and assistant got T's. "I'm ejected from the game as head coach. I take my board, and I take it like a frisbee and throw it off the wall. Then I'm ejected from the building. I

guess they shoot two for me, two for the assistant, two for Kenny Wilson, and they get the possession and win the game by maybe five. Home cooking. We never went back there. Next year, Johnstown calls us. We go up there and go into the tournament."

Carlisle coach Dave Lebo, Jeff's dad, also remembers Hurley's wife getting a technical, although Hurley couldn't confirm that. In 1985, St. Anthony's carpooled to Johnstown, where it could face Philadelphia public school power Ben Franklin, Western Pennsylvania power Meadville or local Johnstown.

Jerry Walker strolled into War Memorial Arena, where he quickly spotted hanging posters of all-time tournament greats: Overbrook giant Wilt Chamberlain, Overbrook sensation Wayne Hightower, Farrell's Julius McCoy, Catasauqua's Larry Miller, Chester's Horace Walker and Emerson Baynard and on and on, the stars aligned overhead on placards. "I'm going to be up there after the tournament," Walker, the precocious freshman, professed as he pointed at the Chamberlain poster.

St. Anthony's opened against Johnstown. Tom Walter was a starting guard for Johnstown High and a talented baseball player who had competed in the national AAABA baseball tournament in Johnstown. Living in Cambria County and being so close to two national tournaments, Walter had also watched the fantastic Baltimore Dunbar basketball squad in 1982. He'd seen Hollywood star Tom Cruise play Stef Djordjevic in the football movie *All the Right Moves*. Then he played against the great Dobbins Tech team of Hank Gathers and Bo Kimble in the championship game in 1984. He understood the kind of stars who came to Johnstown, especially those who played in the Cambria County Johnstown War Memorial Invitational Basketball Tournament.

"My senior year one of my comical memories of the tournament is my dad before the tournament," said Walter. "He was saying, 'Hey, you're not going to be the best basketball player in this tournament, but you're probably going to be the best baseball player.' Then I found out Willie Banks of St. Anthony's was there. He was the first-round pick of the Minnesota Twins—I think he went third. Turns out I wasn't the best baseball player either."[183] The year before that, St. Anthony's and Hurley had future major leaguer John Valentin on their basketball roster too. Banks pitched in the major leagues for nine years.

Jerry Walker opened the Johnstown Tournament by backing his boast. He scored 17 points, grabbed 10 rebounds and doled out 4 assists as the

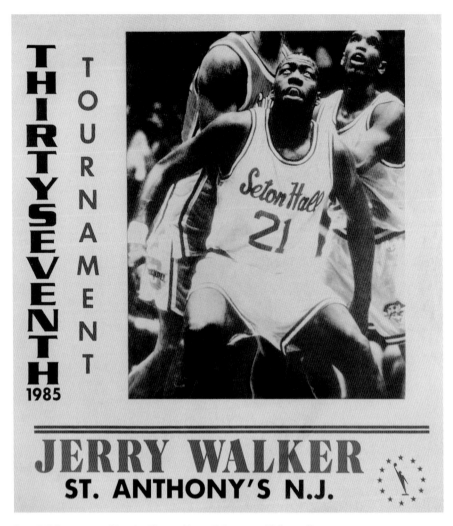

Jerry Walker poster. *Photo by Thomas Slusser,* Johnstown Tribune-Democrat.

Friars defeated the home team 67–51. Ben Franklin, with a frontcourt stacked with players six-foot-five or taller, edged Meadville 57–55 in the other opening game. Michael Burnette scored 26 for Meadville, Booker Holland 22 for Franklin.

BEN FRANKLIN FROM PHILADELPHIA, like St. Anthony's, was angling to raise its national profile in the 1980s. The year before their visit to Johnstown, Ben Franklin had sent point guard Jerome "Pooh" Richardson to UCLA.

With Pooh running the point, Franklin was the lone team to topple national champion Baltimore Dunbar. Franklin coach Ken Hamilton wisely capitalized on his Philly connections. He'd become great friends with former Overbrook star and UCLA legend Walt Hazzard. Hamilton became business partners with Hazzard's former Overbrook High teammate Wali Jones. Now Hamilton was maneuvering to make Ben Franklin a top-billing program.

Ben Franklin had already defeated Philadelphia's top-ranked program, Simon Gratz. Hamilton's program had grown exponentially since his first season, when he sought to build a program like the one Joe Goldenberg ran at West Philly High. In fact, Goldenberg offered helpful advice to Hamilton in the early years. Then Roman Catholic High coach William "Speedy" Morris went out of his way for Hamilton. Hamilton recounted his tenuous but pivotal first week as head coach:

> *I got the job on Nov. 1. It was a big controversy. They weren't sure if I was gonna be the guy. The AD handed me the schedule that the old coach had made. That was Monday. That same Friday there's a scrimmage against Roman Catholic. Speedy Morris. I'd been a coach for four days. Roman is on Broad Street, about four blocks from Franklin. We walked up the steps to Roman's gym. All my kids were seniors and had played the year before. This is one of Speedy's down years. We played six quarters. Two of the quarters, we got shut out. We never came closer than 20 points. Afterwards, I sent my kids back to their neighborhoods. We had just lost six quarters and none of them are closer than 20 points. I have my head down, thinking, You know, maybe this isn't for you.*

Speedy noticed Hamilton's frustration: "Coach, are you OK?"

"No! I sure would like to know what you just did to me," Hamilton confessed.

"You got time?" Speedy asked. "I'll finish sweeping up the gym, and you can come down to my office." At the time Speedy owned a bar. "Manischewitz wine was on the counter," Hamilton recalled. "He opens up the refrigerator, and there is every kind of beer you could want."

"What do you want to know?"

"'Everything.' He hands me a copy of what he does in practice every day for the entire season, and how you lead up to putting the defense in and when you put the offense in. Then I ask him, 'How'd you get a layup every time against us?'"

Said Morris, "You always have to have somebody in the back door."

"The next Monday, when I started back to practice, everything I'm doing is totally different from what I'd been doing before. The public and Catholic leagues never played each other in the regular season. He sets me up to play all these Catholic schools. I was one of his sons. Phil Martelli was one of his sons. And John Griffin was one of his sons."

Hamilton had the systems of two of Philadelphia's greatest prep coaches: Joe Goldenberg at West Philly and Speedy Morris at Roman Catholic. When Hamilton later noticed Goldenberg's West Philly Speedboys wearing flashy uniforms, he asked him where he got them.

"Let me introduce you to Sonny Vaccaro," Goldenberg said.

The Dapper Dan All-Star game was Pittsburgh promoter Sonny Vaccaro's baby. Vaccaro, in charge of basketball at Nike, also provided gear and merchandise to elite high school programs. Vaccaro supplied Ben Franklin with what Hamilton needed, and then Sonny asked Hamilton to coach in his showcase tournament, the first African American head coach.

"Mike Jarvis coached the other team with Patrick Ewing," Hamilton said. "Now I'm getting all these sneakers and warmup suits. These super kids from north Philly now didn't have a reason to go to West Philly. First time I made the semis at the Palestra, they killed us by maybe thirty-five or forty points. After the game my wife and I are sitting there. Joe walks by with his wife."

"Don't worry," he said. "Your team is coming. You're going to be all right."

"I think it was two years later we beat them!" said Hamilton.

"I knew you were coming," Goldenberg said, "but I didn't expect it to be this fast!"

"A lot of it had to do with him."

So here was Ben Franklin facing New Jersey titan St. Anthony's for the Johnstown 1985 tournament title. Hurley's Friars dominated the second quarter to take a 27–16 halftime lead. Franklin pressured hard to take a 37–35 lead in the fourth quarter. Hamilton's team was coming back! Hurley's boys responded with 9 straight points, followed by Franklin's 6-point run to move to within 44–43. Willie Banks canned four of five free throws and blocked a key shot to preserve the victory.

"He would have been a Division I shooting guard if he didn't have baseball," Hurley said.

Jerry Walker flirted with a double-double with eight points and nine rebounds to make all-tournament. Mike Thomas led the Friars with eighteen points. Walker didn't get his face on a tournament banner for being the MVP, but he did for making the all-tournament team. Mark Horner of

Paul Schmidt poster. *Photo by Thomas Slusser,* Johnstown Tribune-Democrat.

Johnstown was named MVP, making him the third Johnstown Trojan to claim the award after Paul Schmidt and Don Maser.

The Johnstown Tournament title kicked off a dominant era of St. Anthony's basketball. They'd go 91-2 the next three seasons. One of the freshmen point guards who didn't make the trip to Johnstown—Bob's son Bobby—would be needed later that season and beyond.

"I didn't bring Bobby up to Johnstown," Bob Hurley said. "He was playing JV at this point. We had a couple guards who got injured. We brought him up 10 to 12 games after Johnstown against the school I went to, St. Peter's Prep. He hit his first three shots. By the state final, I think he had 10 points, 10 assists. We were playing with a freshman center and a freshman point guard."

"His last three years we were 91-2," continued Coach Hurley. "We lost two regular season games [both to Ferris High]. We were No. 1 in the country one year, beat Tolentine. A week went by, and we lost to Ferris and lost to them again the following year. We won against every school nationally in the tournaments we played in but lost twice to the same school at 4:00 p.m. in a gym close to home."

Hurley's 1988–89 team—with Walker, Bobby Jr., Terry Dehere and Rodrick Rhodes—went undefeated. Four Division I stars on one high school team. Four future pros.

Upon retirement in 1991, Ferris coach Tom Favia had the most wins in Jersey City public school history and a respectable record against Bob Hurley.

When Walker and Bobby Hurley were juniors, St. Anthony's traveled to Honolulu, Hawaii, where they beat a Tolentine team loaded with stars: Brian Reese (North Carolina), Adrian Autry (Syracuse) and Malik Sealy (St. John's). The Friars continued their national expansion, but they never returned to Johnstown.

When the Naismith Basketball Hall of Fame inducted Coach Hurley in 2020, his career numbers were astronomical: four-time *USA Today* national champion, three-time *USA Today* national Coach of the Year, twenty-eight state titles (nine consecutively) and eighteen undefeated seasons.[184] His son Bobby Jr. would win two NCAA national titles as Duke's point guard. Younger son Danny won consecutive NCAA national titles at UConn as head coach. In 1985, Johnstown got a glimpse of that historic Hurley basketball lineage.

Meadville High, which had been sent packing from the Johnstown Tournament in 1954 to accommodate Wilt Chamberlain, went 0-2 in 1985. They lost by 2 to Ben Franklin and by 14 to Johnstown. In the spring of 1986, the Bulldogs would lose in the state tournament's western final. In 1987, they would reach the state championship but lose to Billy Owens's Carlisle team 48–47. By then, Meadville's Mike Burnette was being hailed as a Jordanesque leaper. He'd score 1,194 points at St. Bonaventure.

WEST VIRGINIA

West Virginia became the ninth state to land a team in the Johnstown Tournament when they arrived in 1989. The tournament that had opened to Pennsylvania's elite programs in 1949 and for most of the 1950s expanded incrementally but significantly.

It went from a field of elite Pennsylvania teams in the 1950s to an eastern tournament. New Jersey (Camden) joined the fray in 1959. The District of Columbia's DeMatha made its first appearance in 1961, followed by New York's Power Memorial in 1969. Ohio representative John F. Kennedy High broke through in 1972, followed by Virginia (T.C. Woodson) in 1979, Maryland (Cardinal Gibbons) in 1980 and Kentucky (Henry Clay) in 1987. Martinsburg, West Virginia, rounded out the list of states in 1989.

Martinsburg handled the suburban Pittsburgh area's top team, Penn Hills, 90–73. Martinsburg would face another D.C. power, Calvin Coolidge High, in the final. Martinsburg led by 15 midway through the third quarter. With star Marsalis Basey scoring 22 first-half points, Martinsburg took command. But Coolidge started trapping the five-foot-eight guard and making him expend his energy bringing the ball up court. The Colts also utilized their height in the second half. As *Tribune-Democrat* reporter Paul Husselbee noted, Coolidge scored almost half of its 26 fourth-quarter points on putbacks. With the game tied at 74, Eric Pratt drove the length of the court for the winning basket. He missed, but John Stuckey grabbed the rebound and finished the game off with his putback with two seconds remaining. He still remembers the night he won the Johnstown

Tournament in the closing seconds. It took decades for him to get back to the site of his heroic basket.[185]

"I did marketing for a motorcycle rally in Johnstown," he said. "So I came back to the arena, and it brought back the memories of high school. I still have the clip from the newspaper article when we played there."[186]

Stuckey finished with twenty-nine points, Basey with twenty-eight. Basey got the tournament MVP trophy. Stuckey, a six-foot-four junior, was a volume dunker and rebounder. Basey, a five-foot-eight senior, was a lynx in transition. Stuckey would go on to play at Hartford University, where he'd team up with Vin Baker, a seven-foot emerging phenom who would become a first-round draft pick. Basey would star at West Virginia University for Coach Bob Huggins. Built more like a middle infielder than a professional basketball player, Basey lasted four years in the minor leagues.

Basey's high school coach, David Rogers, owns a West Virginia–best 852-225 record in forty-five seasons at Martinsburg, his alma mater, including three state championships and five runner-up finishes. He's West Virginia's all-time wins leader. His assistant coach today is Marsalis Basey. Rogers's greatest win came in the 1994 state title victory over DuPont High with Randy Moss and Jason Williams. "They also had Bobby Howard, who played linebacker at Notre Dame and for the Chicago Bears," said Rogers.

"We weren't supposed to beat them that year. No question they had more talent. We outrebounded them 50 to 25 that night and beat them by 7."[187]

PART V

THE 1990s

Philly Powers, Dunbar Overload
and Tournament Demise

DUNBAR SQUARED

In 1990, Johnstown lured two Dunbar High basketball teams to the tournament. The more famous of the two to basketball fanatics was the one in Baltimore, Maryland, where Bob Wade produced the greatest team in high school history in 1982–83. Before that, Baltimore Dunbar turned out Skip Wise and David Wingate—later on, Sam Cassell, Donta Bright and Michael Lloyd.

But the more historic Dunbar belongs to the one in Washington, D.C. You could step outside of the school and see American government. "We were three blocks from the nation's capitol," said former coach Mike McLeese. "You can see the Capitol Building from the Dunbar that I coached at. They have a brand-new building now. You can't see the Capitol Building now."

D.C. Dunbar was America's first public high school for Black students. Founded in 1870 as the Preparatory High School for Colored Youth, D.C. Dunbar also took on the name of the great African American poet Paul Dunbar, as the one in Baltimore had. Paul Dunbar the man moved to Washington, D.C., later in life and attended Howard University. One of D.C. Dunbar's principals was the first Black graduate of Harvard College. Its prestigious alumni range from surgeon Charles Drew, who developed better methods for blood storage, to Tuskegee airmen to other poets. In the 1950s, 80 percent of D.C. Dunbar's graduates went to college. "It was kind of a rivalry because D.C. and Baltimore are rivals in everything because we're only thirty-five miles up the parkway," said McLeese.[188]

McLeese's ascent in coaching occurred incrementally. He'd coached his fraternity team in college, and then he moved on to coach at elementary and junior high schools. He became the head coach of the D.C. Dunbar girls' varsity team. McLeese learned about the boys' basketball opening at D.C. Dunbar from Georgetown coach John Thompson, whose summer basketball camps McLeese had worked.

"He was instrumental in me getting the Dunbar job," said McLeese. "We were playing cards, and he told me the Dunbar job was open. I was coaching the girls at Dunbar. He said, 'Mac, are you interested in the boys job?' He made the call to the principal. She hired me on the spot right there. That's why I say he had a very profound effect on my career."

John Thompson would figure into another big break for McLeese. In 1988, Big John was the U.S. Olympic basketball coach, whose team would compete in Seoul, South Korea. It was the last time the United States sent amateurs, a precursor to the Dream Team of 1992. With George Raveling and Craig Esherick as assistants, the 1988 team finished third, earning a bronze medal. Thompson invited McLeese along on the trip, and the young coach's basketball education accelerated as he observed Thompson and Raveling running their team while being exposed to international basketball. McLeese served as the D.C. Dunbar boys' coach from 1987 to 1994, winning 180 games and losing 40 in seven seasons before becoming the coach at Howard University, where Paul Dunbar himself had studied.

McLeese brought his D.C. Dunbar squad to the loaded 1990 Johnstown Tournament, which featured eleven preseason All-Americans in the field. D.C. Dunbar had four starters between six-foot-five and six-foot-eight. They were huge and talented, but they'd also already lost to Baltimore Dunbar twice that season.

BALTIMORE DUNBAR ALSO HAD a new coach in 1990. After posting a record of 341-25 in this decade, including two unbeaten national championship seasons (1982–83 and 1984–85) and a 59-0 run from 1981 to 1983, Bob Wade moved on to coach at the University of Maryland, where he was given the task of rehabilitating a program stricken with the sudden death of superstar Len Bias. Carmie "Pete" Pompey took over at Baltimore Dunbar. He would generate his own 57-game winning streak and the school's first state title in 1992 after the program merged into the Maryland Public Secondary Schools Athletic Association (MPSSAA).

Under Pompey, Baltimore Dunbar would win the Johnstown Tournament in 1990 over D.C. Dunbar, 58–45, as Michael Lloyd scored 17 and Donta Bright 10. James "Scoop" Marshall of D.C. Dunbar was named MVP. Baltimore Dunbar would finish another special season at 27-1. D.C. Dunbar would win the public school championship before losing to DeMatha in the city championship game. The only teams to defeat the Crimson Tide and prevent them amassing more hardware were Baltimore Dunbar (thrice) and DeMatha.

"For us growing up in the city," said Marshall, "basketball was the only chance we had to travel. There was no AAU or anything like that. The nostalgia of the town, like going back in time, was kind of cool because I didn't get to see that before."

Thanks to a sneaker deal with Reebok, D.C. Dunbar traveled in fashion, adorned in high-end merchandise: four or five pairs of sneakers, sweatsuits, socks, mouthpieces, underwear and more. Said Marshall, "We didn't have to pay for nothing."

Rising D-I players like Johnny Rhodes and Mike "The Animal" Smith were drawing recruiters. Smith would spend seven years in the NBA.

In addition to Johnstown, D.C. Dunbar also traveled to Las Vegas and Alaska for tournaments. The basketball team earned mentions in *Sports Illustrated*. The whole program "changed our lives," according to Marshall. And in one case, it probably saved at least one player's life, back when D.C. was the murder capital of the country. "One of our players was driving his brother's car to practice," Marshall recalled, "and these people who had an issue with him thought it was his brother driving. When the kid came out after practice, the guys jumped out with guns. Coach Mac came out and jumped in the middle of it. He saved the player's life."

In 1991, Baltimore Dunbar returned to Johnstown and nipped rising superpower Simon Gratz of Philadelphia in the finals. Lloyd was still on Dunbar's roster. On a team that had everything, Lloyd could do everything. No. 3–ranked national power Gratz led the game 43–39 with 3:39 remaining. In the next minute, Lloyd drained a 3-pointer and Bright added a layup for a 44–43 lead. Dunbar rode its defense from there. Lloyd's steal and layup gave the Poets a 50–47 lead. Gratz's Jamahal Redmond drove in for a layup to trim the margin to 1. Then the Poets forced a Gratz turnover, resulting in Booth's clinching layup.[189]

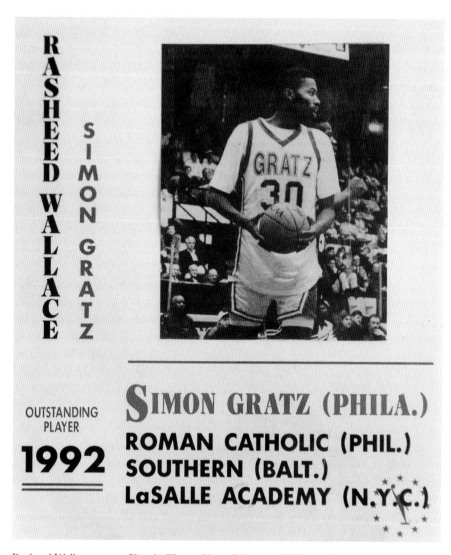

Rasheed Wallace poster. *Photo by Thomas Slusser,* Johnstown Tribune-Democrat.

Bright (20) and Lloyd (12) once again paced the Poets. Gratz center Rasheed Wallace scored 14 points, none in the fourth quarter as he tended to injuries. Shawn "Red" Smith led the Bulldogs with 17 points. Redmond added 10.

GRATZ'S LEGENDARY COACH BILL Ellerbee is a basketball gym rat who's been around Philadelphia hoops his entire life. He watched Wilt Chamberlain play in person as a kid. Ellerbee could walk to the Penn Palestra to watch double- or triple-headers when elite college teams clamored for media attention. He watched Catasauqua's Larry Miller play as Miller evolved into a high school All-American. Bill Ellerbee has lived Philadelphia Public League basketball. Knowing Pennsylvania basketball history, Ellerbee also knew that he'd get a second shot at Dunbar in a few weeks in another tournament if all fell right. "They beat us in overtime by a bucket when we played them again down in Myrtle Beach," he said. "They beat us in overtime by two points. They were the national champions for 1991–92."[190]

Gratz rallied late to defeat Jason Kidd's St. Joseph Notre Dame team from California in the Beach Ball Classic semifinals, 60–53. Baltimore Dunbar downed St. Raymond's from New York, 89–81, as All-American Donta Bright and Keith Booth each registered double-doubles. All-American Michael Lloyd chipped in 23 points as the Poets extended their winning streak to thirty-three games. Once again, you had two inner-city public schools—one from Baltimore, one from Philadelphia—squaring off in a faraway gym for a title.

"Basketball was almost like a religion in the inner city," said Ellerbee, who won 452 games and lost 100 games at his alma mater, "and the kids wanted to play it. You could get them to do anything, including their schoolwork and their homework and things of that nature."

Gratz's players from the 1980s were obsessed with basketball, which allowed Ellerbee to develop his juggernaut. Gratz's team was the defending Beach Ball Classic champion, having beaten a team from Cleveland, Ohio, when Rasheed Wallace was becoming the No. 1–ranked sophomore in America. The 1991 Beach Ball Classic final would be played on December 30 in Myrtle Beach, South Carolina. The Poets came out inspired, grabbing a 42–24 halftime cushion. But the Bulldogs, ranked tenth nationally, fought back. They tied the game at 53 late. Dunbar scored on its final possession. After Lloyd missed a jump shot, Donta Bright grabbed the rebound, looked around to see where Rasheed Wallace was lurking and then put the game-winner in at the buzzer. Since Wallace had established a record with 16 blocks earlier in the tournament, offensive post players were hypervigilant of his whereabouts. Bright processed that he had room to maneuver and put back the deciding shot on a day he would describe as the greatest in his life.

Dunbar wouldn't lose a game all year. Lloyd would enroll at Syracuse, Bright at UMass. Gratz would reload and come into the next season as the new top-ranked program in America.

SIMON SAYS "GRAZIE!"

The 1992 Johnstown Tournament managed to accomplish what Philadelphia schedulers couldn't: match up Philly superpowers Roman Catholic against Simon Gratz, one a Catholic league giant and the other a stalwart from the Public League.[191]

From 1980 to 2008, Philadelphia ceased its city championship games that pitted the Catholic champion against the Public League. Despite local fans clamoring for a Gratz-Roman showdown at some point during any season, the game couldn't be wedged into the schedule when both teams were loaded with players.

In 1992, Gratz featured the top-ranked team in America. After national top recruit Rasheed Wallace, the Bulldogs also had future D-I center Lynard Stewart, who had transferred into Gratz from Lincoln High for his junior year. Rondell Turner, at six-foot-eight, transferred in for his senior year from University City, where he was the top scorer. Coach Bill Ellerbee also had a roster filled with Division I guards. In the Johnstown opener, Gratz stretched a 4-point halftime lead into a 15-point cushion after three quarters to down Baltimore Southern, 61–44.

Roman Catholic struggled in dispatching LaSalle High of New York, which featured blue-chip guard Shammgod Wells—whose birth name was actually God Shammgod—and six-foot-ten Eddie Elisma. Roman's six-foot-nine center Marc Jackson won his matchup with Elisma by scoring 22 points and pulling 13 boards in a 57–47 decision.

Roman Catholic coach Dennis Seddon was new to Johnstown. His team was ranked in the top 20 in the nation and rising. The career playground director had established strong relationships with ballers all over the city. "I always coached on the playground level," he said. "I probably coached a good 1,000 games before I got to high school. I had my own little farm system."[192]

When Seddon's 1990 Roman team won the Catholic League championship, it was future NFL superstar Marvin Harrison making the winning shot. "Marvin loved basketball, like football, but he realized his future was in football," said Seddon. "Six-foot guards are a dime a dozen, but he was recruited by Phil Martelli at St. Joe's for basketball."

Basketball getaways opened the world to Seddon and his urban roster. He never knew what he might encounter or learn. "I remember getting dressed in the hockey locker room at Johnstown because one of the signs when you walked in there was a sign that said, 'Put your hockey sticks here!'" he said. "The court itself reminded me of the old Boston Garden. You would dribble the ball, and there were dead spots in the wood. You might dribble the ball and guess what? It's not coming back up. It just added to the whole flavor of the thing."

Gratz was playing here for the second time in three seasons. The balance of its scoring in the opener was a testament to its Barry White–deep bench. Jamahal Redmond scored 14 points, Wallace 11 more to go with 11 rebounds. Turner had 10, Stewart 7.

"It was one of the first tournaments I was in," said Stewart, who went on to play for John Chaney at Temple and is the current head coach at Simon Gratz. "It was my first time traveling for basketball. I didn't play AAU or anything like that. Being able to be involved with that was great. Those guys were used to traveling. We took a bus up to Johnstown. It was important for us to start the season off the right way, being No. 1."[193]

And on day two, Stewart found himself in a tournament final as well as entwined in a big-city rivalry four hours from Philadelphia. "People in Philly were mad because they said, 'Why do you have to go to Johnstown to play the game when you could play in the Palestra and pack the place?'" said rising Roman guard Chris McNesby, now the head coach at Roman Catholic.[194]

While Roman may have been the four-time defending Catholic League champions, they weren't stacked throughout the roster quite like Simon Gratz. Roman managed to get Wallace into early foul trouble, but it didn't matter. The Bulldogs bulldozed the Cahillites 16–5 after one quarter en route to a 60–29 demolition. Marc Jackson scored 19 of Roman's 29 points; the rest of the team produced only 10. Today, Jackson's sons play for Coach McNesby at Roman.

Wallace stuffed the stat sheet for Gratz with fourteen points, fifteen boards and three blocks. Turner added ten points. "Everybody on this team would be the man if they were at a different school," Redmond told Associated Press writer Mike Owen. "But we want to win, so that's why everybody comes here."[195]

Gratz won every game in 1992–93. Ellerbee polished off a 30-0 season and mythical national championship. Wallace would be off to the University of North Carolina. Turner, who didn't even start for the Bulldogs as a senior, went to play at the University of Rhode Island. But another talented Gratz team would return to play in Johnstown yet again, in December 1993.

BY 1993, ST. RAYMOND's High coach Gary DeCesare ran his program like a college program. He coached at the New York school from 1986 to 2002, going 290-133, playing in gyms across North America and beyond.[196]

"We played in Alaska twice; Missouri; Arkansas; Tennessee; the Bahamas; New Jersey; New York; D.C.; Hawaii; Orlando; Las Vegas; Pennsylvania; Louisville; San Diego; Springfield, Massachusetts; Miami; and Texas," he said. "We went on the road to play anybody to prepare us for our league. I thought the New York State Catholic High School Athletic Association was the best league in the country. We won four state championships." DeCesare also coached in Division I at Richmond and DePaul, so treating St. Ray's like a college program was only natural.

At Johnstown in 1993, St. Raymond's opened with a 78–61 win over St. John's of D.C. St. Ray's guards Eric Harris and Kareem Reid didn't need to travel the tournament circuit to face upper-echelon talent, but travel they did. *Newsday* featured the St. Raymond's tandem of Harris and Reid in its article titled the "Odd Couple."[197] Reid was the flashy five-foot-eight scoring guard, Harris the six-foot-one shutdown defender. They'd already won a state championship together.

In the other semifinal, Gratz dusted the Canterbury School and high-scoring junior Louis Bullock, who would set his school mark with 57 points in one game. Against Gratz, Canterbury's entire team didn't score 57 points in an 87–45 dismantling. Stewart posted 25 points and 17 rebounds for the Bulldogs. Mike Blunt added 23 more.

In the championship game, Gratz guard Shawn "Red" Smith scored 25 points to go with 12 rebounds, inspired by the matchup with Reid and Harris. The Bulldogs won handily, 66–41. Stewart was named MVP. Smith and Stewart spent the season as co-stars, as both averaged over 15 points per game for the season.

Checkball magazine owner Littel Vaughn has followed Philly hoops for decades. He said the other Bulldog post player, Rondell Turner, had the skills to become a veteran pro basketball player had things turned out differently. Smith, too, was elite. He outplayed two elite guards—including Reid—during the national schedule, establishing himself as a blue-chipper.[198]

Following the 1993–94 season, Ellerbee's record stood at 265-61. In the Public League final, Gratz blew a late seven-point lead against Franklin Learning Center, losing by one point. That dropped Ellerbee's record over the previous five seasons to a still remarkable 136-13.[199] The key play in the game was when Gratz missed a layup, then Stewart tried to dunk the follow. He, too, missed and was assigned a technical foul for hanging on the rim, giving life to FLC.

St. Raymond's voyages to tournaments resulted in Kareem Reid getting noticed by Arkansas coach Nolan Richardson, who quickly recruited him after watching Reid at the King Cotton Classic. Harris would go on to play point guard at Minnesota and lead Clem Haskins's Gophers to the 1997 Final Four.

Coach DeCesare preferred the smaller tournaments like Johnstown's four-team setup to the huge, sixteen-team mega-tournaments. "When you got those small towns and played in their tournaments, they got so much backing," he said. "The Tournament of Champions in Springfield, Missouri—now it's Missouri State—had a ten-thousand-seat arena. You're like the major league team in that city. I remember Missouri State playing a one o'clock game on a Saturday. I took my team to their game. The place would be sold out, then they'd empty it, and they'd have a high school tournament that sold out—probably the same ten thousand fans that saw the college game."

ROMAN SHADE

The scuttlebutt around Johnstown in December 1994 centered on the possibility that the great Johnstown Tournament could end—or, more precisely, would end. "As it got close to the tournament," Roman Catholic junior Donnie Carr said, "people were saying this could be the last one."

The banners in War Memorial Arena still hung in the concourse with care, hoping that a tournament savior would appear. The 1994 tournament was different in many ways. First, rather than between Christmas and New Year's, the tournament was played the second week of December. Next to newspaper blurbs about the basketball tournament were prominent state championship game stories…for football.

But Johnstown Tournament fans had basketball on the brain. Roman Catholic was ranked No. 1 in Pennsylvania and in the top ten nationally. In 1994, the second-ranked team in Washington, D.C., D.C. Dunbar, returned along with Blackhawk High from suburban Pittsburgh, as well as local entry Johnstown High.

Two years earlier, D.C. Dunbar had been 33-1 and No. 3 in America. In 1994, D.C. Dunbar was ranked behind national No. 1 DeMatha Catholic in the Washington, D.C. polls.

Roman opened with a 91–30 dousing of host Johnstown. If this was the tournament's final year, it was the worst way for the Trojans to exit stage left. D.C. Dunbar outlasted Blackhawk 70–54, leaving a championship matchup of Philly versus D.C.

Roman figured to have a clear edge over Dunbar. Center Lari Ketner was six-foot-nine and immovable on the low block. Carr was starting for the

Dante Calabria coaches his Bethel Park High team in a playoff game at Hershey High. *Photo by Bradley A. Huebner.*

second year. He would face off in epic one-on-one showdowns with Kobe Bryant in Philadelphia prep games.

Blackhawk was a young squad featuring sophomore guard Archie Miller, Coach John Miller's second son. They were young and missing starter Steve Dickinson, who was injured. Coach John Miller was happy to be in Johnstown despite being short-handed. His 1991–92 team had played in Johnstown when John's older son, Sean, was on the team. That year, Blackhawk was without two starters in Johnstown, who were still playing in the PIAA football state championship game. That Cougars team lost to a Baltimore Dunbar team that would finish 29-0, mythical national champions. In the subsequent consolation game, North Carolina–bound Dante Calabria of Blackhawk scored 32 points in an 82–74 win over Johnstown. That Blackhawk team went on to win the first of four state titles under Miller. And Calabria would wind up in Chapel Hill, North Carolina, playing with Rasheed Wallace.

IN 1994, ROMAN RANKED seventh in the nation and had already beaten No. 1 DeMatha 71–70. The Cahillites were the clear favorite to win the Johnstown championship. It was a long way from where the program sat when Dennis Seddon became the coach.

In 1986, with Cahillite basketball continuing its ascent, Roman Catholic hired Seddon while it was considering closing its doors, much like St. Anthony's in New Jersey had to consider several times before finally shutting down. Seddon remembers receiving the grim prognosis.

"The archdiocese says, 'You have to recruit 250 kids for September class by February 1,'" Seddon said. "We had a contract to play in the Beach Ball Classic. We get a letter around Valentine's Day. They said we're taking back our invitation because Roman's going to close. Well, we get 274 kids. May 1, they tell us the school's going to stay open. [Head Coach] Barry Brodzinski leaves in June. I get the job in July. Myrtle Beach took away our Christmas tournament."

Bill Ellerbee and Simon Gratz changed their minds about going to a tournament in Hawaii, so Roman replaced them. The Cahillites played Camden High from just across the Delaware River for third place. "It was the first time they'd ever played each other," said Seddon. "We're playing in Honolulu at 2 in the morning." Roman won.

Seddon had built his coaching profile by running the playgrounds around Philadelphia, and he'd coached the Roman Catholic JVs to a 60-3 record in three seasons. Under Seddon, Roman's varsity took the program national every chance it got. "In my career we were in Hawaii eight times," he said. "We played in roughly 30 different states, up and down the East Coast, California, Vegas….We played against some really, really good players. I like to tell people about our all-tournament team based on the way people played against us."

Bobby Hurley. Joe Smith. Rasheed Wallace. Jason Kidd from California. Kobe Bryant in Philly. But the greatest opponent was a skinny kid from Farragut Academy in Chicago. "This team had a 6-11 freshman who came in," Seddon remembered. "He moved to power forward as the game rolled along. He was the small forward, then he was the two guard. They were beating us pretty good, and we got back in the game. They moved him to point guard. I'm telling everybody about this guy, and nobody heard of him." Seddon called Kevin Garnett the best player Roman ever played against when he was the coach.

The final day of the 1994 Johnstown Tournament—and the tournament's farewell—turned into a doubleheader of blowouts. Roman Catholic drubbed

D.C. Dunbar 77–52. Carr had 18 points and 10 rebounds. Ketner scored 15. Blackhawk drilled Johnstown 77–48 in the consolation game.

Donnie Carr played with three pros while at Roman: Ketner, guard Rasual Butler and Eddie Griffin. Butler died tragically in a car accident. Ketner died young from cancer. The players were all close, friends beyond Roman Catholic, although that's where it all began.

As a young, rising player, Carr had to choose where he'd play high school basketball. Simon Gratz came calling. So did Roman.

"I'm a proud alumnus," said Carr, now a college assistant coach at LaSalle University. "It was the best decision of my life because of my experience winning the championships I won, the relationships I built, the connections, the teammates, the friendships."

And unless something changed, Carr would be playing in the final Cambria County Johnstown War Memorial Invitational Basketball Tournament, which had run from 1949 to 1994. The tournament had survived the Korean War, the Vietnam War and the war in the Persian Gulf. It had survived the third of three floods. But it was taking on water.

JOHNSTOWN DOWN

It took the local teams in AAABA baseball seventy-four years to win a tournament title. In 2018, Johnstown's Martella's Pharmacy won the championship that had seemed impossible for a local to attain. In 2023, another Johnstown team, Mainline Pharmacy, won it. Beyond the mostly full stadium for the live championship, more than one thousand people watched the live feed remotely.

The baseball tournament that began four years before the Johnstown Tournament has endured, and the rewards have finally arrived. Johnstown baseball teams can compete with and beat the best from other states!

Baseball has been especially good to the townspeople even beyond the AAABA tournament. In 2023, former son Tom Walter led his Wake Forest University team to the No. 1 national ranking, earning Walter Coach of the Year in the vaunted Atlantic Coast Conference. Native son Randy Mazey also has led West Virginia University's program to winning ways, including advancing to the super regional in 2024. The Johnstown native was twice named Big 12 Conference Coach of the Year before retiring in 2024. His shortstop was drafted seventh overall in the Major League Baseball draft. The trend in baseball has gone from mostly steady to peaking.

A FEW BLOCKS AWAY at War Memorial Arena—now 1ˢᵗ Summit Arena—so much recent disappointment has squelched the hopes of locals, starting in 1994 when the famed basketball tournament folded. The inclined plane

The former War Memorial Arena sitting in the dark, waiting for another tournament to begin in the future. *Photo by Bradley A. Huebner.*

behind War Memorial Arena/1ˢᵗ Summit Arena that transports people both away from and back toward the downtown at a 71 percent slope experienced technical issues in 2024, forcing it to be shut down for repairs. Basketball teams visiting for the Johnstown Tournament often rode that plane, even in snowy conditions, giving them a helicopter view of the city.

Former DeMatha High player and coach Pete Strickland remembers riding the inclined plane in the 1970s when the Stags played here. "The incline was like visiting the seven wonders of the world," he said. "The travel and everything was so new to us. We were probably the first high school to do the travel like that. The arena was always packed, and everything was abuzz."

D.C. Dunbar coach Mike McLeese remembers the inclined plane from his visit in 1990. "We did a tour of the Flood Museum," he said. "We also saw the inclined plane. That was the first time I had ever seen anything like that. I didn't have any idea what that was."

Never mind that Pittsburgh has two inclined planes on Mount Washington. The Johnstown plane is not far from the Stone Bridge, where the wreckage and people and fires from the 1889 great flood crashed and settled in a night of horror and agony. Construction began on a mechanism that would save people in another calamity. It's not only a tourist attraction but also a lifesaving lift that rises 895 feet to a restaurant and to a Southmont neighborhood rife with stately mansions.

"On March 17, 1936, when flood waters again ran through Johnstown, the Inclined Plane proved its worth by carrying almost 4,000 residents to safety," the inclinedplane.org website noted. "In the most recent flood to hit Johnstown on July 20, 1977, the Inclined Plane once again carried people to the safety of higher ground, as well as carrying boats, emergency personnel, and equipment down to the valley to aid in rescue operations."[200]

Even the current basketball promotions at War Memorial Arena/1st Summit Arena have fallen apart. On February 23, 2024, just hours before their performance, the Globetrotters canceled their game after finding court conditions not to their liking. Nonetheless, the Highlands Community College basketball team that had planned to attend the Globies' game used the newly vacant court to scrimmage.

And on May 6, 2024, legendary Johnstown High basketball coach Paul Litwalk passed away.

How did the local basketball scene plummet so precipitously? By 1994, the signs were everywhere. Not the posters of past tournament greats and future NBA players, but the metaphorical signs that the tournament was teetering. Some blamed the escalating costs to run the tournament. Others said that the novelty and interest in it had diminished. Still others argued that competing against other big-sponsor, sixteen-team national tournaments all over America became too difficult. Getting newspapers around Pennsylvania to commit enough column inches to publicize the tournament had grown taxing too, as regional holiday tournaments proliferated throughout Pennsylvania, about thirty every December in the surrounding counties.

Go back through the old issues of the *Tribune-Democrat*. Financial problems plagued the arena and the tournament. Several times thieves broke into the arena and stole the financial gate. In the middle of the 1970s, the arena asked the city to contribute $50,000 for operating expenses. In 1976, the city agreed to help with the arena's $400,000 tax debt "to meet the bond-redemption payment," as reported by John McHugh.[201] In the 1980s, a local Arby's signed on as the first corporate sponsor for one year. In the new millennium, large amounts of money disappeared from War Memorial Arena coffers into other bank accounts, as reported in 2010. "Promoters for two sporting events were so worried about losing profits at the Cambria

County War Memorial Arena that they brought in their own ticket collectors for two nights, a step that eventually sparked a state police probe."[202]

And yet locals lobbied to find a way to sustain the basketball tournament. One editorial in February 1976 captured the need to maintain War Memorial Arena and its signature events despite escalating costs:

> *Although not everyone has been, or ever will be, happy with the operation of the arena over the years, without a doubt it is one of the city's and the county's major assets. It may never be a money maker, but value can be calculated in terms other than monetary. And the War Memorial stands in tribute to the county's war dead while it stands as the county's prime host for major events for today's and future generations.*

In the final consolation game in Johnstown Tournament history, John Miller's Blackhawk High team defeated Johnstown 77–48, a fitting ending because rather than closing the tournament with "Blackhawk Down," as in the war movie, you could close with the apt phrase "Johnstown Down"—the entire tournament. A pre-COVID attempt to restart the tournament with a local focus was made but soon was scrapped. And don't look to football to inspire civic pride. Athletic director Kerry "KoKo" Pfeil sees better days ahead, but the Trojans have won one game in their last fifty-nine.[203] They're searching for "some" of the right moves.

That downhill commute into Johnstown's business district that basketball fans once eagerly undertook would no longer be for watching elite high school basketball teams, coaches and players. You could still make the downward sloping journey to see minor-league hockey, professional wrestling, concerts or the Globies (most years). But the great basketball tournament that began back in 1949 would disappear, like the A-listers from *Slap Shot* and *All the Right Moves*, who came, scintillated and split.

If you want to see an elite basketball tournament today, Farrell High still offers its four-team holiday showcase. In 2023, three of the teams were Pennsylvania traditional powers that had played in the Johnstown Tournament at some point. There have been other respected regional tournaments. Nearby Altoona often played in the Jaffa Mosque, which seated more than three thousand fans and would invite strong teams from outside central Pennsylvania. Even Altoona's girls' team was bringing in elite squads from as far away as California for its tournament back when Coach Art Taneyhill was winning *USA Today* mythical national championships. Farther north, Erie Cathedral Prep continues to run its Burger King Classic.

In 2023, it celebrated its fortieth season. It most resembles Johnstown, with a four-team elite field funneling to championship and consolation games.

Looking back at the history of the Burger King Classic, Erie Prep AD Bill Flanagan said that three teams still stand out. Coach Bob Hurley's 1989 St. Anthony's Friars went unbeaten with Jerry Walker, Bobby Hurley, Terry Dehere and freshman Rodrick Rhodes. They would win the mythical national title.

"That '89 season saw St. Anthony win three national tournaments and defeat teams from 10 different states, most notably Miami Senior (FL) in a come-from-behind victory with Bobby Hurley limited by an ankle injury, and a convincing win over Flint Hill Prep (VA)," wrote Jason Bernstein of the *Jersey Journal*. "Throughout it all was a seemingly endless trail of television cameras and national media to follow the group of Jersey City kids without a gym to call their own."

Flanagan also remembers the great Tim Thomas from Paterson Catholic and the uber-talented St. Patrick's squads from New Jersey. Thomas, at six-foot-ten, was the second-ranked player in America behind Kobe Bryant. And Rice High of New York sent several strong teams to Erie with players like Kemba Walker and Felipe Lopez. Erie Prep is built to host such a tournament. It has multiple facilities with several gyms within a few blocks, six locker rooms to accommodate four teams and a Burger King nearby where players can eat.

"It's harder and harder to do these every year," Flanagan admitted. "You can pick any reason why. You go year by year and hope it continues. I've always viewed these as like mom-and-pop events. I had friends of mine and classmates of mine who played in it."

One state over, Atlantic City, New Jersey, still runs its Seagull Classic, which began in 1971. It rose to elite status in the Garden State and then took a Rip Van Winkle–esque twenty-eight-year snooze before returning. While Johnstown holds claim to being America's First and Pennsylvania's Finest elite tournament, other tournaments have branched out to be worthy of the claim as biggest. Kentucky has its King of the Bluegrass Tournament. Director Lloyd Gardner readily admits that the Bluegrass modeled itself after the Kingdom of the Sun tournament in Ocala, Florida. The City of Palms in Florida, which advertises itself as "Future NBA on Display," is another premier event.

Even a long-established postseason tournament like the Alhambra Catholic Invitational Tournament (ACIT) in Maryland has fought for survival. After sixty-three years, the tournament shut down in 2023 due to costs and other factors. Most tournaments paused during the COVID epidemic, which gave them time to evaluate the benefits and costs of continuing.

"The gate won't pay the bills anymore," Gardner said. "I raise enough sponsorship to make sure we have everything good and nice—$19,000 for referees and security before I ever open the door. One time in forty-three years the gate receipts paid the expenses. We used to have four out-of-state teams forever, but the rooms went sky high even with the break. I give them six rooms at least, two meals a day and $1,000 or so. Every school that plays in my tournament gets a check."

It's not hyperbolic to call what visionaries like Clayton Dovey III and Charles Kunkle Jr. created in Johnstown a minor miracle. They lured some of the nation's best programs, coaches, teams and players to a remote steel town. Many laughed at Walt Disney when he proposed a theme park that families would drive one thousand miles to enjoy, but Disneyland and Disneyworld have been annual destinations for many Americans. Attracting Hall of Famers like Morgan Wootten and Wilt Chamberlain and Len Elmore to a steel town in cold and snowy December to entertain the residents, and to expose Johnstown boys to elite basketball, was a lofty goal, but it was met.

For Johnstown to find its way back to those halcyon days, to point the trajectory of the slope upward once again, it will need an infusion of risk-takers, big thinkers, financial backers, like those who appeared after World War II. Such an ascending slope is fueled by imagination and fosters widespread hope. Remember, Greater Johnstown Area High made it to a Pennsylvania state final in 2005. The last batch of Johnstown Tournament games lasted forty-six years. Hope and a rising slope become symbiotic. Same for despair and a downward slope. They feed off each other, good and bad.

Looking back at the brackets from 1949–94, several schools that trekked to Johnstown have disappeared altogether just like the tournament: Ben Franklin (New York), Rice, Tolentine, Johnstown Catholic (now called Bishop McCort), Johnstown Tech, Yeadon, Fifth Avenue and St. Anthony's (D.C. and New Jersey), to name a few.

Clearly Cambria County's decision makers appreciate the value of sports. In 1992, the Greater Johnstown Cambria County Business Hall of Fame honored two basketball visionaries in its first class: Kunkle and Picking. Years later, former Johnstown High and Pitt-Johnstown basketball star Carl Sax was inducted. They are men raised on sports who have given back to Johnstown.

In 2024, Carl Sax attended the Sunnehanna Amateur Golf Tournament a few blocks from his house. In its seventy-first year, it was appreciating with age. Sax, at eighty-nine, raved about the competition like an excitable teenager, effusive in his hometown pride, the way he does when he reminisces about winning the Cambria County Johnstown War Memorial Invitational Basketball Tournament in the 1950s.

There's always hope. But there's also a budget to meet. The river walls need refurbishing. The rivers need to be dredged. Cost estimates range from $500,000 to $1 million in "Biden's economy." And as Johnstown natives know best, preparing for a rainy day takes priority.

NOTES

Part I

1. National Park Service, "The South Fork Dam," June 13, 2024, https://www.nps.gov/jofl/learn/historyculture/the-south-fork-dam.htm.
2. History, "A Flood Hits Johnstown—Again | July 20, 1977," https://www.history.com/this-day-in-history/second-great-flood-hits-johnstown.
3. Grandview Cemetery, October 16, 2023, https://www.grandviewjohnstownpa.com.
4. AAABA Tournament, Johnstown, Pennsylvania, March 27, 2024, https://aaabajohnstown.org.
5. "1958–2015 Big 33 Game History," https://big33.org/wp-content/uploads/2016/01/PROGRAM-Big-33-Game-History-1958-2015.pdf.
6. Jim Dent, *The Kids Got It Right: How the Texas All-Stars Kicked Down Racial Walls*, 1st ed. (New York: Dunn Books, St. Martin's Press, 2013).
7. Carl Sax (Johnstown alumnus and resident), in discussion with the author, April 2023.
8. Todd Thiele, "Who Knew Charles Kunkle Jr. Well?" Facebook, March 20, 2024, https://www.facebook.com/search/top/?q=Charles%20Kunkle.
9. Sports Mike, "WHS to Play in State's Most Modest Arena," *Williamsport Sun Gazette*, December 12, 1950.
10. Herb Sendek Jr. (Cambria County native and basketball coach), in discussion with the author, July 2023.
11. Herb Sendek Sr. (Cambria County resident), in discussion with the author, July 2023.
12. Hershey Harrisburg Sports & Events Authority, https://www.hhsportsandevents.com/listings/hersheypark%C2%AE-arena/2991.

13. Jimmy Calpin, "Regard Old Forge, Sharon as Likely Finalists in State Court Tournament," *Scrantonian Tribune*, December 28, 1952, https://www.newspapers.com/image/530044441/?match=1&terms=Johnstown%20Old%20Forge.

14. *Latrobe Bulletin*, "Greensburg Bows to Johnstown," December 31, 1952, https://www.newspapers.com/image/447984270/?match=1&terms=Johnstown%20basketball.

15. *Pittsburgh Post-Gazette*, "PIAA Tourney Reaches Semi-Finals Tonight," March 21, 1953, https://www.newspapers.com/image/87861771/?match=1&terms=Johnstown%20basketball%20to%20face%20Sharon.

16. Associated Press, "Overbrook Can Play in One Tourney," December 16, 1954, https://www.newspapers.com/image/540630608/?match=1&terms=Overbrook%20can%20play%20in%20one%20tourney.

17. Jim Raykie, "Philadelphia Overbrook at Farrell (Pa.) High in 1954," May 17, 2020, 22:57, YouTube, https://www.youtube.com/watch?v=24u3Ey5XPA0.

18. PA Football History, "Pennsylvania High School Football Players in the NFL Draft," April 27, 2023, https://pafbhistory.com/2023/04/27/pennsylvania-high-school-players-in-the-nfl-draft/#:~:text=Bethlehem%20Liberty%20(15)%2C%20Allentown,Harrisburg%20one%20draft%20selection%20each).

19. Lanny Van Eman (McKeesport basketball player and college and NBA coach), in discussion with the author, 2022–24.

20. Gene Danko (McKeesport High basketball alumnus), in discussion with the author, June 2022.

21. *Life*, "The Giants of Schoolboy Basketball" (February 21, 1955): 59–62, https://books.google.com/books?id=LFQEAAAAMBAJ&pg=PA59&source=gbs_toc_r&cad=2#v=onepage&q&f=false.

22. Associated Press, "Overbrook Wins; Chamberlain, 46," December 31, 1954, https://www.newspapers.com/image/175399553/?match=1&terms=Overbrook%20Noses%20McKeesport.

23. Doug Leaman (Overbrook High basketball player), in discussion with the author, May 2022.

24. Cecil Mosenson, *It All Began with Wilt* (Mustang, OK: Tate Pub & Enterprises, 2008).

25. Will Mega TV, "Wilt Chamberlain's Basketball Coach Cecil Mosenson Part 2," 2023, 0:46, YouTube, https://www.youtube.com/watch?v=62TeiaW7U6Q&list=PL44Pr1sxcjXfCArLesW4rGjd04AC_QFrI.

26. Greg Markovich (son of McKeesport and Michigan State basketball player), in discussion with the author, March 2024.

27. Officialhoophall, "Zigmund J. 'Red' Mihalik's Basketball Hall of Fame Enshrinement Speech," November 3, 2017, 9:23, YouTube, https://www.youtube.com/watch?v=vSuIV1iHO0A.

28. Ford City Borough, "History," https://fordcityborough.org/sample-page/history.

29. Fred Lucas, "America's Top 20 Cities for Crime, and What Party Runs Them," *Daily Signal*, June 26, 2020, https://www.dailysignal.com/2020/06/24/americas-top-20-cities-for-crime-and-what-party-runs-them.

30. Alana Winkler, "Crozer Theological Seminary," Clio, December 14, 2021, https://theclio.com/entry/143551.

31. Benny Walker (former Chester High basketball player), in discussion with the author, February 4, 2024.

32. *Republican and Herald*, "Late Rally by McKeesport Clinches 'A' Crown," March 28, 1955.

33. Bo Ryan (Chester High former athlete and Hall of Fame basketball coach), in discussion with the author, January 30, 2024.

34. Rich Pagano, "Speaking of Sports, Emerson Baynard: A Legend," Spirit News, December 7, 2022, https://myspiritnews.com/articles/sports/speaking-of-sports-3.

35. Larry DeFillipo, "June 16, 1961: Lew Krausse Jr. Twirls Debut Shutout 10 Days After High-School Graduation," Society for American Baseball Research, https://sabr.org/gamesproj/game/june-16-1961-lew-krausse-jr-twirls-debut-shutout-10-days-after-high-school-graduation.

36. *Delaware County Times*, "Nanticoke Jolts Chester; Baynard Is Selected MVP," December 30, 1960.

37. Skipper Patrick, "'I Pitched Like My Dad Told Me,' Bonus Baby Says After Win," Associated Press, June 1, 1961.

38. Bill Fisher, "42,964 Fans Saw Steelton," *Lancaster New Era*, March 13, 1965.

39. Rich Westcott, "Sports Scope," *Delaware County Times*, March 12, 1965.

40. Don Hennon (former Wampum High guard), in discussion with the author, May 2, 2024.

41. *Greenville Record Argus*, "Altoona Snaps Farrell Win Streak at 99," December 15, 1956.

42. *Monongahela Daily Republican*, "'Hounds Dominate MVC Title Scene," February 24, 1955.

43. Jim "Mouse" Chacko (former Charleroi High athlete), in discussion with the author, November 14, 2023.

44. *Delaware County Times*, "Yeadon Squeezed Out, 75–74," December 29, 1956.

45. Ben Jenkins (Charleroi sports historian), in discussion with the author, March 19, 2024.

46. Matt Zabitka, "Clippers Mop Up Everything but the Ball Game," *Delaware County Times*, December 28, 1957.

47. Wali Jones (former Overbrook High, Villanova University and NBA basketball player), in discussion with the author, June 2, 2020.

48. *Philadelphia Inquirer*, "Court Tourney to Overbrook," December 29, 1957.

49. *Stockton Evening and Sunday Record*, "Kansas Lures Another Wilt," June 25, 1958.

50. Ron Paglia, "Chacko Family Sports Legacy Got Its Start Decades Ago," *TribLive*, October 4, 2009, https://archive.triblive.com/news/chacko-family-sports-legacy-got-its-start-decades-ago.

51. Ben French, "Farrell Wins State Title, 63–55, as McCoy Scores 29," *Oil City Derrick*/Associated Press, March 31, 1952.

52. 1998 Blair County Sports Hall of Fame, "Jim Curry Introduced by Oscar Robertson," June 1, 2017, 3:35, YouTube, https://www.youtube.com/watch?v=MsQcdDlg-rQ.

53. *Allentown Morning Call*, "Catasauqua Wins in Overtime, 77–72," December 28, 1963.

54. Tom Ponton (DeMatha Catholic development director), in discussion with the author, May 8, 2024.

55. Bill Ruback (former DeMatha Catholic basketball player), in discussion with the author, June 6, 2024.

56. Charles "Hawkeye" Whitney (former DeMatha Catholic basketball player, N.C. State, NBA), in discussion with the author, May 20, 2024.

Part II

57. Chester Zaremba (Nanticoke area historian), in discussion with the author, March 9, 2024.

58. Jack Dudrick (former Nanticoke High basketball player), in discussion with the author, March 9, 2024.

59. Duane Ford (former Nanticoke High basketball player and state championship basketball and softball coach), April 26, 2024.

60. *Delaware County Times*, "Nanticoke Jolts Chester; Baynard Is Selected MVP," December 30, 1960.

61. Dan Rodenbach (former Bethlehem High and Princeton basketball player), in discussion with the author, April 16, 2024.

62. Billy Packer (former Bethlehem High and Wake Forest basketball player, Final Four announcer), in discussion with the author, June 24, 2019.

63. William C. Kashatus, *One-Armed Wonder: Pete Gray, Wartime Baseball, and the American Dream* (Jefferson, NC: McFarland, 1995).

64. *Gettysburg Times*, "Nanticoke 5 Welcomed by Town Folks," March 27, 1961.

65. *Wilkes-Barre Times Leader*, "Basketball Controversy: ACON Club Requests PIAA Investigation," March 21, 1969.

66. Ray Saul, "Speaking of Sports," *Hazleton Standard-Speaker*, March 17, 1969.

67. Don Rodenbach (former Bethlehem High and Princeton basketball player), in discussion with the author, April 16, 2024.

68. *Morgan Wootten Legend*, published by DeMatha Catholic, 2009.

69. Joe Wootten (Wootten Camp director and Bishop O'Connell coach), in discussion with the author, June 2003.

70. Sonny Vaccaro (Dapper Dan Tournament founder, former Nike and Adidas basketball shoe division head), in discussion with the author, April 25, 2023.

71. *Washington Daily News*, "DeMatha in Johnstown Final," December 30, 1961.

72. Johnny Jones (DeMatha Catholic basketball player), in discussion with the author, May 11, 2024.

73. Jim Williams (former Abington High and Temple basketball player), in discussion with the author, July 24, 2023.

74. David Falk (NBA super-agent), in discussion with the author, December 17, 2023.

75. Joe Kennedy (former DeMatha Catholic and Duke basketball player), in discussion with the author, May 6, 2024.

76. Mike Brey (former DeMatha Catholic player and coach, former Delaware and Notre Dame head coach), in discussion with the author, August 15, 2023.

77. Bob Petrini (former DeMatha Catholic and Pitt basketball player), in discussion with the author, December 18, 2023.

78. Morgan Wootten and Bill Gilbert, *A Coach for All Seasons* (New York: Masters Press, 1997).

79. Joe Nastasi (former Northern Cambria basketball player), in discussion with the author, February 13, 2024.

80. Greg Kuhn (former Northern Cambria basketball player), in discussion with the author, February 29, 2024.

81. Paul A. Kurtz, "Cambria Tourney Shows Top Teams," *Pittsburgh Press*, December 15, 1964.

82. Jack Kropp, "Northern Cambria Tops Coraopolis," *Pittsburgh Press*, March 13, 1965.

83. *Uniontown Evening Standard*/AP, "No. Cambria Wins Title; Lifts Pressure from Montrose," March 22, 1965.

84. Frank Frontino (Northern Cambria basketball player, Pittsburgh Pirates pitcher), in discussion with the author, April 27, 2024.

85. A.J. Nastasi (Northern Bedford basketball player), in discussion with the author, April 23, 2024.

86. Mario Parascenzo, "Schenley High Spartans Have Timber for Title," *Pittsburgh Post-Gazette*, December 10, 1965.

87. Steve Smear (Bishop McCort multi-sport athlete and Penn State football player), in discussion with the author, May 16, 2024.

88. Mario Parascenzo, "Schenley Bench Proved Big Factor in Triumph," *Pittsburgh Post-Gazette*, March 28, 1966.

89. *Somerset Daily American*, "Four Team Invitation Hoop Meet at Cambria County War Memorial on Dec. 28–29," December 8, 1966.

90. Anonymous source who wished not to be identified, Johnstown trip, July 31, 2023.

91. Petey Gibson (Schenley High point guard with Kenny Durrett), in discussion with the author, July 17, 2023.

92. Ed Salmon (Millville High, New Jersey basketball coach), in discussion with the author, December 26, 2023.

93. Bill Hughes (Millville High basketball player), in discussion with the author, June 20, 2023.

94. *Sports Illustrated*, "The Best Basketball Player in America," cover story, February 16, 1970, https://vault.si.com/vault/1970/02/16/if-you-want-tom-easy-does-it.

95. Alan Shaw (Millville High and Duke basketball player), in discussion with the author, June 1, 2023.

96. Jim Hobgood (Laurel Highlands and Virginia basketball player), in discussion with the author, August 11, 2023.

97. Pat DiCesare (music promoter and childhood neighbor to Sonny Vaccaro), in discussion with the author, June 22, 2023.

98. Bob Vosburg, "Basketball Fan Gets His Kicks with 'Top 100,'" *New Castle News*, December 5, 1969.

99. Len Elmore (Power Memorial and Maryland basketball player), in discussion with the author, February 6, 2024.

100. Japeth Trimble (Power Memorial and Maryland basketball player), in discussion with the author, August 22, 2023.

101. *Sunbury Daily Item*, "Mansfield Cagers Suffer 1st Loss," December 31, 1969.

102. Fred McMane, "Maryland Wins with 5 Sophs," *El Paso Herald-Post*, March 27, 1972.

Part III

103. Steve Berkowitz, "Basketball Is Family Affair for Thompsons," *Washington Post*, March 21, 1989.

104. Bill Campion (Rice High and Manhattan basketball player), in discussion with the author, October 31, 2023.

105. Jeff Samuels, "Hopewell and Upper St. Clair Losers in Johnstown Tourney," *Pittsburgh Press*, December 30, 1971.

106. Pete Mollica, "Sligh's 50 Points Help Sink 'Canes," *New Castle News*, February 2, 1972.

107. Gerard J. Pelisson and James A. Garvey III, *The Castle on the Parkway: The Story of New York City's Dewitt Clinton High School and Its Extraordinary Influence on American Life* (Scarsdale, NY: Hutch Press, 2009).

108. Bob Piano (Dewitt Clinton High assistant basketball coach), in discussion with the author, May 14, 2024.

109. Steve "The Bear" Sheppard (Dewitt Clinton and Maryland basketball player), in discussion with the author, January 27, 2024.

110. Vince Leonard, "New Castle Bows in Hurricane Final," *Pittsburgh Post-Gazette*, December 31, 1971.

111. Charlie Rayman, "Tonies Say 'Goodbye, Mr. T.' with a Victory," *Washington Daily News*, March 20, 1972.

112. Aaron Long (St. Anthony's D.C. and Georgetown basketball player), in discussion with the author, May 13, 2024.

113. Tim Lambour (Bishop Guilfoyle and Georgetown basketball player), in discussion with the author, December 29, 2023.

114. Jeff Thompson, "Dickinson Basketball vs. Georgetown, 1973," Dickinson College Archives and Special Collections, https://archives.dickinson.edu/sites/all/files/files_document/I-ThompsonJ-2021-1_1.pdf.

115. Mark Edwards (former DeMatha and Georgetown basketball player), in discussion with the author, May 11, 2024.

116. *Delaware County Times*, "Chester Draws Ohio Team in Opener at Johnstown," December 26, 1972.

117. National Civic League, "All-American City Winners," https://www.nationalcivicleague.org/america-city-award/past-winners.

118. *Delaware County Times*, "Chester Advances into Johnstown Finals," December 30, 1972.

119. Don Maser (former Johnstown and Duquesne basketball player), in discussion with the author, July 17, 2023.

120. Paul Litwalk (former Johnstown High basketball coach), in discussion with the author, July 23, 2023.

121. Steve Kittey, "PIAA Playoffs," *Latrobe Bulletin*, March 20, 1973.

122. Herman "Helicopter" Harris (former Chester High and Arizona basketball player), in discussion with the author, May 22, 2024.

123. Joe Goldenberg (former Overbrook High basketball coach), in discussion with the author, May 30, 2023.

124. Mary Flannery, "Banks to Find Out If Wayne Is the Real McCoy," *Philadelphia Daily News*, January 23, 1976.

125. Gary Smith, "Banks' Intensity Rose Above Stars," *Philadelphia Daily News*, December 1, 1976.

126. Joe Goldenberg (former coach at West Philadelphia), in discussion with the author, May 30, 2023.

127. *Binghamton Press and Sun-Bulletin*, "Whirl of Sports," January 28, 1976.

128. Mary Flannery, "Banks Reaches Summit," *Philadelphia Daily News*, January 26, 1976.

129. Gene Banks (former West Philly, Duke, NBA basketball player), in discussion with the author, August 11, 2023.

130. Dick "Hoops" Weiss (basketball writer), in discussion with the author, November 13, 2023.

131. James "Bruiser" Flynt (former Kentucky assistant basketball coach), in discussion with the author, June 14, 2023.

132. Eddie Biedenbach (former North Carolina State assistant coach), in discussion with the author, October 7, 2022.

133. David "Puffy" Kennedy (former Brashear High and Cincinnati basketball player), in discussion with the author, June 1, 2023.

134. Joey Crawford (former NBA referee from Philadelphia), in discussion with the author, November 14, 2023.

135. Ricky Tucker (former Overbrook High and Providence basketball player), in discussion with the author, October 23, 2023.

136. Mike DeCourcy (Sporting News and Big Ten Channel reporter), in discussion with the author, June 27, 2023.

137. Pete Strickland (former DeMatha Catholic and Pitt basketball player), in discussion with the author, July 18, 2023.

138. D.J. Kennedy (former Schenley High and St. John's basketball player), in discussion with the author, June 2, 2023.

139. Cody McDevitt and Bruce Siwy, "A City Imperiled: Johnstown River Walls at Risk of Failure," *Somerset Daily American*, June 8, 2019, https://apnews.com/general-news-94fd064f6a884efd983a9fc41c2c044f.

140. Clarence Robson (Johnstown native), in discussion with the author, July 31, 2023.

141. Chad Fetzer (Johnstown resident and owner of Fetz's), in discussion with the author, July 31, 2023.

142. Deb Kiner, "Flood in 1977 Was Third to Devastate Johnstown," Pennlive, July 19, 2019, https://www.pennlive.com/life/2019/07/flood-in-1977-was-third-to-devastate-johnstown.html.

143. Greg "Dutch" Morley (former DeMatha Catholic and Maryland basketball player), in discussion with the author, April 17, 2024.

144. Paul Litwalk (former Johnstown High basketball coach and resident), in discussion with the author, July 18, 2023.

145. Tim Rigby (former Johnstown WJAC-TV sports broadcaster), in discussion with the author, October 14, 2022.

146. Tom Ponton (DeMatha Catholic director of development), in discussion with the author, May 23, 2024.

147. Dwight Collins (former Beaver Falls High basketball player and Pitt football player), in discussion with the author, January 17, 2024.

148. Dereck Whittenburg (former DeMatha High and N.C. State basketball player), August 19, 2023.

149. Ted Silary, "DeMatha Falls but 'Brook Gains Finals," *Philadelphia Daily News*, December 29, 1978.

150. Steve Kittey, "Beaver Falls Prevails," *Latrobe Bulletin*, March 20, 1970.

151. Max Levin (former Overbrook High basketball coach), in discussion with the author, May 23, 2024.

152. *Philadelphia Inquirer*, "Overbrook Tops DeMatha; W. Phila. Falls to Gibbons," March 10, 1979.

153. Pete Holbert (former W.T. Woodson and Maryland basketball player), in discussion with the author, May 30, 2024.

154. Paul "Red" Jenkins (former W.T. Woodson High basketball coach), in discussion with the author, February 7, 2024.

155. *Centre Daily Times*, "Ben Franklin Wins," December 31, 1979.

Part IV

156. Johnny Dawkins (former Mackin Catholic, Duke basketball player; Central Florida coach), in discussion with the author, October 5, 2023.

157. Curtis "Smiley" Moore (former Mount Vernon High and Nebraska basketball player), in discussion with the author, January 12, 2024.

158. Tony Fiorentino (former Mount Vernon coach and Miami Heat basketball personality), in discussion with the author, September 8, 2023.

159. Gerry Dulac, "'Best in Country' Upholds Rep in Johnstown," *Pittsburgh Press*, December 31, 1981.

160. Bill Travers, "Franklin Wins, 52–48," *New York Daily News*, March 14, 1982.

161. Al Harvin, "Franklin Tradition Fades Out," *New York Times*, December 22, 1981.

162. Jaime Diaz, "There's a Berry in the Bushes: Once St. John's Prize Recruit, Walter Berry Is Now Ripening at a J.C.," *Sports Illustrated* (January 30, 1984), https://vault.si.com/vault/1984/01/30/theres-a-berry-in-the-bushes.

163. Bob White, "Dunbar Can Play Up to Its Top Ranking, DeMatha Coach Says," *Louisville Courier-Journal*, December 16, 1982.

164. Jim Calhoun (former Northeastern and UConn basketball coach), in discussion with the author, August 11, 2023.

165. Bob Wade (former Baltimore Dunbar and Maryland basketball coach), in discussion with the author, December 26, 2024.

166. Herman "Tree" Harried (former Baltimore Dunbar and Syracuse basketball player), in discussion with the author, August 11, 2023.

167. Paul Dunbar, "Sympathy," Poetry Foundation, https://www.poetryfoundation.org/poems/46459/sympathy-56d22658afbc0.

168. Steve Geuther (former Bay High basketball player), in discussion with the author, January 10, 2024.

169. Tyrone "Muggsy" Bogues (former Baltimore Dunbar and Wake Forest basketball player), in discussion with the author, December 26, 2023.

170. Reggie Williams (former Baltimore Dunbar and Georgetown basketball player), in discussion with the author, December 26, 2023.

171. Frank Lawlor, "Mourners Bid Farewell to William Penn Player," *Philadelphia Inquirer*, December 9, 1993.

172. Dave Lebo (former Carlisle High basketball coach), in discussion with the author, January 15, 2024.

173. Darryl "Heat" Gates (former Dobbins Tech High basketball player), September 12, 2023.

174. Linda Page, *Love, Pain, and Passion: The Heart of a Champion* (Bloomington, IN: AuthorHouse, 2010).

175. Ray Parillo, "Here Come Holidays, There Go Teams," *Philadelphia Inquirer*, December 16, 1984.

176. Lloyd Gardner (King of the Bluegrass tournament director), in discussion with the author, May 23, 2024.

177. Bob White, "Kimbro's 38 Futile: Seneca Drops Final to Tech," *Louisville Journal-Courier*, December 23, 1984.

178. Mike Kern, "Dobbins, Coatesville Are 'Polls' Apart," *Philadelphia Daily News*, December 29, 1984.

179. Bo Kimble, *For You, Hank* (New York: Dell, 1993).

180. Ken Hamilton (former Ben Franklin High of Philadelphia basketball coach), in discussion with the author, June 20, 2023.

181. Bob Hurley (former St. Anthony's High of New Jersey basketball coach), in discussion with the author, June 21, 2023.

182. Jeremiah Walker (former St. Anthony's and Seton Hall basketball player), in discussion with the author, June 21, 2023.

183. Tom Walter (former Johnstown High athlete and current Wake Forest baseball coach), in discussion with the author, December 14, 2023.

184. Naismith Memorial Basketball Hall of Fame, "Robert 'Bob' Hurley Sr.," https://www.hoophall.com/hall-of-famers/bob-hurley-sr.

185. Paul Husselbee, "Coolidge Rallies for Title," *Johnstown Tribune-Democrat*, December 31, 1989.

186. John Stuckey (former Calvin Coolidge High and Harford basketball player), in discussion with the author, June 5, 2024.

187. Dave Rogers (former Martinsburg High basketball player and current coach), June 14, 2024.

Part V

188. Mike McLeese (former D.C. Dunbar and Howard University basketball coach), in discussion with the author, May 17, 2024.

189. Scott Newman, "Gratz Falls Short in a Heartbreaker," *Philadelphia Inquirer*, December 8, 1991.

190. Bill Ellerbee (former Simon Gratz basketball coach), in discussion with the author, July 9, 2020.

191. Frank Lawlor, "Roman, Gratz to Meet in Tourney Final," *Philadelphia Inquirer*, December 5, 1992.

192. Dennis Seddon (former Roman Catholic basketball coach), in discussion with the author, December 3, 2023.

193. Lynard Stewart (former Simon Gratz basketball player and current Gratz coach), in discussion with the author, September 5, 2023.

194. Chris McNesby (former Roman Catholic basketball player and current head coach), in discussion with the author, December 17, 2023.

195. Mike Owen, "Gratz Just Good Basketball Team," Associated Press/*Carlisle Sentinel*, February 27, 1993.

196. Gary DeCesare (St. Raymond's basketball coach), in discussion with the author, September 18, 2023.

197. Michael Dobie, "Odd Couple," *New York Newsday*, December 5, 1993.

198. Littel Vaughn (*Checkball* magazine publisher), in discussion with author, May 3, 2024.

199. Ted Silary, "Sub May Surface vs. FLC," *Philadelphia Daily News*, March 3, 1994.

200. Johnstown Inclined Plane, "The History of the Incline," https://www.inclinedplane.org/history.

201. John McHugh, "City Agrees to Help County Settle $400,000 Arena Debt," *Johnstown Tribune*, April 15, 1976.

202. Sandra K. Reabuck, "Details of Arena Probe Emerge," *Johnstown Tribune-Democrat*, August 21, 2010, https://www.tribdem.com/news/local_news/details-of-arena-probe-emerge/article_5de14038-4289-5a14-9dd5-460b56e33fe0.html.

203. Kerry "KoKo" Pfeil (Greater Johnstown Area athletic director), in discussion with the author, June 6, 2024.

ABOUT THE AUTHOR

Bradley A. Huebner is the author of two books about Pennsylvania high school basketball. His first book, *Titles for Our Town*, captures small-town dynasties from the golden age of the 1950s and 1960s. A veteran basketball coach, Huebner grew up playing basketball, baseball and football in Pennsylvania. His father, Richard, played in Johnstown's AAABA tournament in front of fifteen thousand fans in 1952. His grandfather was a repeat golf champion at Lehigh Country Club. Bradley now lives a short drive from Hersheypark Arena, where Wilt Chamberlain famously scored one hundred points in one game, and near Hershey Country Club, where his grandfather learned golf from the great Ben Hogan.